MAKER

COMICS

CONDUCT A SCIENCE EXPERIMENT!

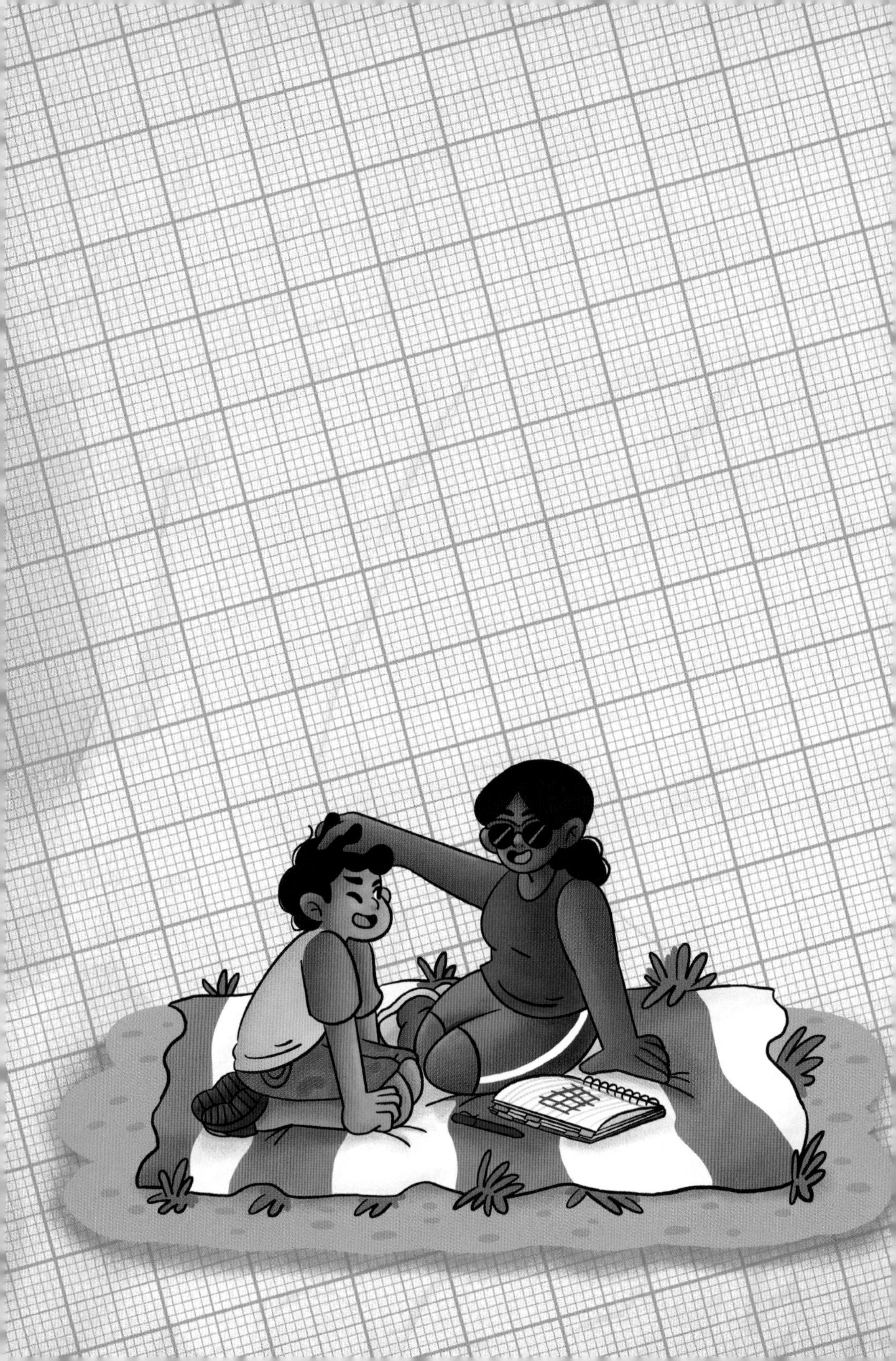

CONDUCT A SCIENCE EXPERIMENT!

Written by Der-shing Helmer
Art by Andrea Bell

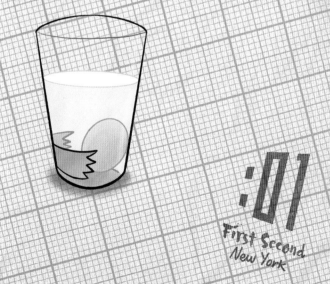

:01
First Second
New York

This book contains instructions on how to carry out scientific experiments and exercises in your own home!

Before getting started, be sure to review this safety warning and the lab safety guide on page 120 to keep you and your experiment fun and safe.

Read the experiment instructions thoroughly before doing the experiment.

The best way to prevent accidents in the lab is to be prepared, and know the procedures beforehand to avoid confusion or mistakes.

No running or roughhousing during the lab.

Many accidents can be prevented simply by behaving maturely in the lab. Unless movement is a part of the experiment, please don't run, poke, tickle, shove, etcetera.

Handle glass carefully.

Glassware can break if dropped or handled improperly! If you break glass in the house, get an adult to help you clean it up right away.

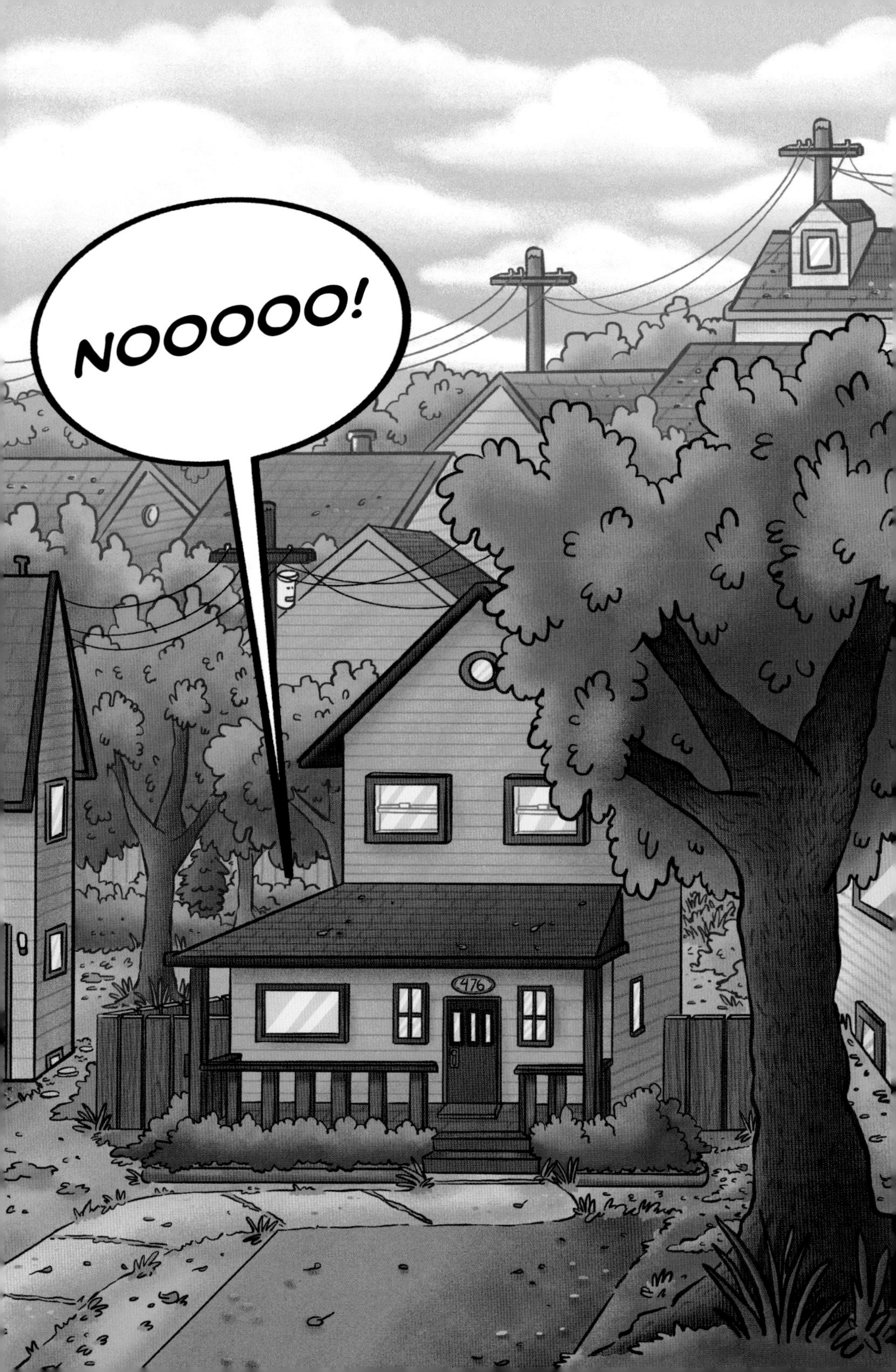
NOOOOO!
476

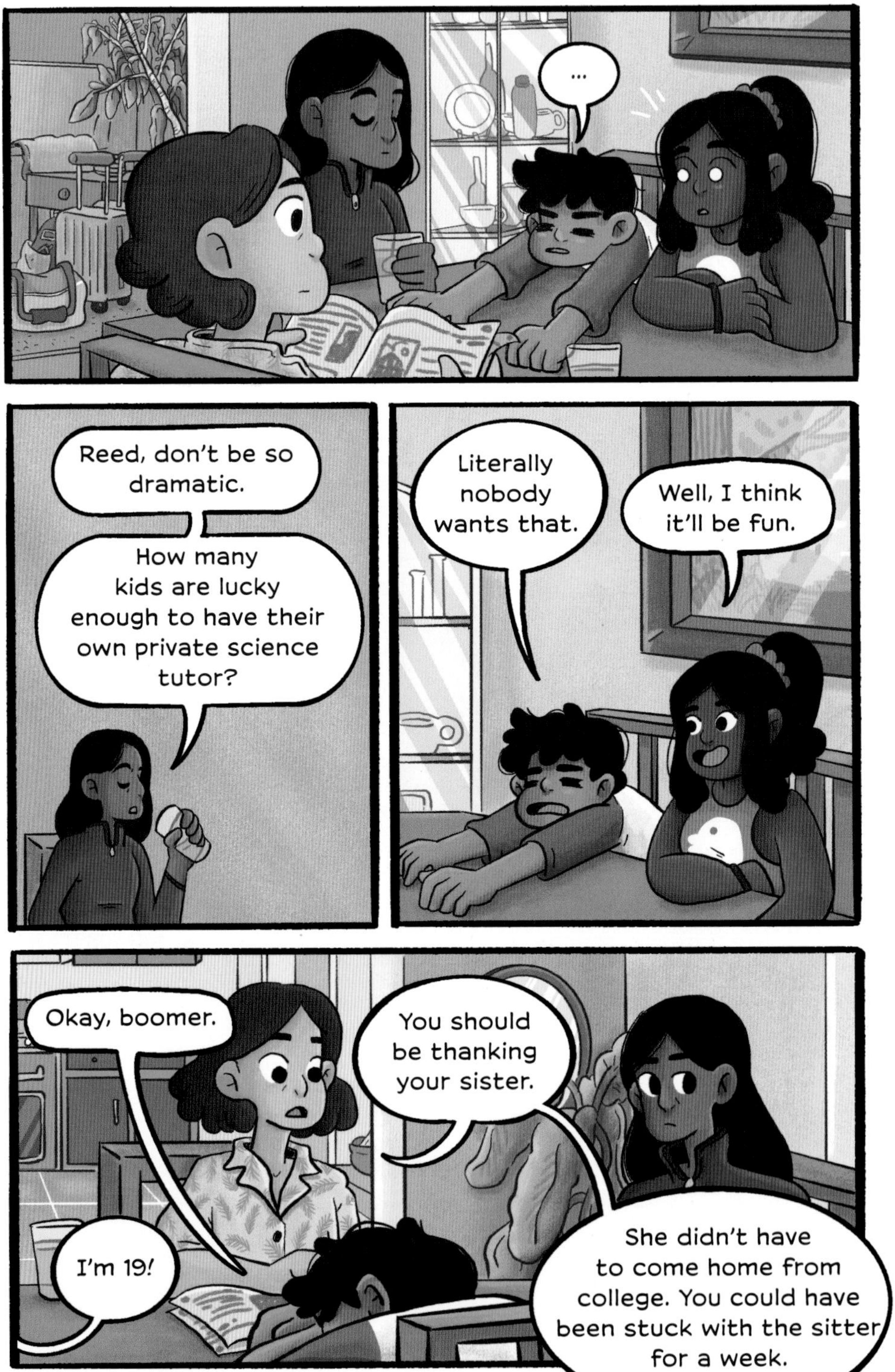
...
Reed, don't be so dramatic.
How many kids are lucky enough to have their own private science tutor?
Literally nobody wants that.
Well, I think it'll be fun.
Okay, boomer.
You should be thanking your sister.
I'm 19!
She didn't have to come home from college. You could have been stuck with the sitter for a week.

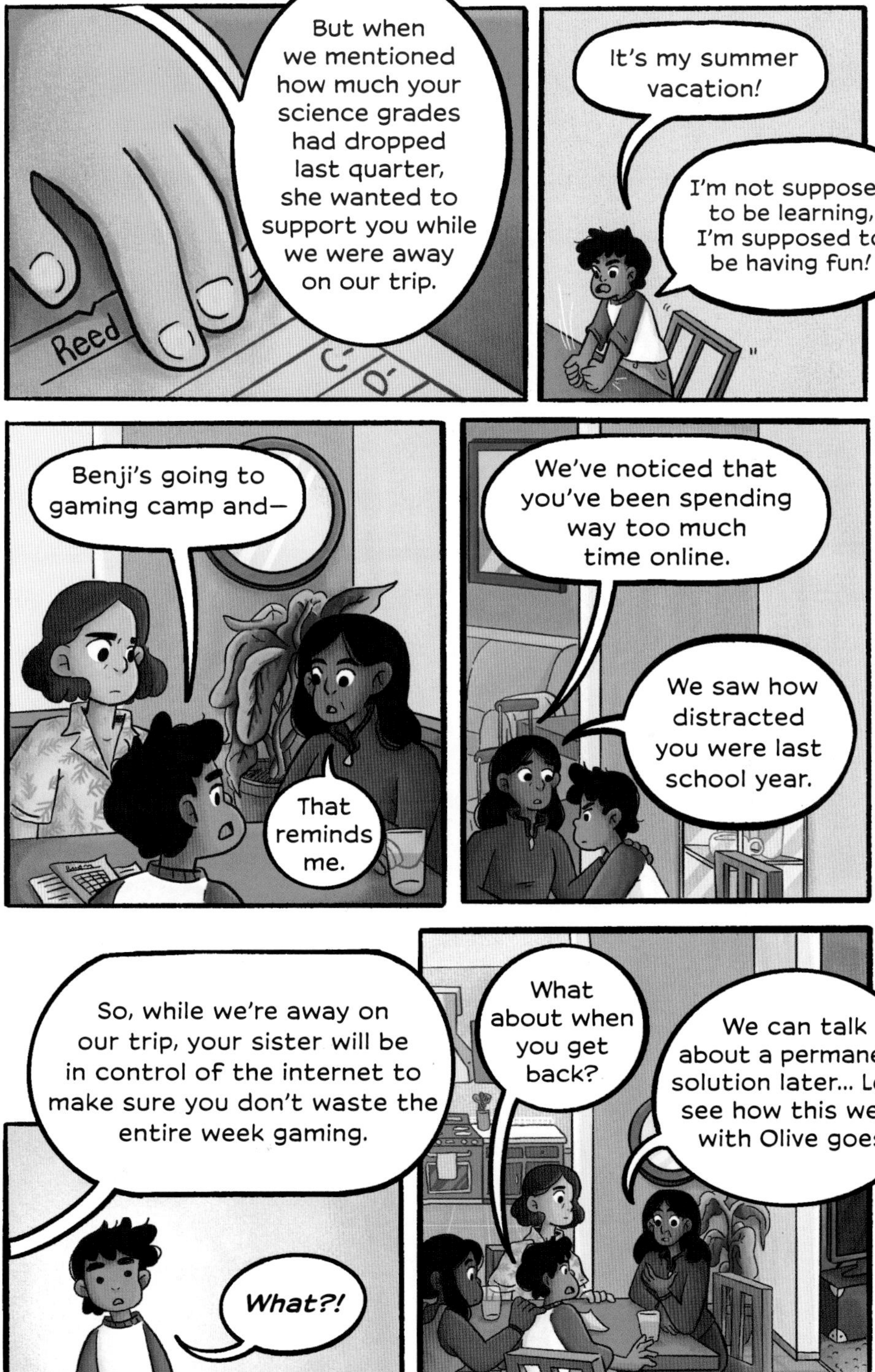
Reed
C-
D-
But when we mentioned how much your science grades had dropped last quarter, she wanted to support you while we were away on our trip.
It's my summer vacation!
I'm not supposed to be learning, I'm supposed to be having fun!
Benji's going to gaming camp and—
That reminds me.
We've noticed that you've been spending way too much time online.
We saw how distracted you were last school year.
So, while we're away on our trip, your sister will be in control of the internet to make sure you don't waste the entire week gaming.
What?!
What about when you get back?
We can talk about a permanent solution later... Let's see how this week with Olive goes.

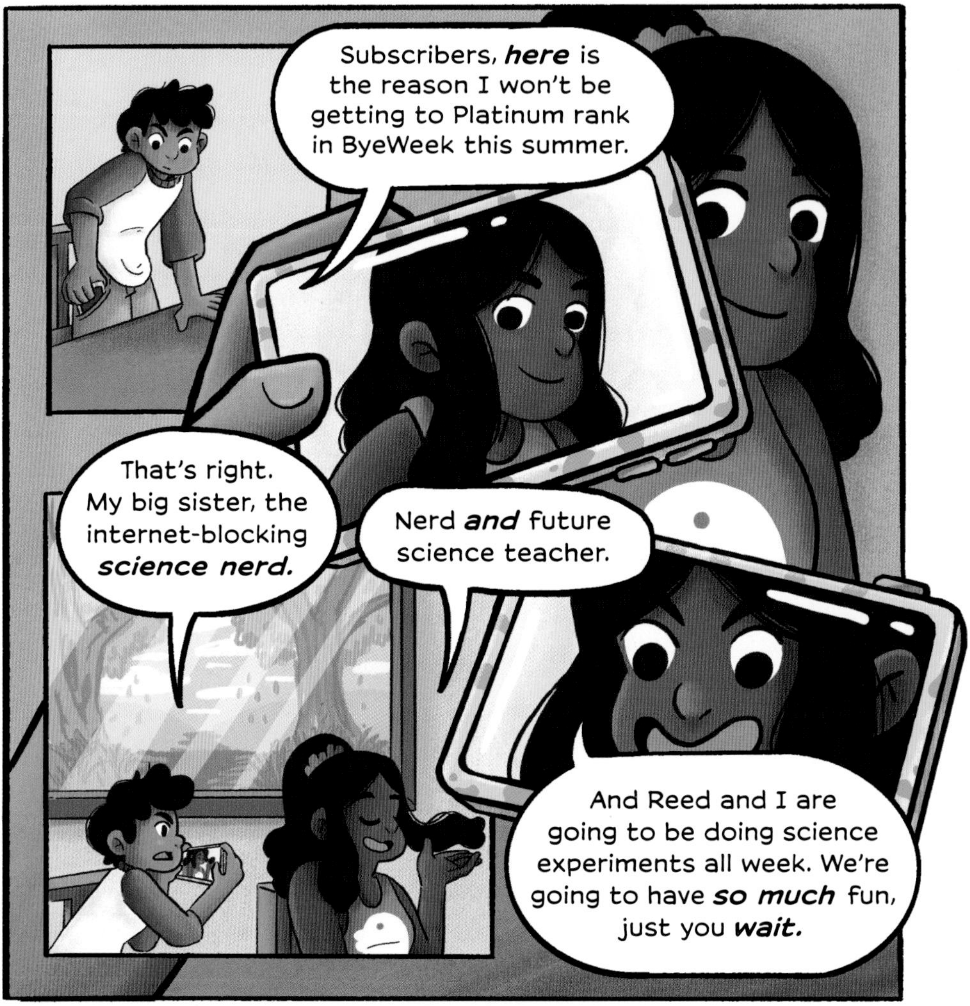
Subscribers, ***here*** is the reason I won't be getting to Platinum rank in ByeWeek this summer.
That's right. My big sister, the internet-blocking ***science nerd.***
Nerd ***and*** future science teacher.
And Reed and I are going to be doing science experiments all week. We're going to have ***so much*** fun, just you ***wait.***

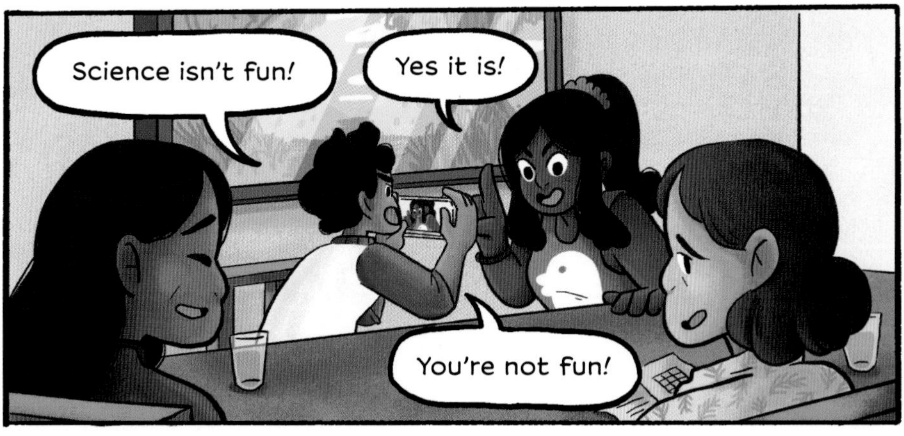
Science isn't fun!
Yes it is!
You're not fun!

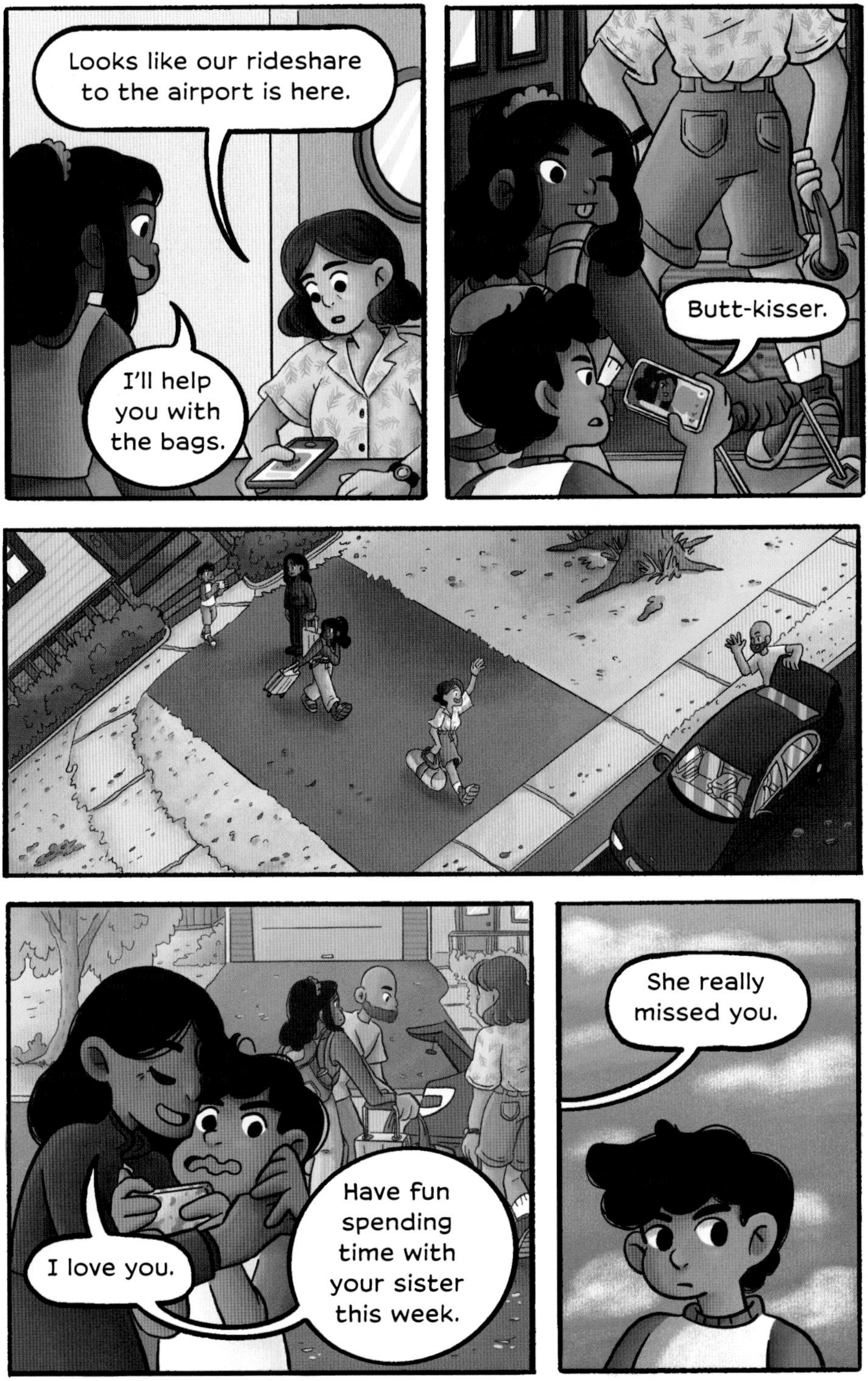
Looks like our rideshare to the airport is here.
I'll help you with the bags.
Butt-kisser.
Have fun spending time with your sister this week.
I love you.
She really missed you.

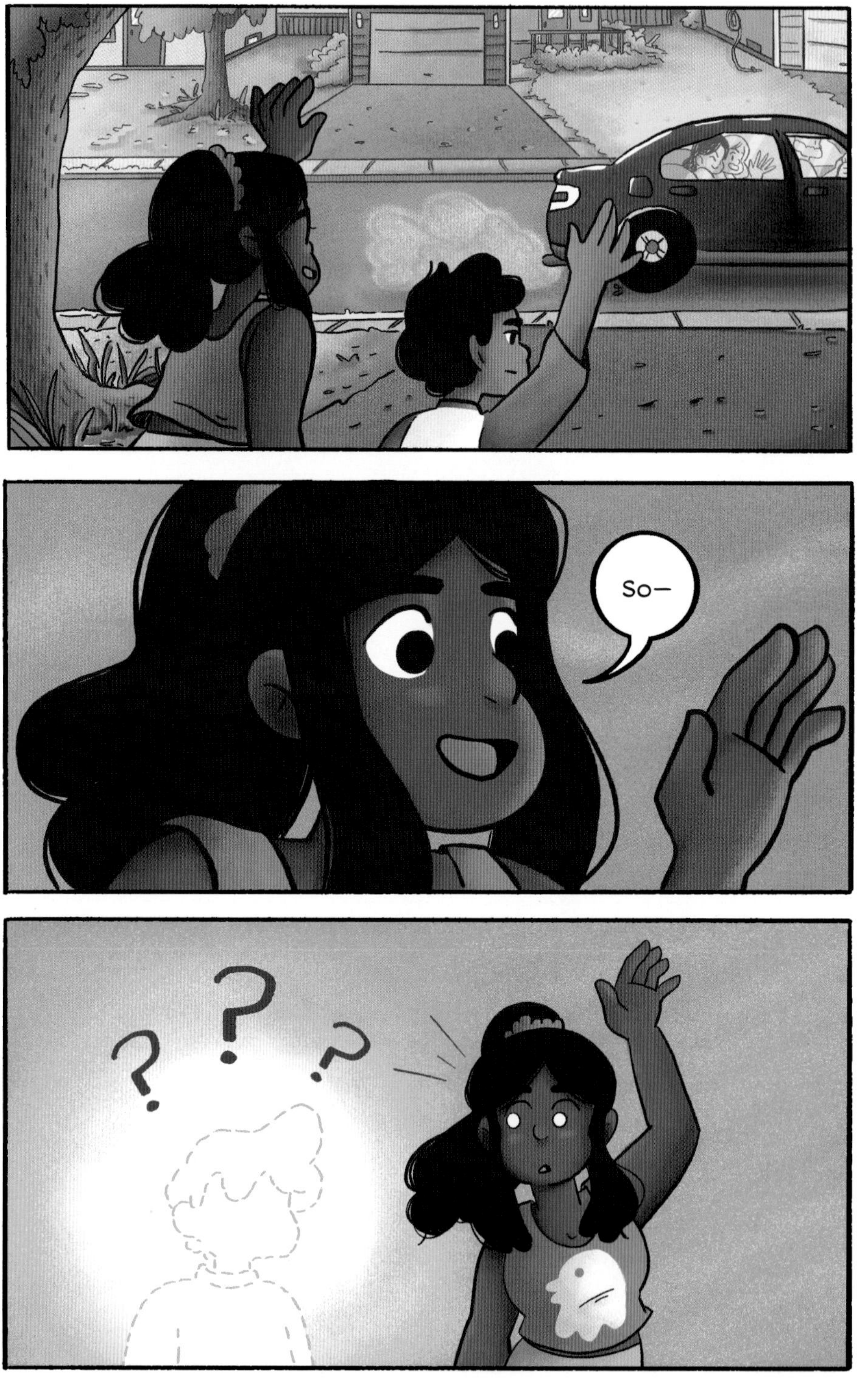
So—
? ? ?

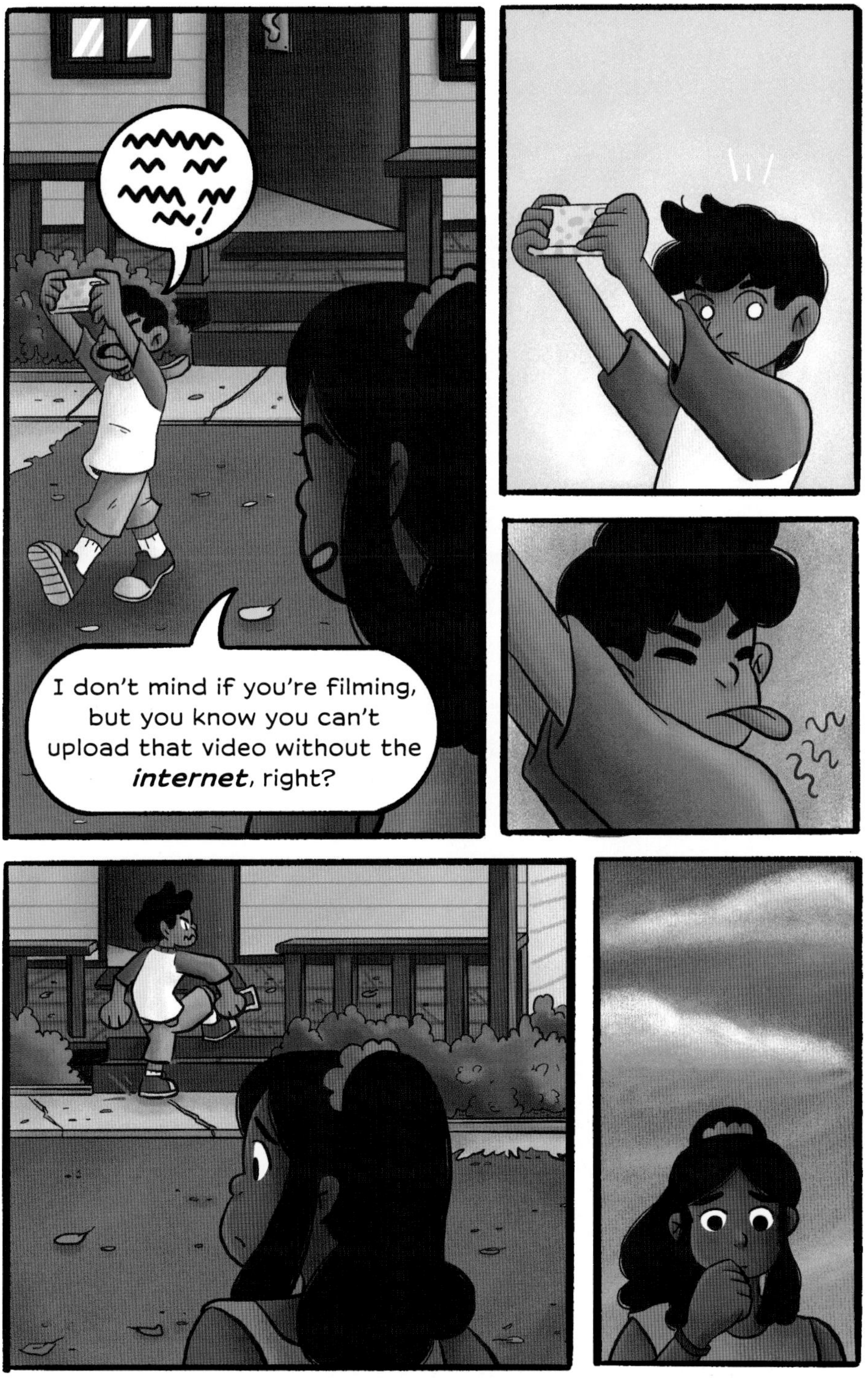
I don't mind if you're filming, but you know you can't upload that video without the ***internet***, right?

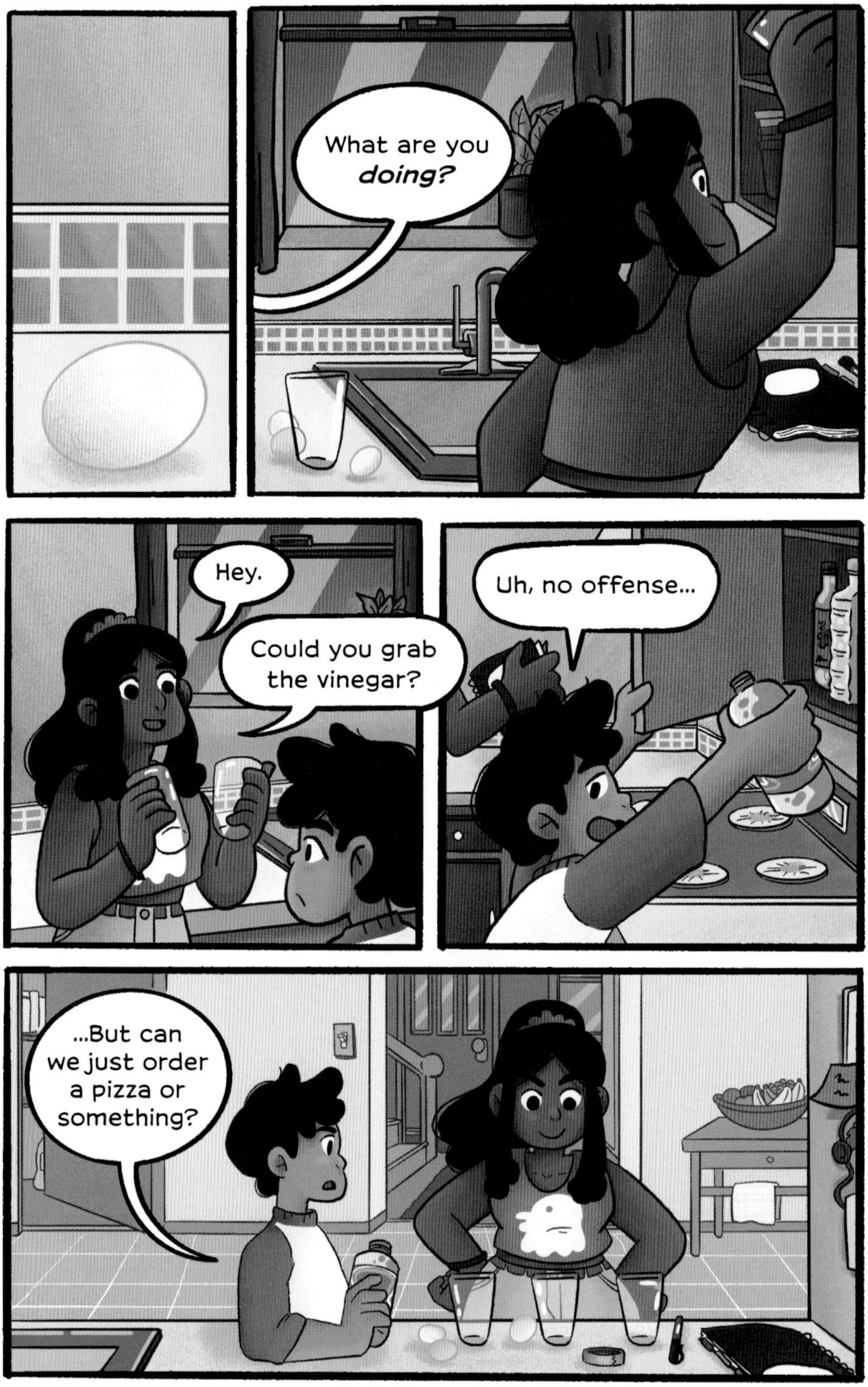
What are you *doing?*
Hey.
Could you grab the vinegar?
Uh, no offense...
...But can we just order a pizza or something?

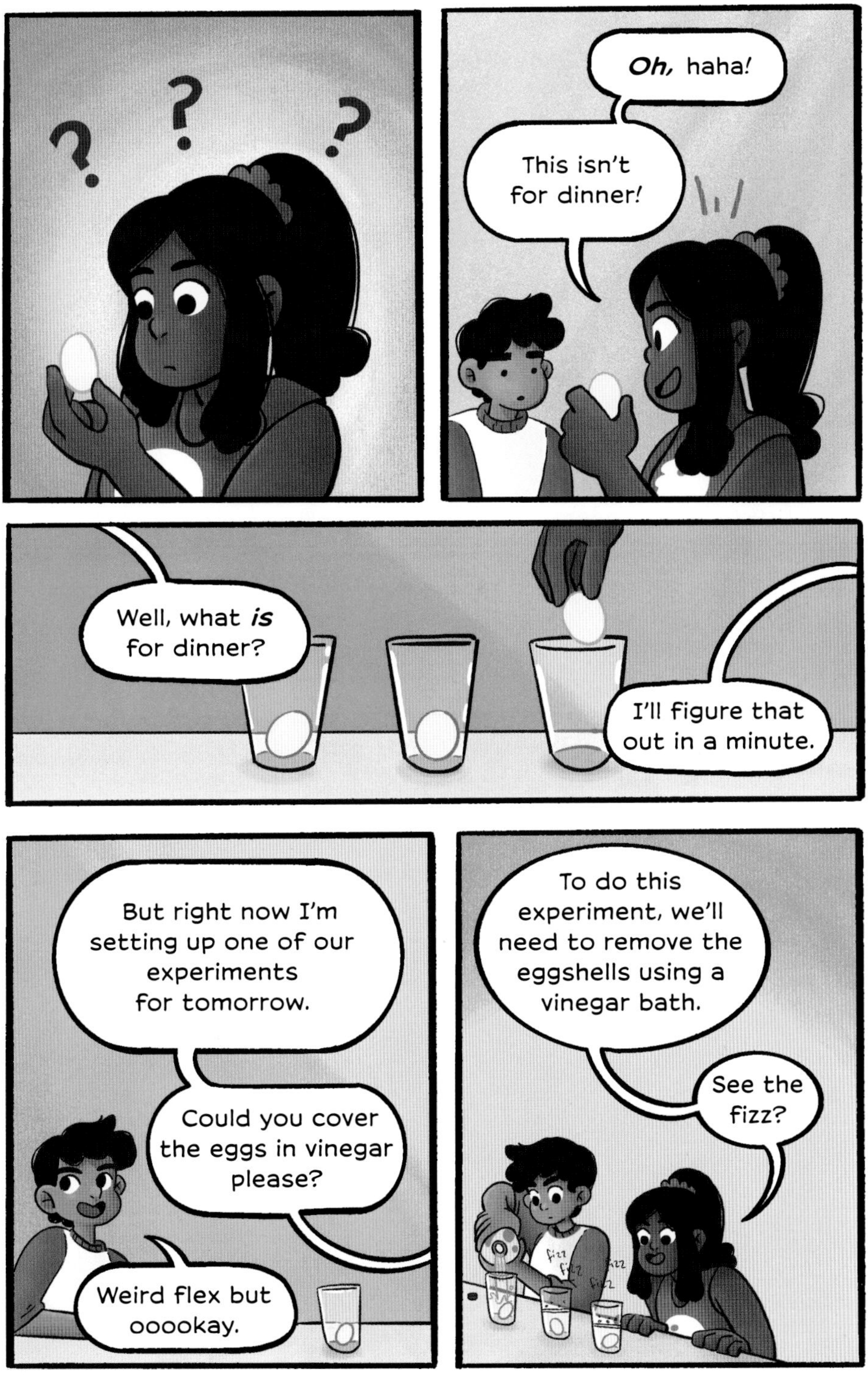
Oh, haha!
This isn't for dinner!
Well, what is for dinner?
I'll figure that out in a minute.
But right now I'm setting up one of our experiments for tomorrow.
Could you cover the eggs in vinegar please?
Weird flex but ooookay.
To do this experiment, we'll need to remove the eggshells using a vinegar bath.
See the fizz?
fizz
fizz
fizz
fizz

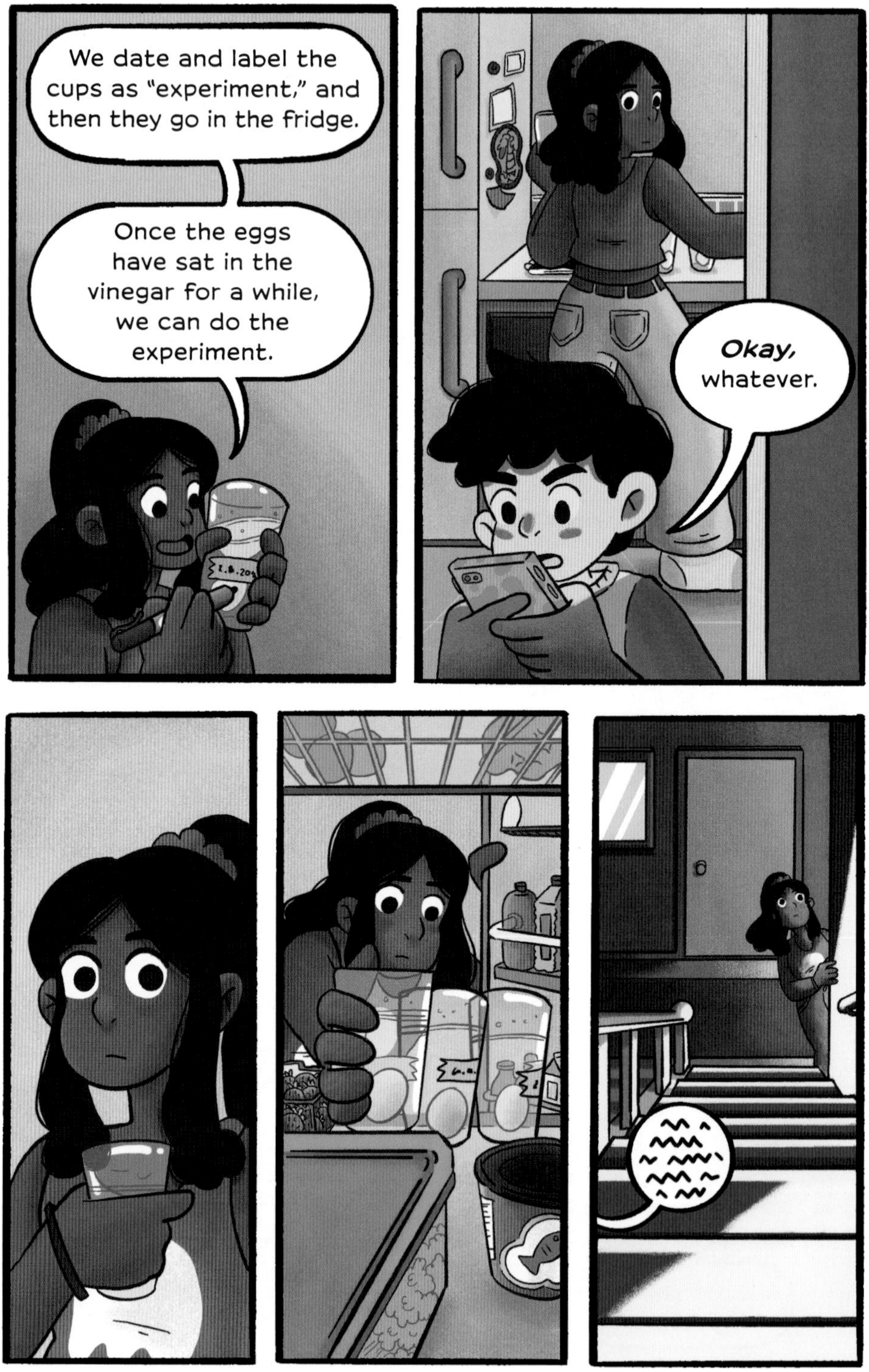
We date and label the cups as "experiment," and then they go in the fridge.
Once the eggs have sat in the vinegar for a while, we can do the experiment.
Okay, whatever.

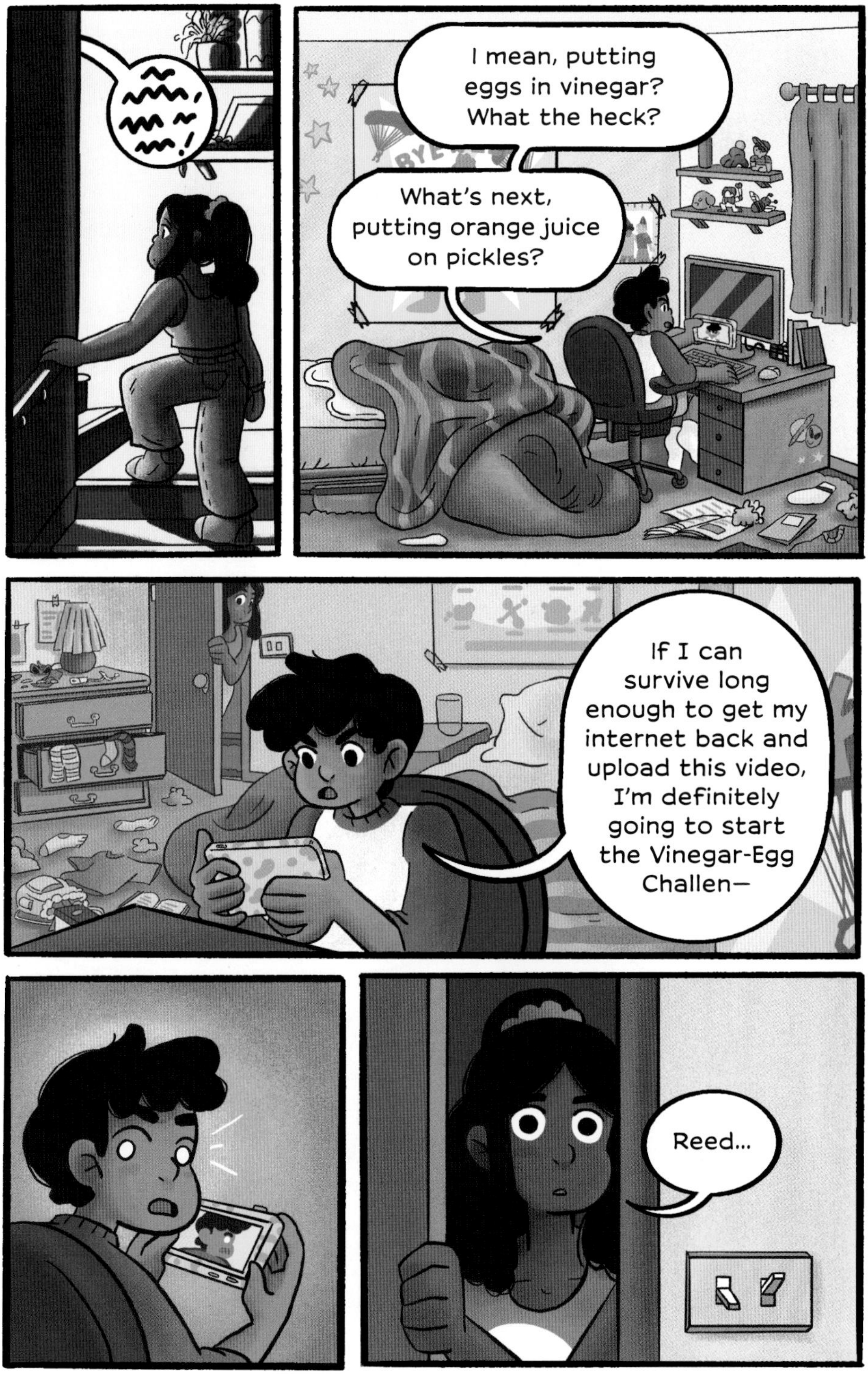
I mean, putting eggs in vinegar? What the heck?
What's next, putting orange juice on pickles?
If I can survive long enough to get my internet back and upload this video, I'm definitely going to start the Vinegar-Egg Challen—
Reed...

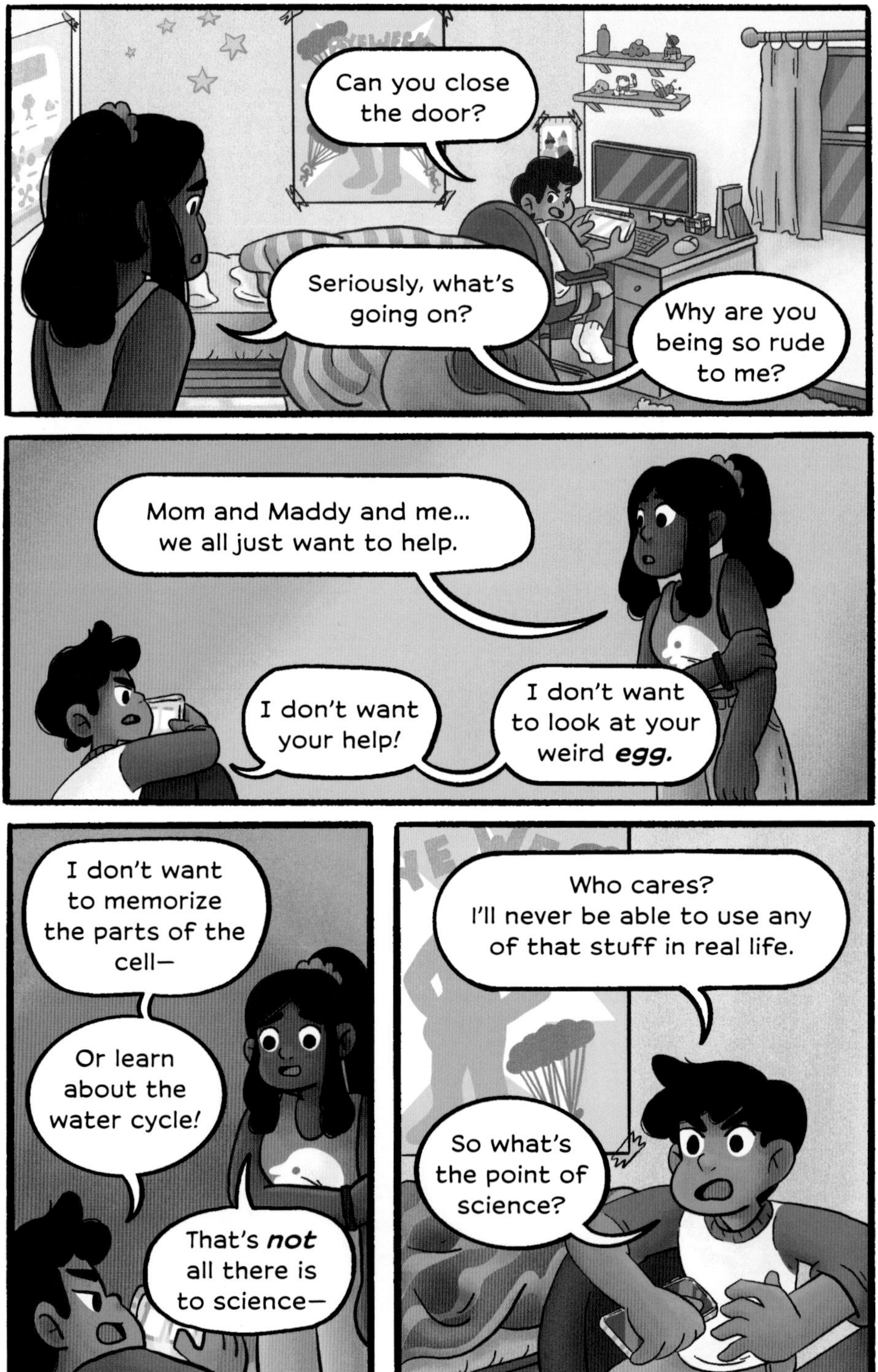
Can you close the door?
Seriously, what's going on?
Why are you being so rude to me?
Mom and Maddy and me... we all just want to help.
I don't want your help!
I don't want to look at your weird ***egg.***
I don't want to memorize the parts of the cell—
Or learn about the water cycle!
That's ***not*** all there is to science—
Who cares? I'll never be able to use any of that stuff in real life.
So what's the point of science?

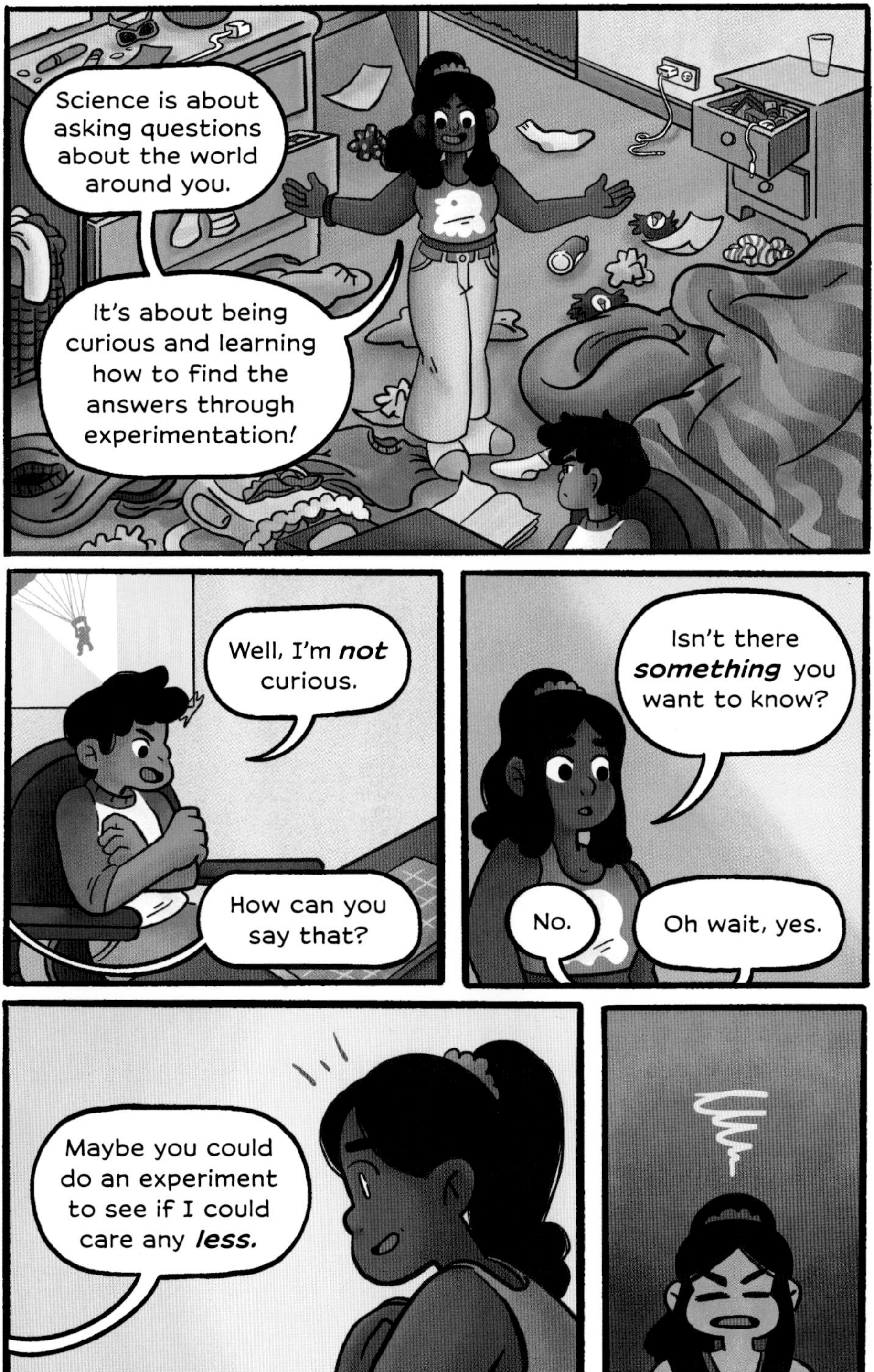
Science is about asking questions about the world around you.
It's about being curious and learning how to find the answers through experimentation!
Well, I'm *not* curious.
How can you say that?
Isn't there *something* you want to know?
No.
Oh wait, yes.
Maybe you could do an experiment to see if I could care any *less.*

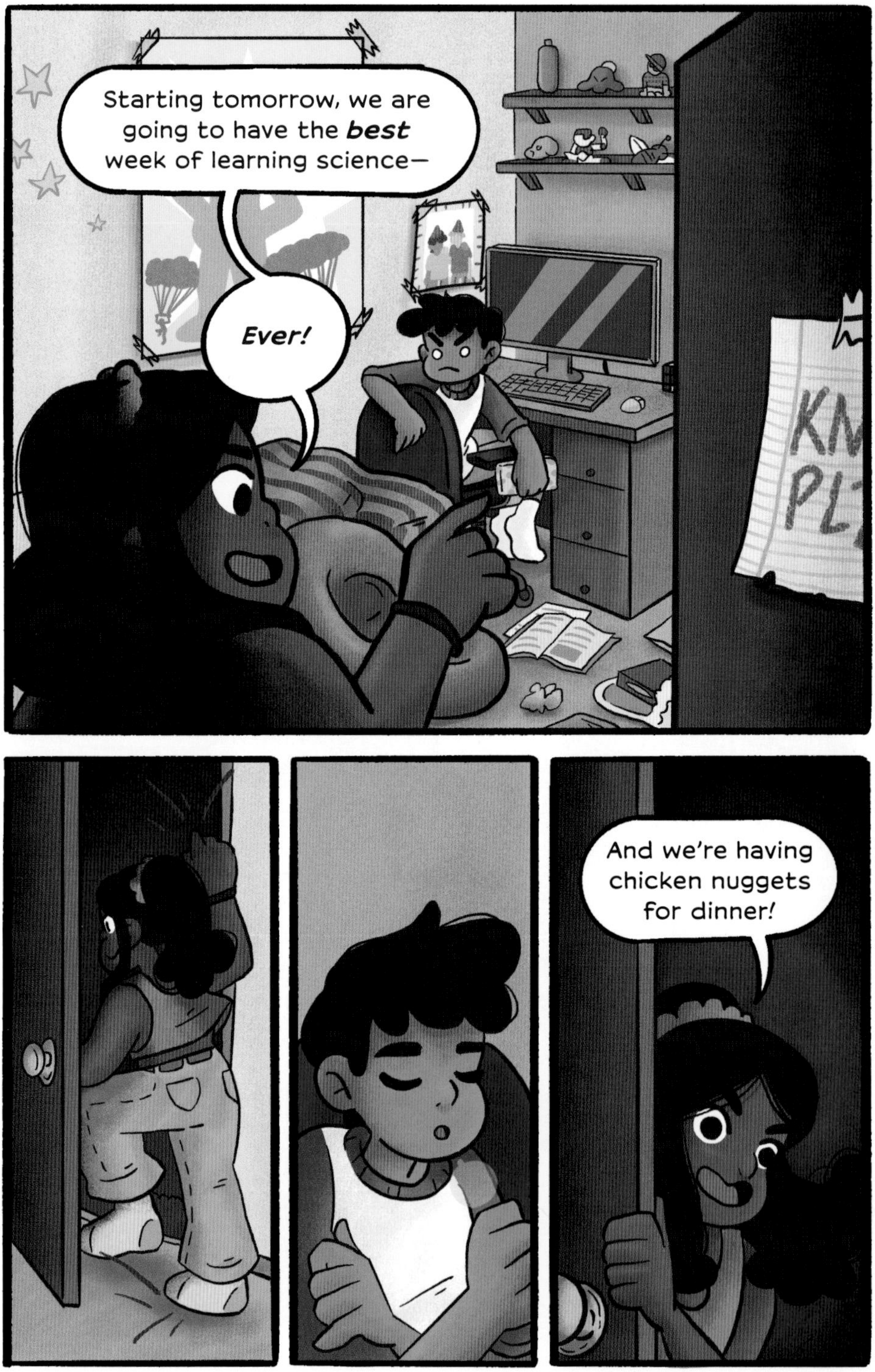
Starting tomorrow, we are going to have the *best* week of learning science—
Ever!
And we're having chicken nuggets for dinner!

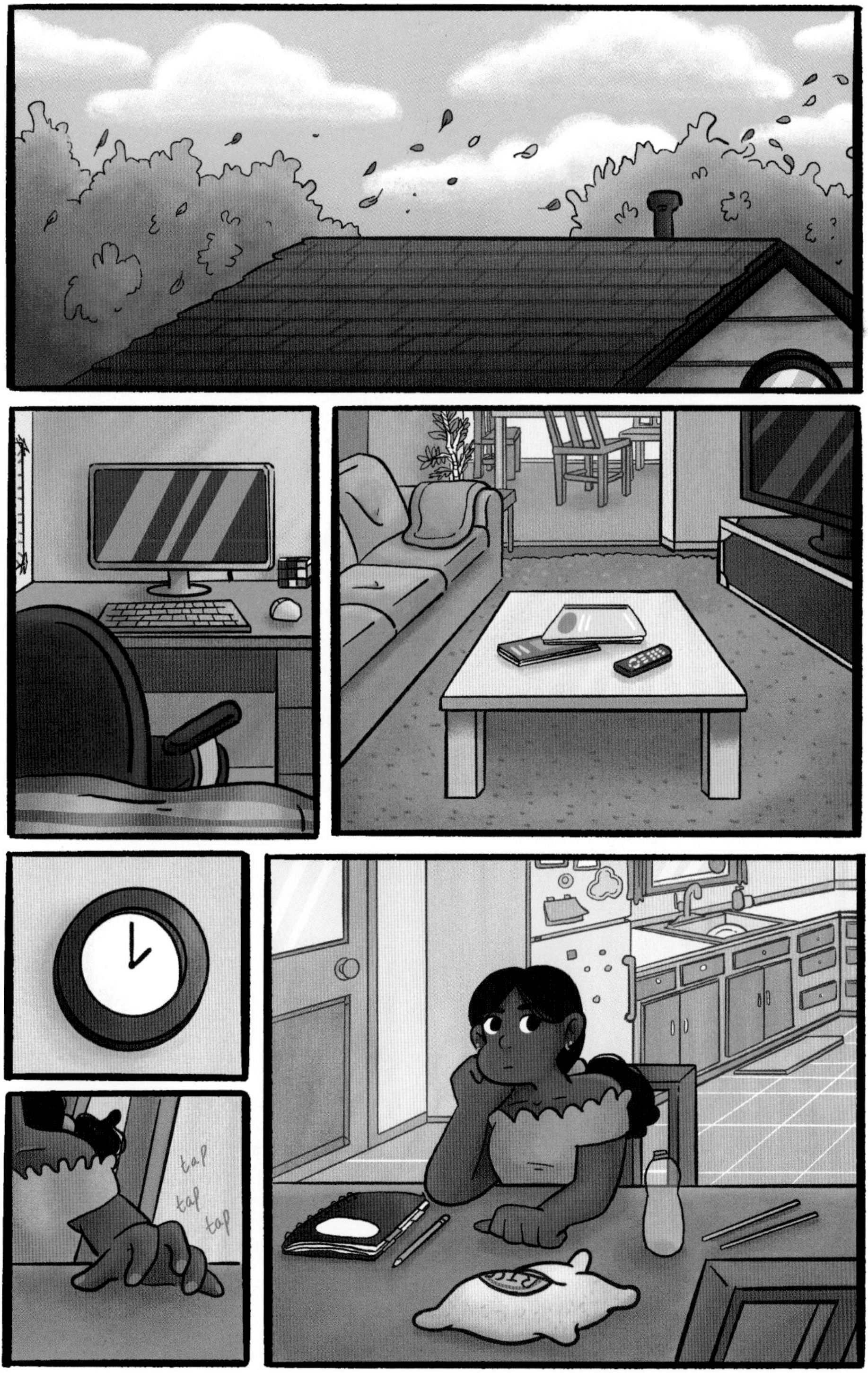
tap
tap
tap

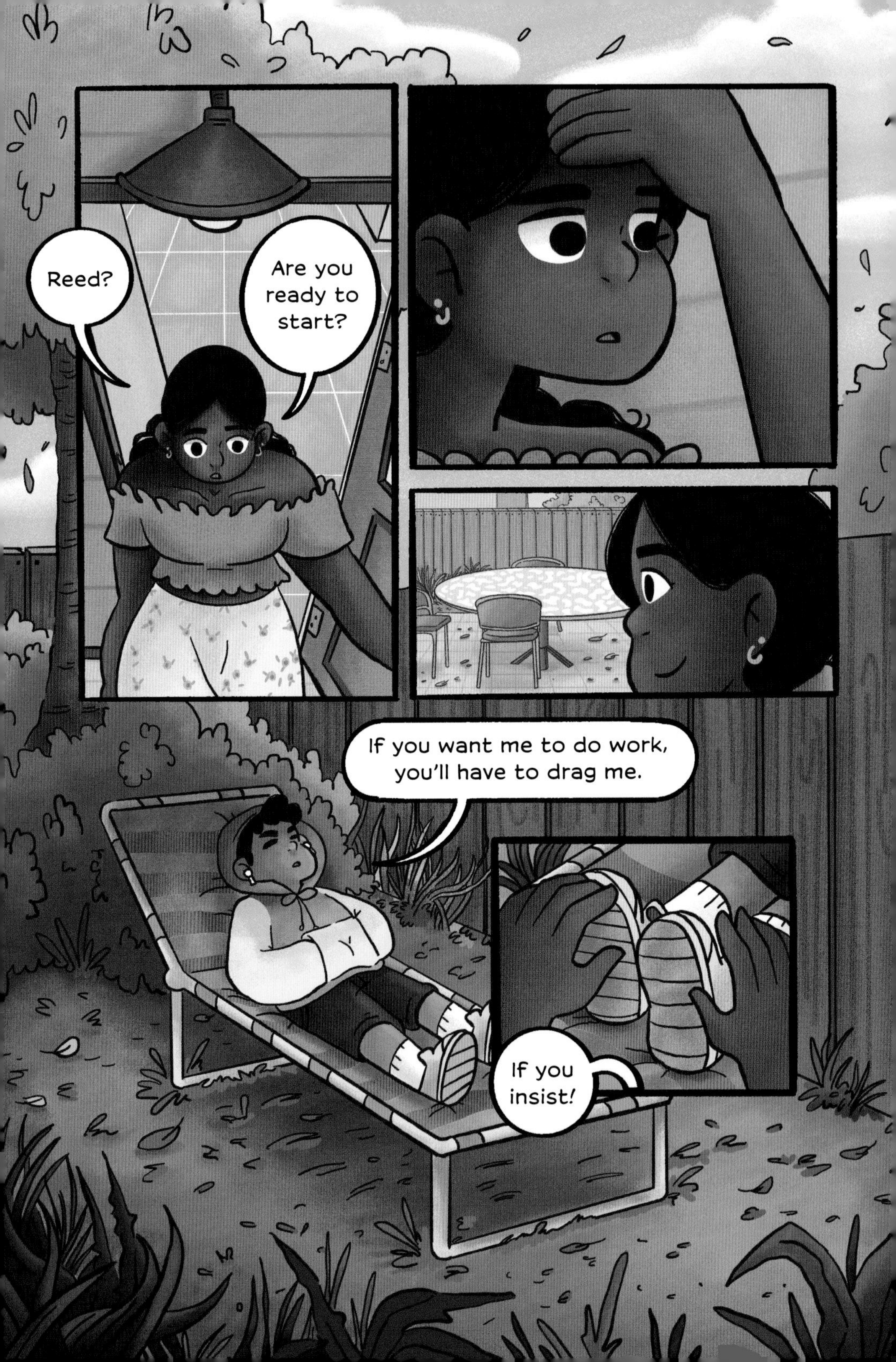
Reed?
Are you ready to start?
If you want me to do work, you'll have to drag me.
If you insist!

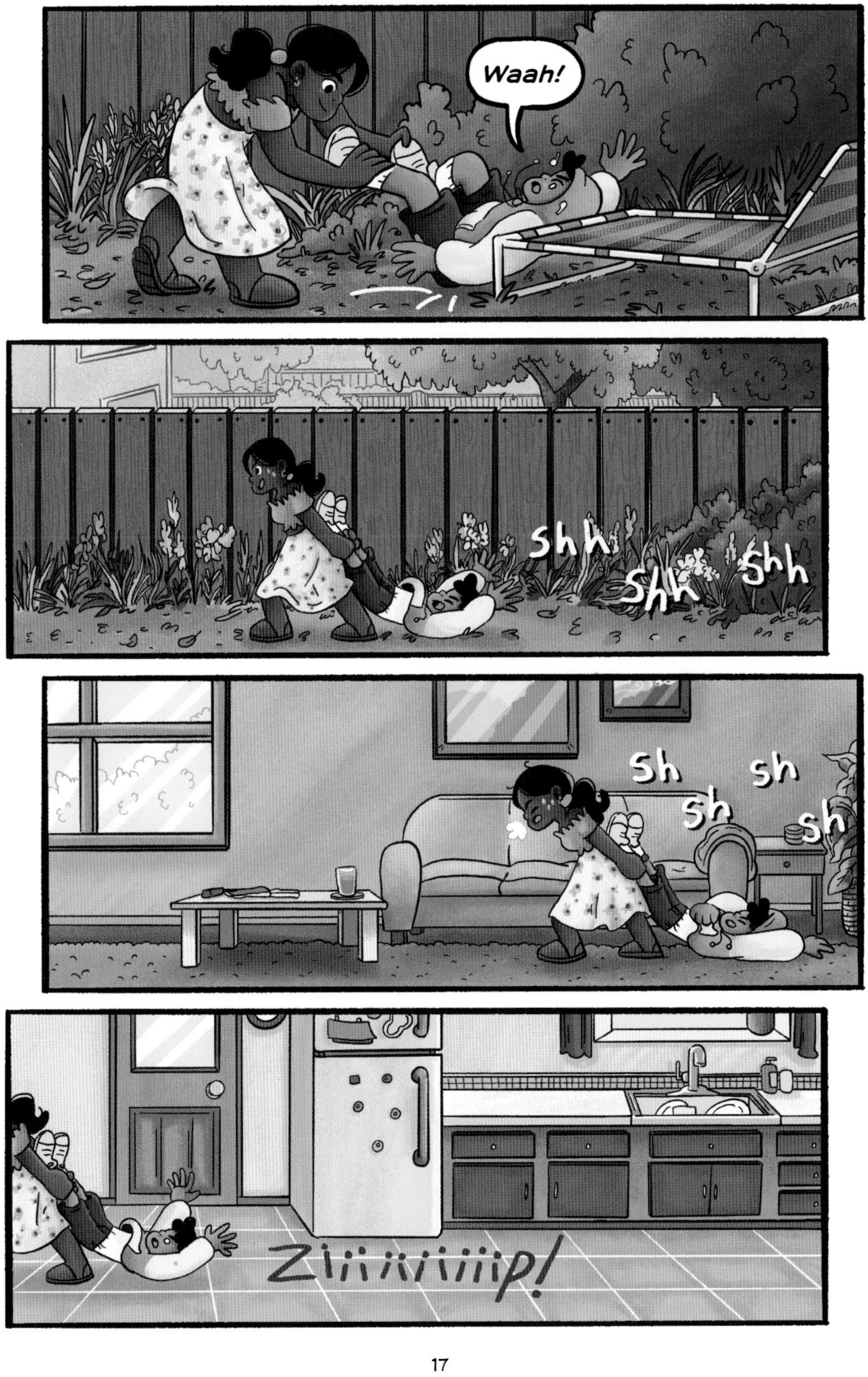
Waah!
Shh
Shh
Shh
Sh
sh
Sh
sh
Ziiiiiiiiiip!

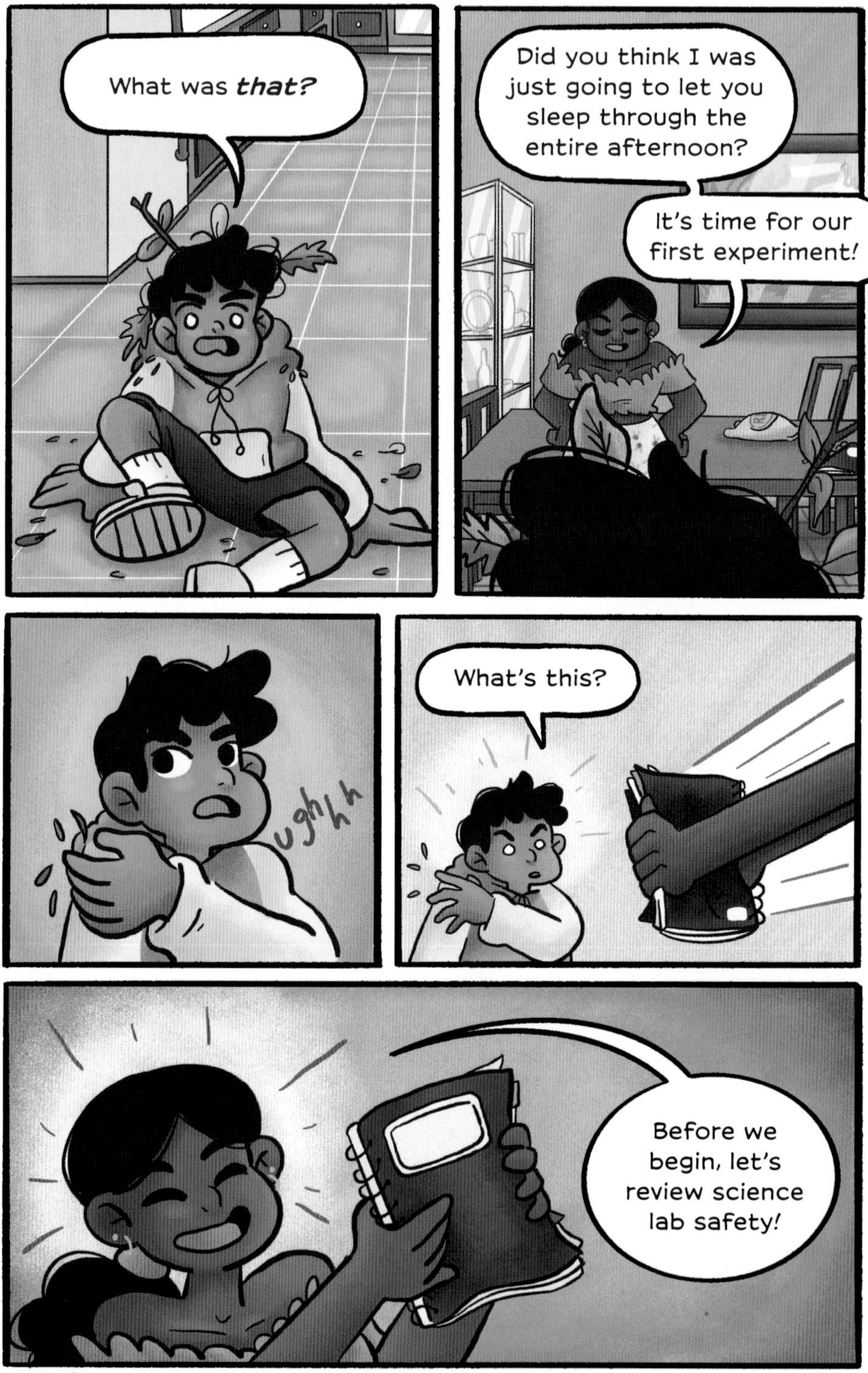
What was *that?*
Did you think I was just going to let you sleep through the entire afternoon?
It's time for our first experiment!
ughhh
What's this?
Before we begin, let's review science lab safety!

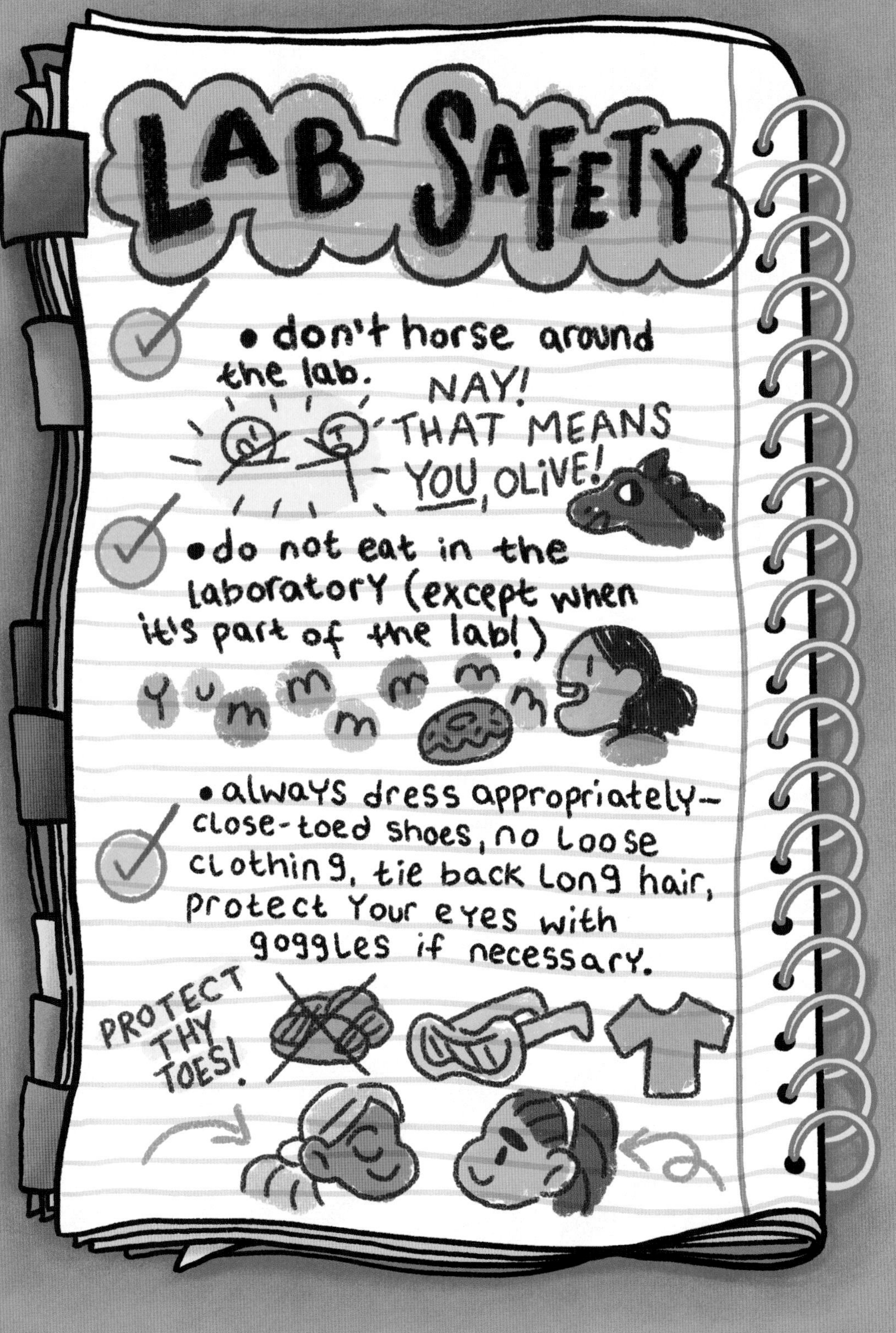
LAB SAFETY
• don't horse around the lab.
NAY! THAT MEANS YOU, OLIVE!
• do not eat in the laboratory (except when it's part of the lab!)
yummmm
• always dress appropriately— close-toed shoes, no loose clothing, tie back long hair, protect your eyes with goggles if necessary.
PROTECT THY TOES!

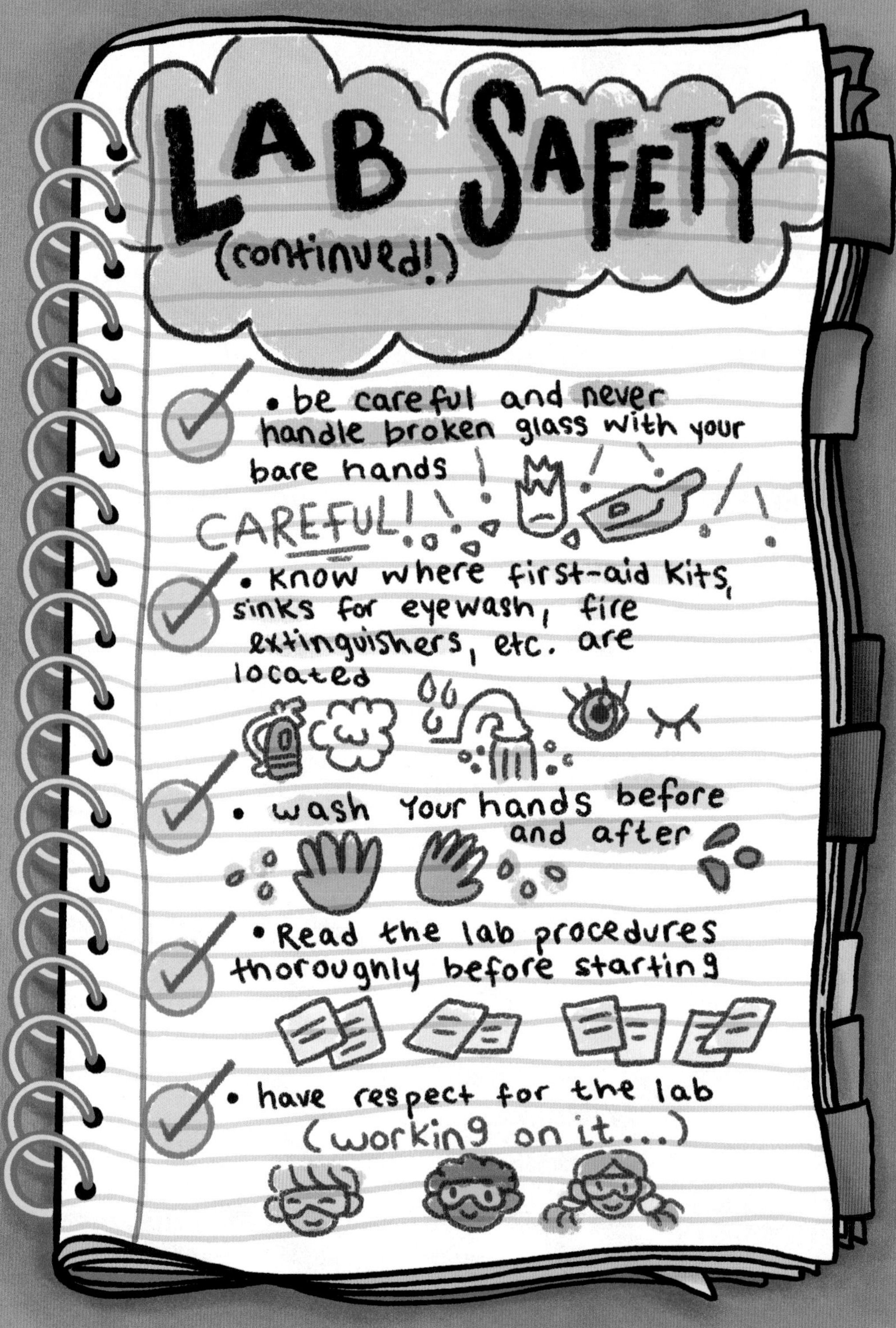
LAB SAFETY
(continued!)
• be careful and never handle broken glass with your bare hands
CAREFUL!
• know where first-aid kits, sinks for eyewash, fire extinguishers, etc. are located
• wash your hands before and after
• Read the lab procedures thorougnly before starting
• have respect for the lab
(working on it...)

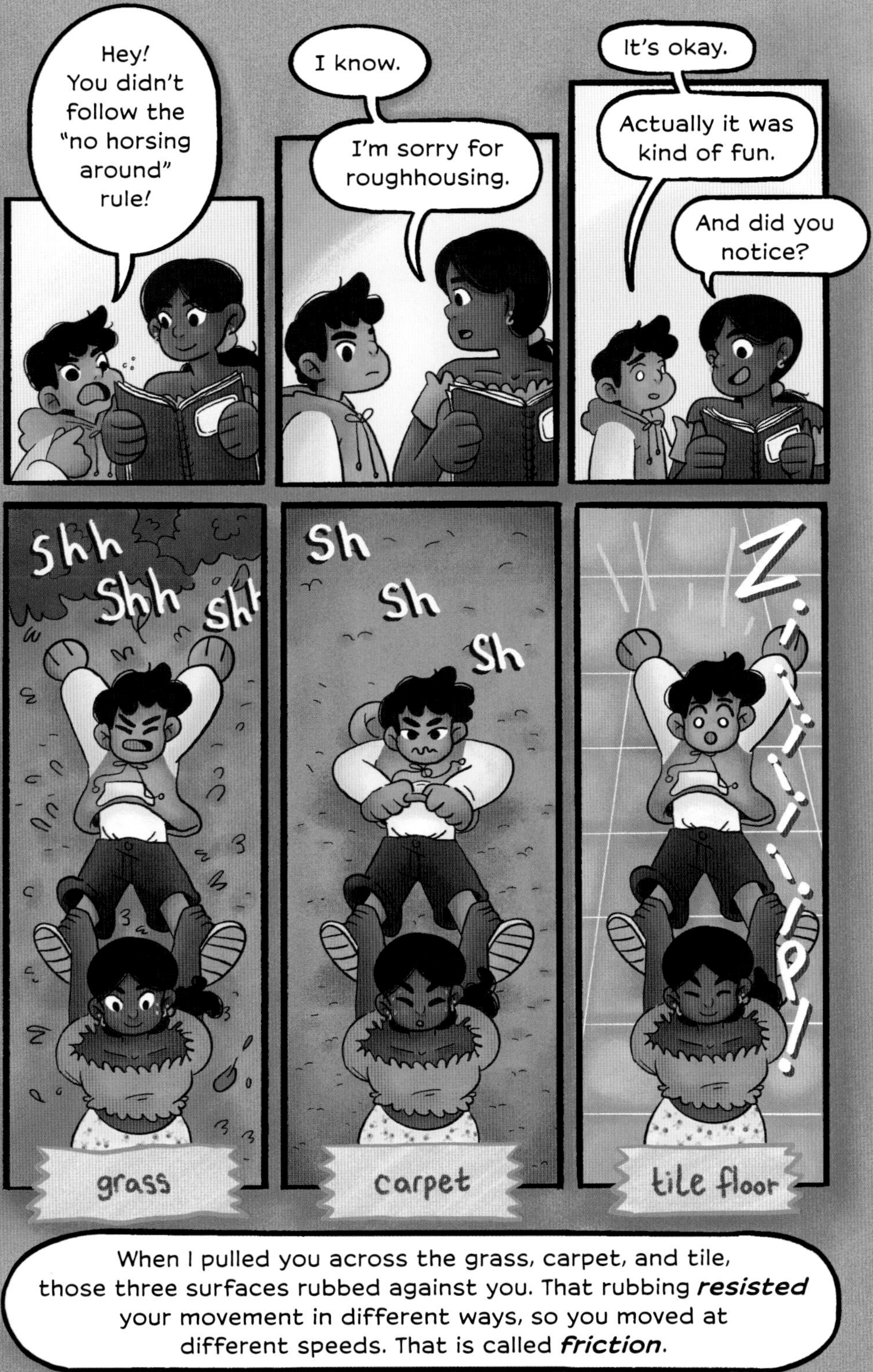
Hey! You didn't follow the "no horsing around" rule!
I know.
I'm sorry for roughhousing.
It's okay.
Actually it was kind of fun.
And did you notice?
Shh
Shh
Shh
grass
Sh
Sh
Sh
carpet
Zi-i-i-i-i-p!
tile floor
When I pulled you across the grass, carpet, and tile, those three surfaces rubbed against you. That rubbing *resisted* your movement in different ways, so you moved at different speeds. That is called *friction*.

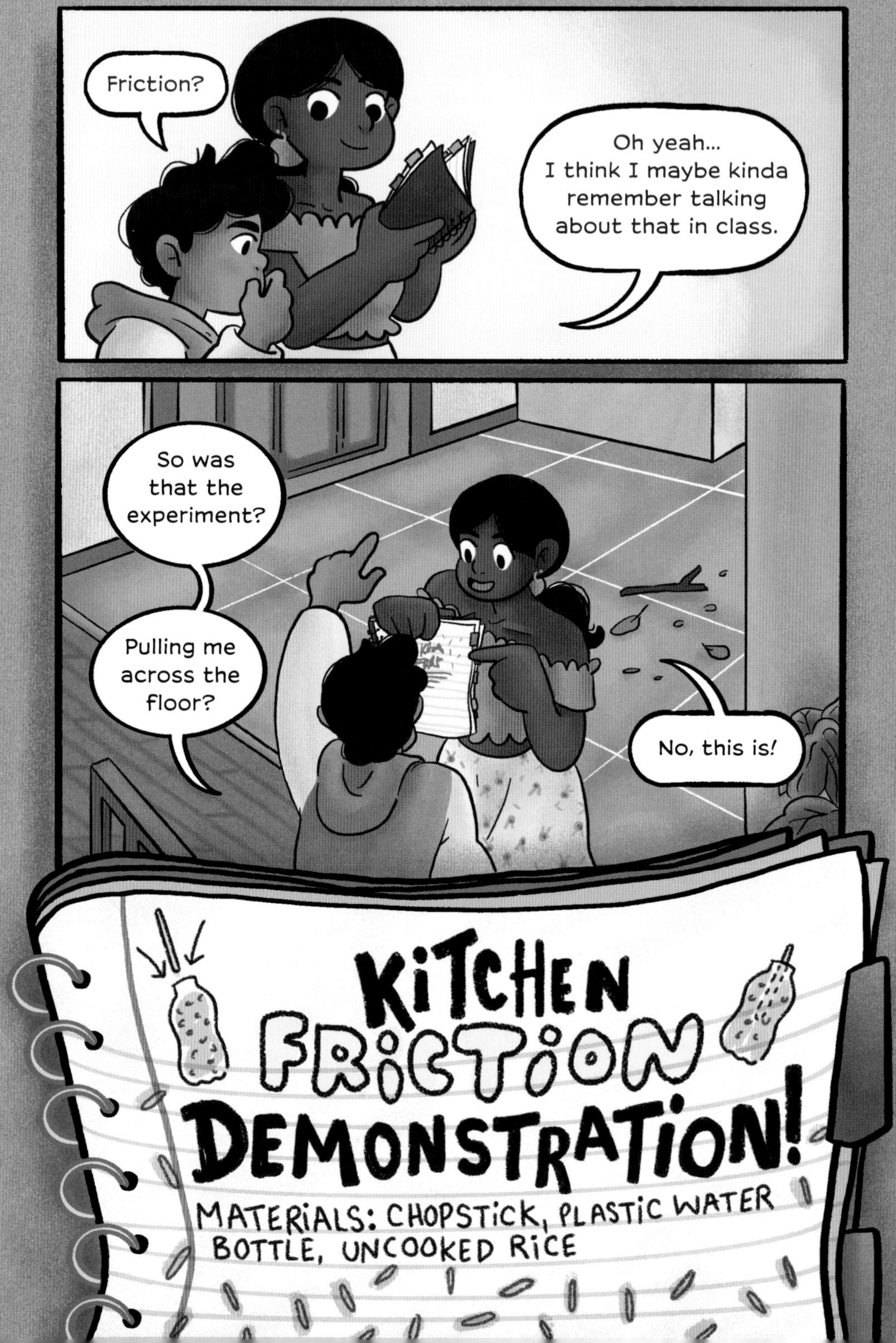
Friction?
Oh yeah... I think I maybe kinda remember talking about that in class.
So was that the experiment?
Pulling me across the floor?
No, this is!
KITCHEN FRICTION DEMONSTRATION!
MATERIALS: CHOPSTICK, PLASTIC WATER BOTTLE, UNCOOKED RICE

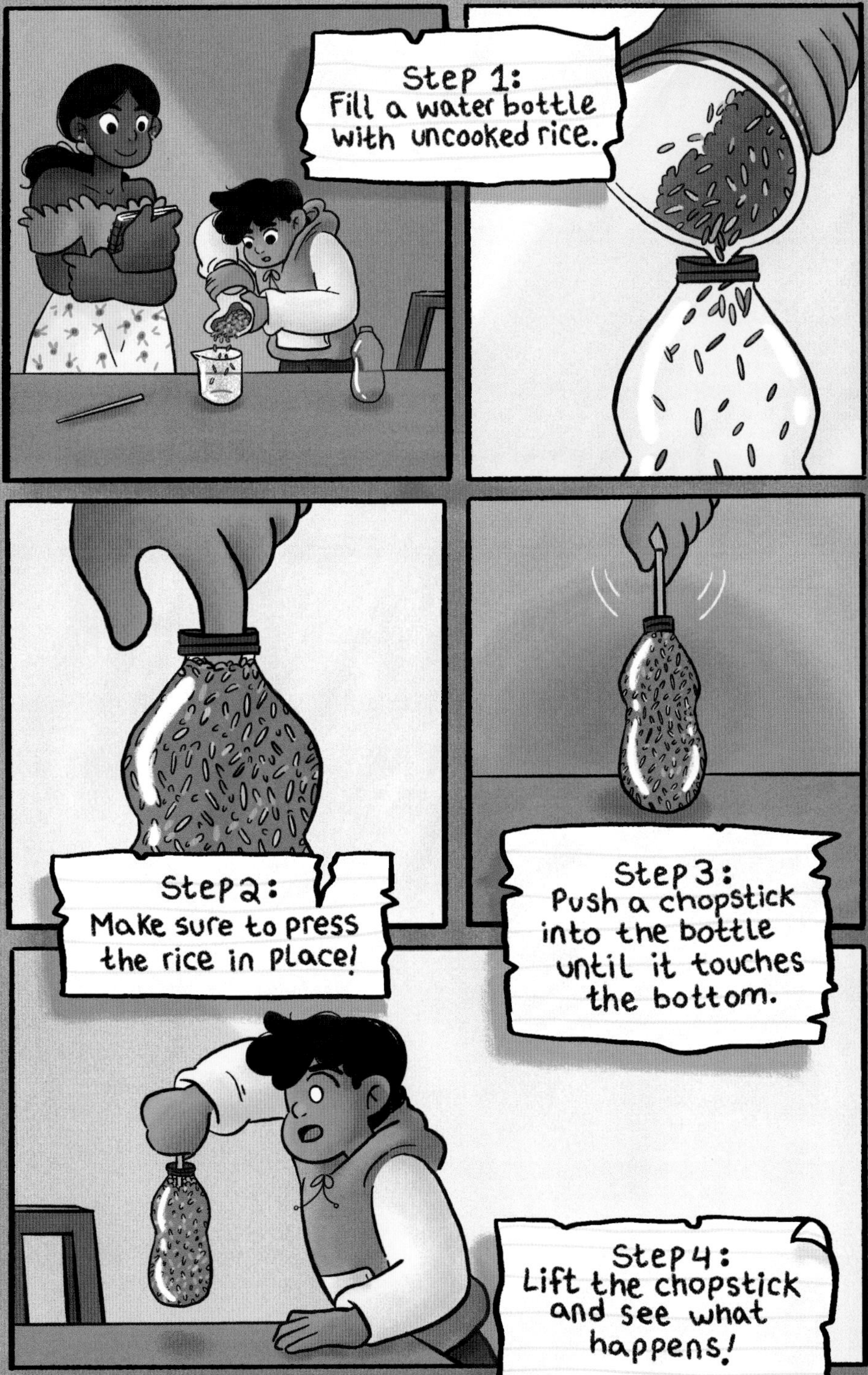
Step 1:
Fill a water bottle with uncooked rice.
Step 2:
Make sure to press the rice in place!
Step 3:
Push a chopstick into the bottle until it touches the bottom.
Step 4:
Lift the chopstick and see what happens!

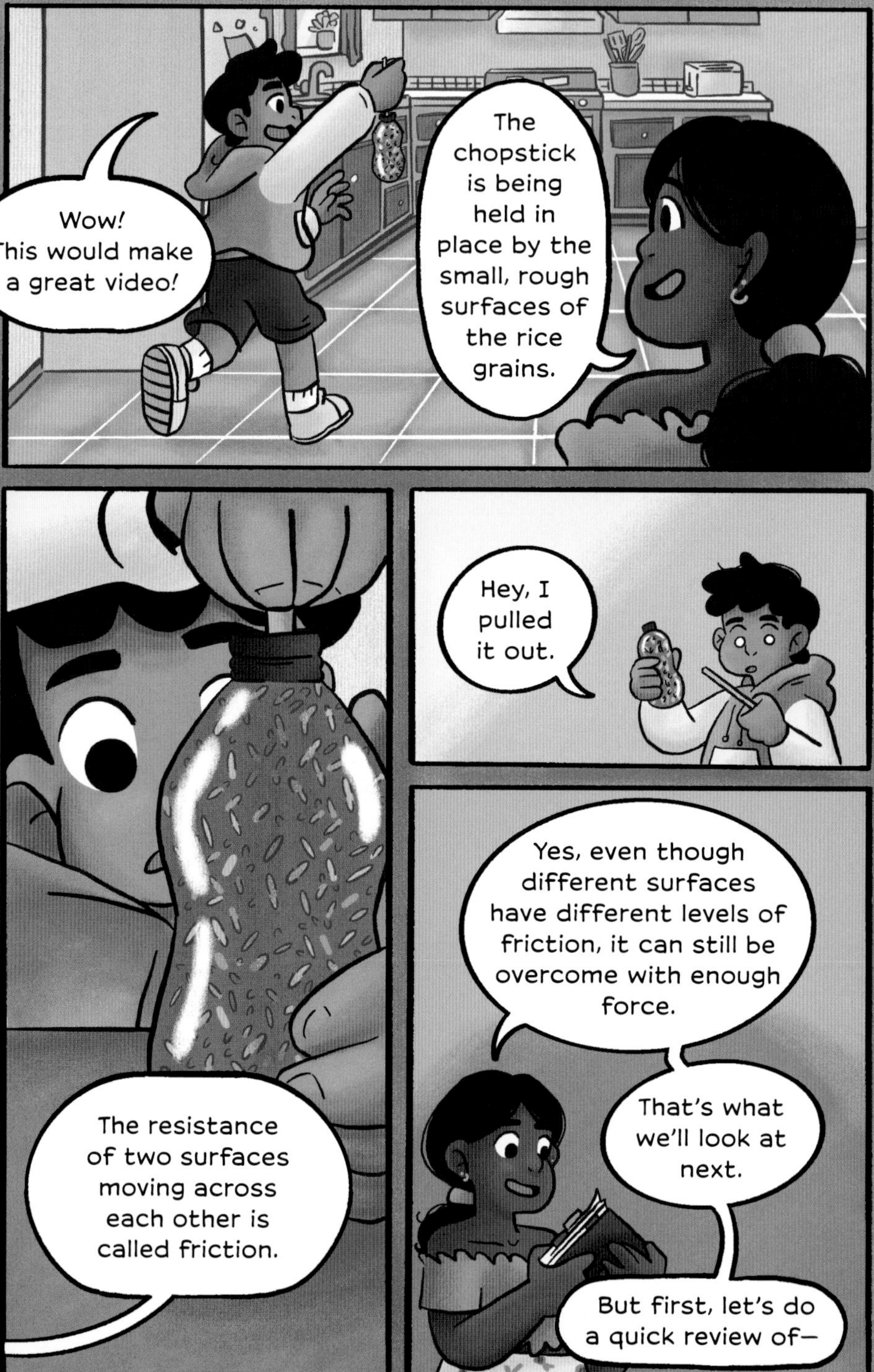
Wow! This would make a great video!
The chopstick is being held in place by the small, rough surfaces of the rice grains.
The resistance of two surfaces moving across each other is called friction.
Hey, I pulled it out.
Yes, even though different surfaces have different levels of friction, it can still be overcome with enough force.
That's what we'll look at next.
But first, let's do a quick review of—

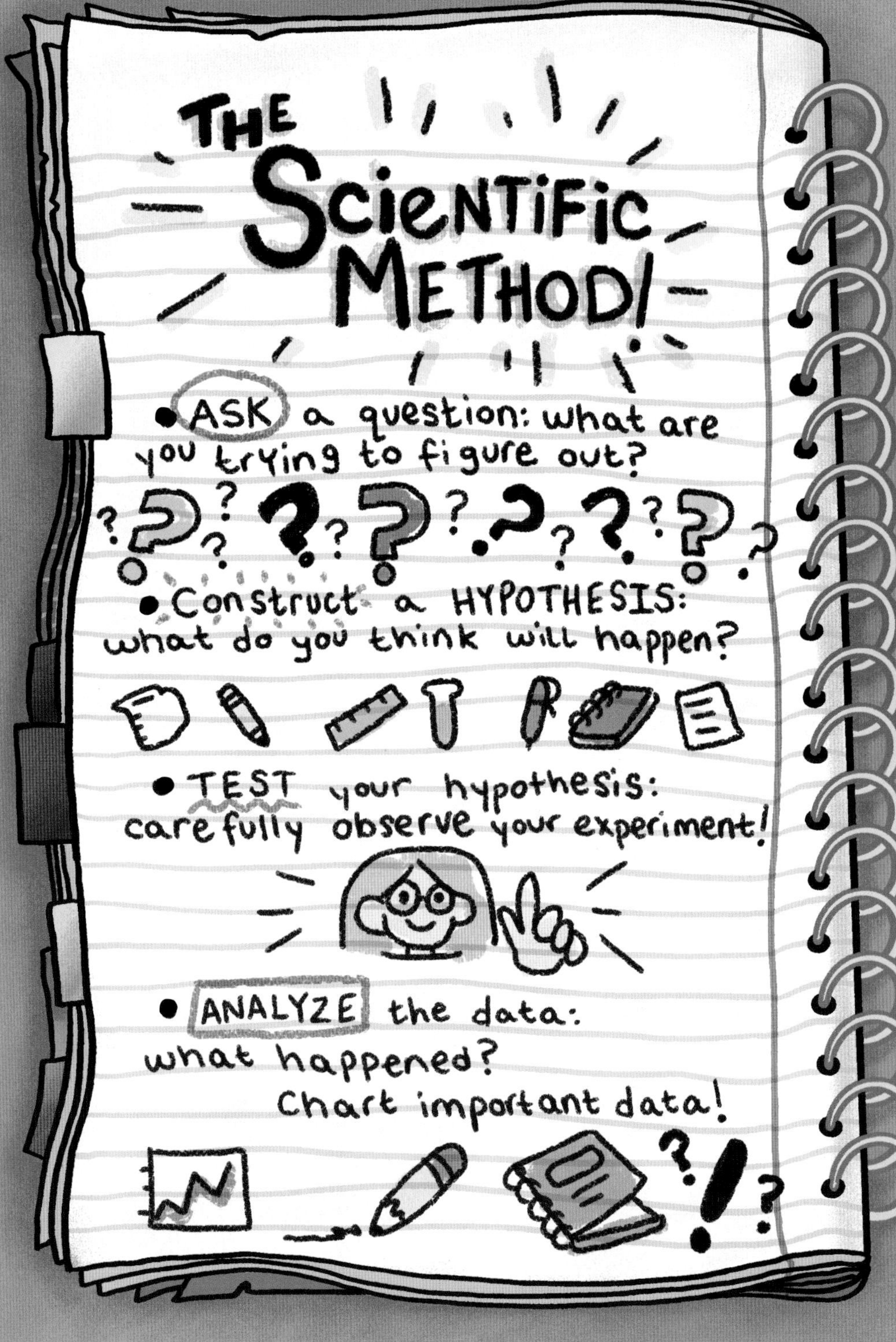
THE SCIENTIFIC METHOD!
• ASK a question: what are you trying to figure out?
• Construct a HYPOTHESIS: what do you think will happen?
• TEST your hypothesis: carefully observe your experiment!
• ANALYZE the data: what happened? Chart important data!

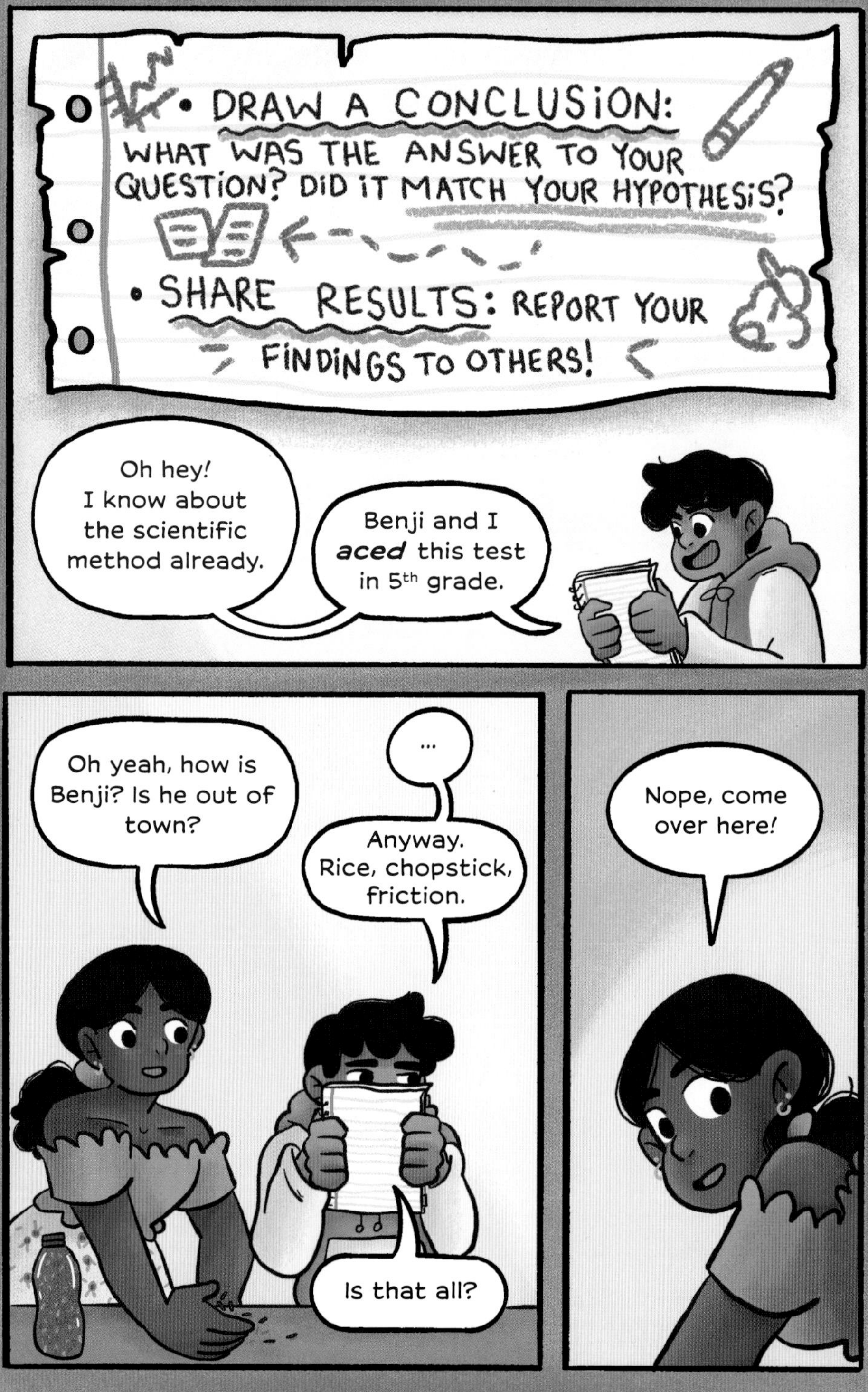
• DRAW A CONCLUSION:
WHAT WAS THE ANSWER TO YOUR QUESTION? DID IT MATCH YOUR HYPOTHESIS?
• SHARE RESULTS: REPORT YOUR FINDINGS TO OTHERS!
Oh hey! I know about the scientific method already.
Benji and I *aced* this test in 5th grade.
Oh yeah, how is Benji? Is he out of town?
...
Anyway. Rice, chopstick, friction.
Is that all?
Nope, come over here!

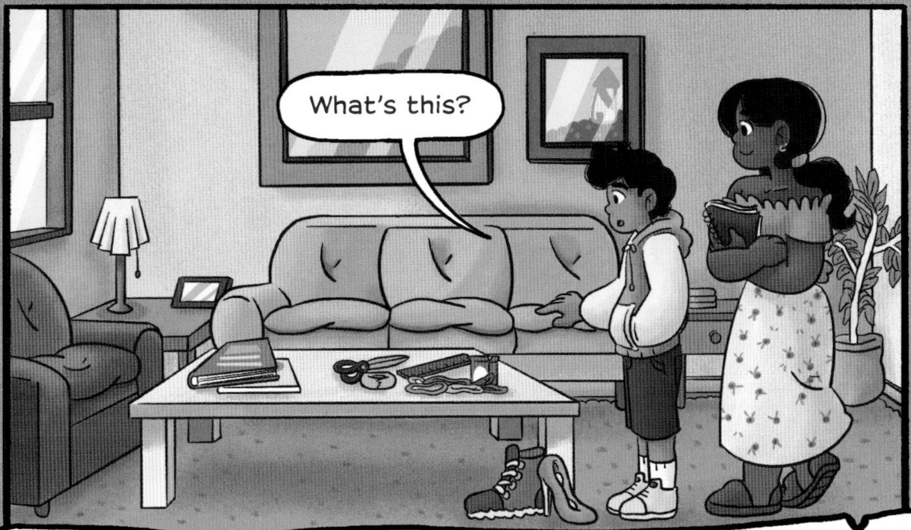
What's this?

GET A GRIP

FRICTION EXPERIMENT

* **Questions:** Do different surfaces affect the amount of friction on a shoe? Which surfaces provide the most and least friction?

* **Materials:** masking tape, several rubber bands of the same size, scissors, shoe(s), different surfaces, ruler

Procedures:

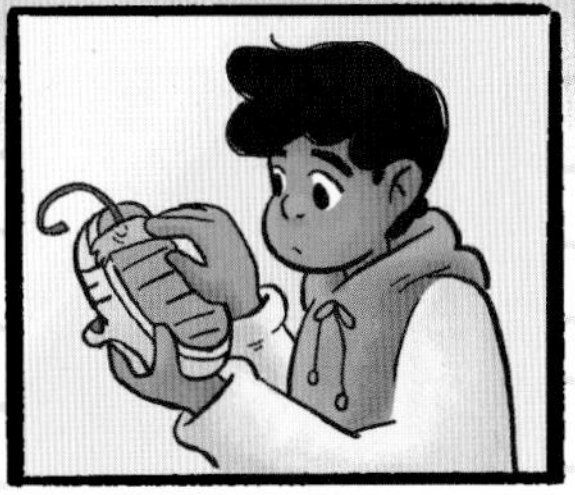

Step 1: cut open a rubber band, then use a piece of masking tape to tape one end to the bottom of a shoe, at the toe.

Step 2: Place your shoe on your first test surface. For example: carpet. Place a ruler next to it.

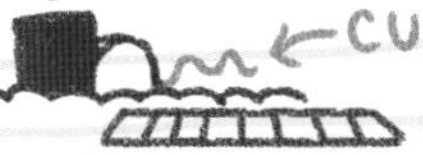
shoe
cut rubber band
ruler

Step 3: Now carefully stretch the rubber band until the shoe moves. How far was it able to stretch before the shoe moved?

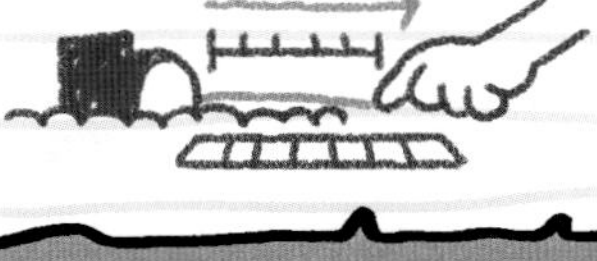
PULL

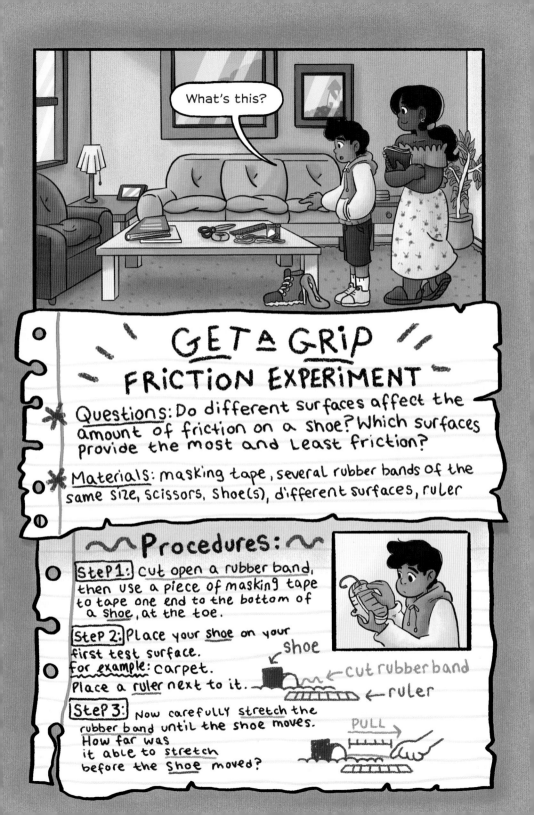

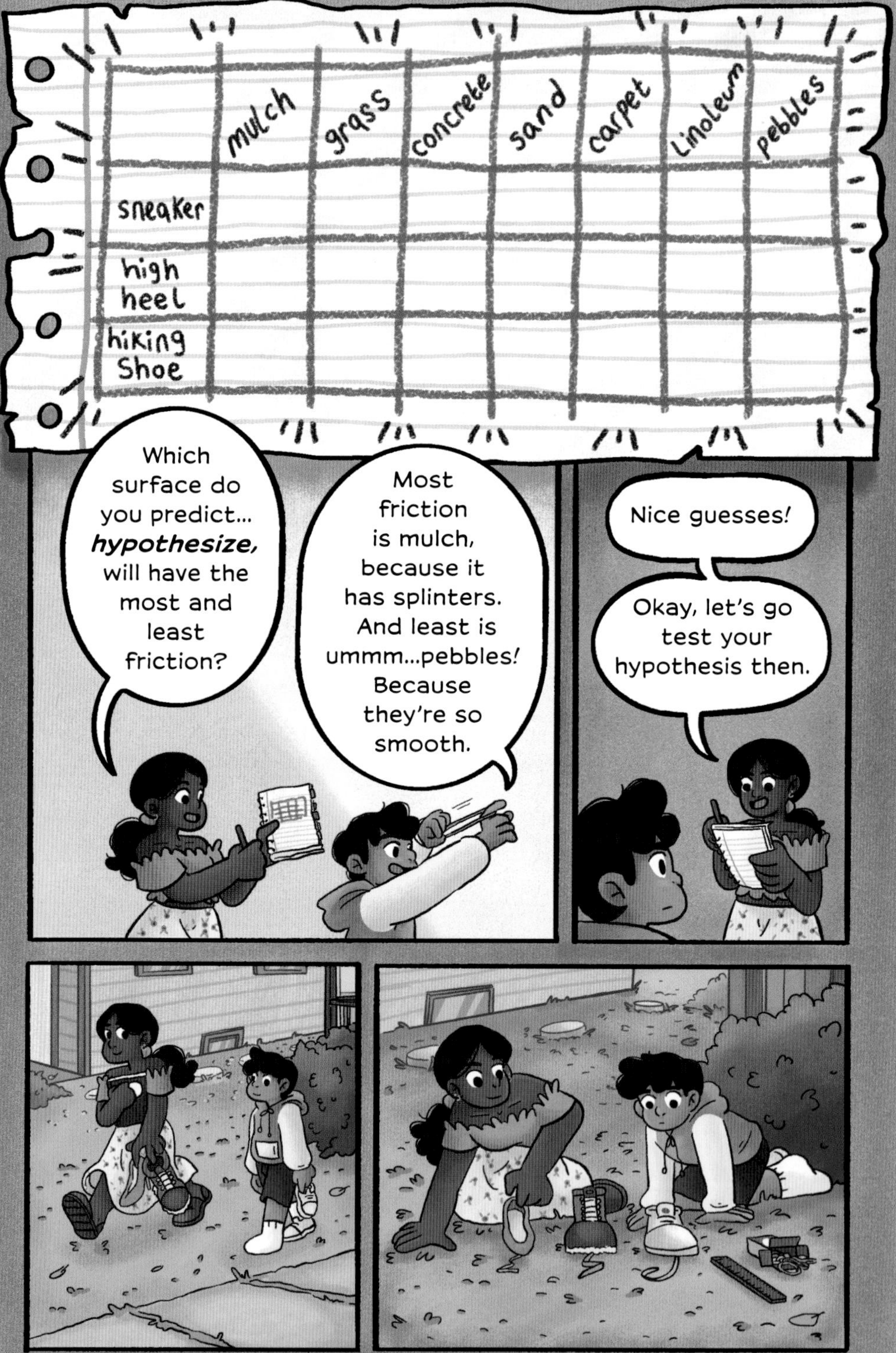
mulch
grass
concrete
sand
carpet
Linoleum
pebbles
sneaker
high heel
hiking Shoe
Which surface do you predict... ***hypothesize,*** will have the most and least friction?
Most friction is mulch, because it has splinters. And least is ummm...pebbles! Because they're so smooth.
Nice guesses!
Okay, let's go test your hypothesis then.

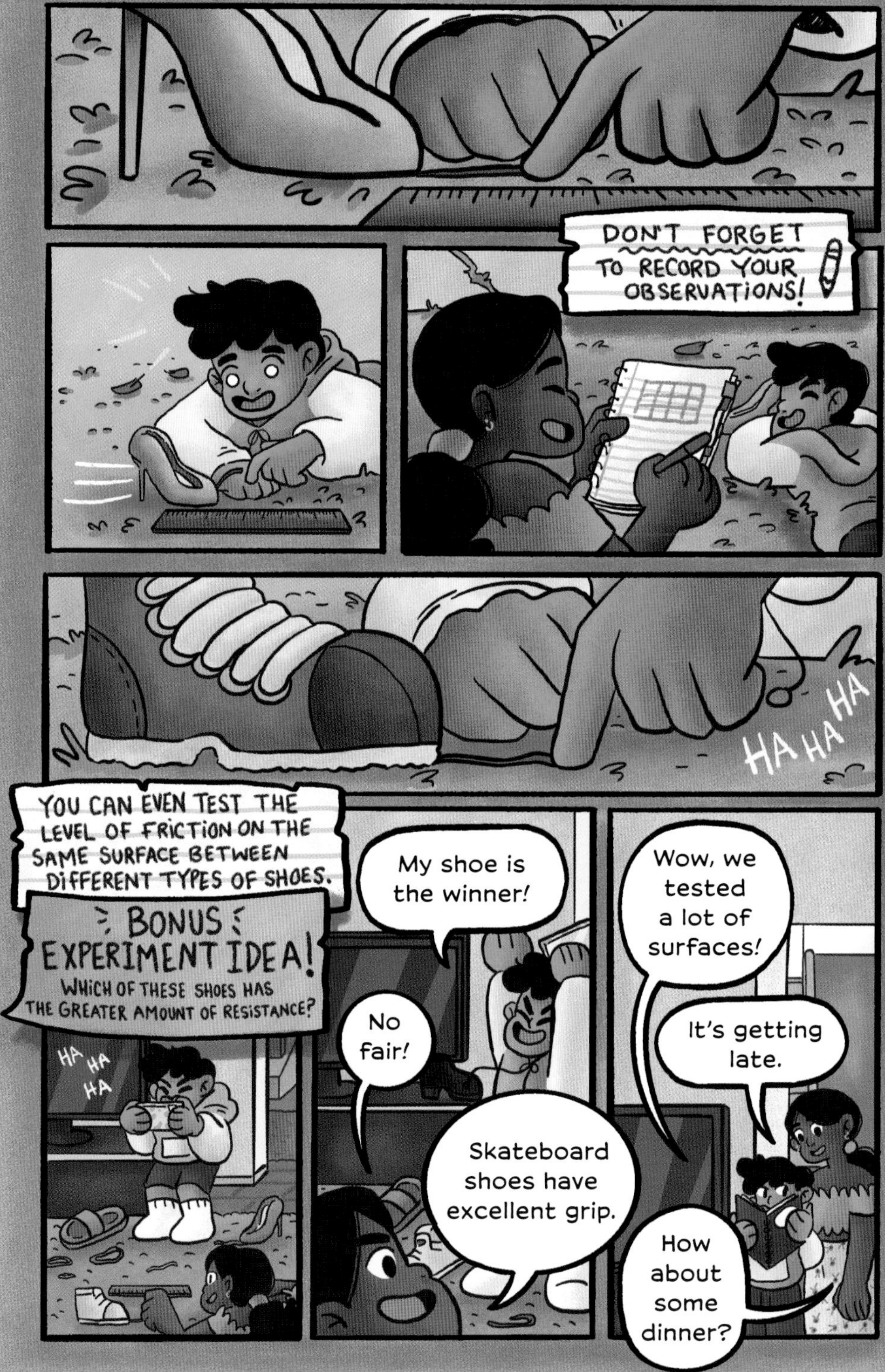
DON'T FORGET TO RECORD YOUR OBSERVATIONS!
HA HA HA
YOU CAN EVEN TEST THE LEVEL OF FRICTION ON THE SAME SURFACE BETWEEN DIFFERENT TYPES OF SHOES.
BONUS EXPERIMENT IDEA!
WHICH OF THESE SHOES HAS THE GREATER AMOUNT OF RESISTANCE?
HA HA HA
My shoe is the winner!
No fair!
Skateboard shoes have excellent grip.
Wow, we tested a lot of surfaces!
It's getting late.
How about some dinner?

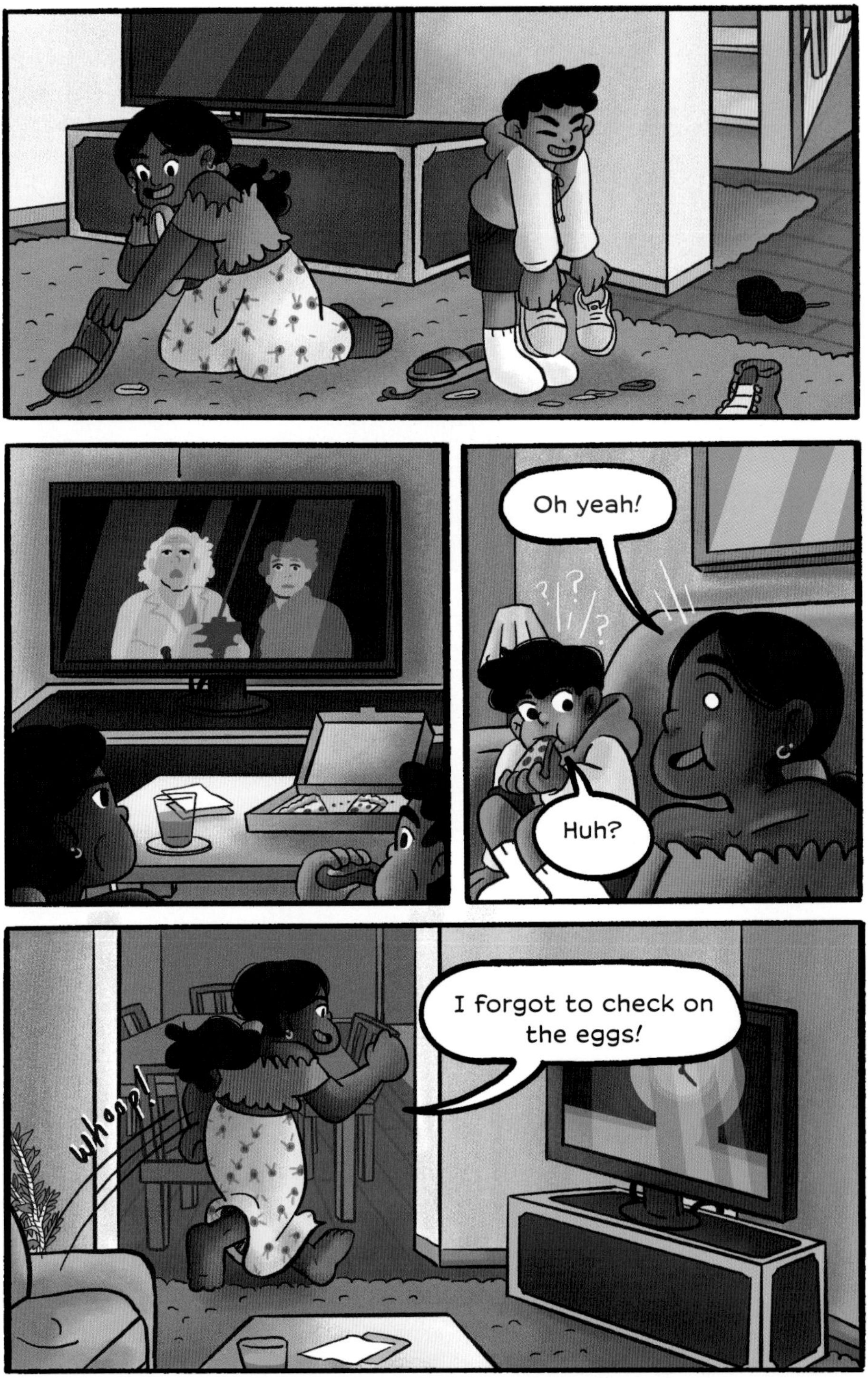
Oh yeah!
Huh?
I forgot to check on the eggs!
Whoop!

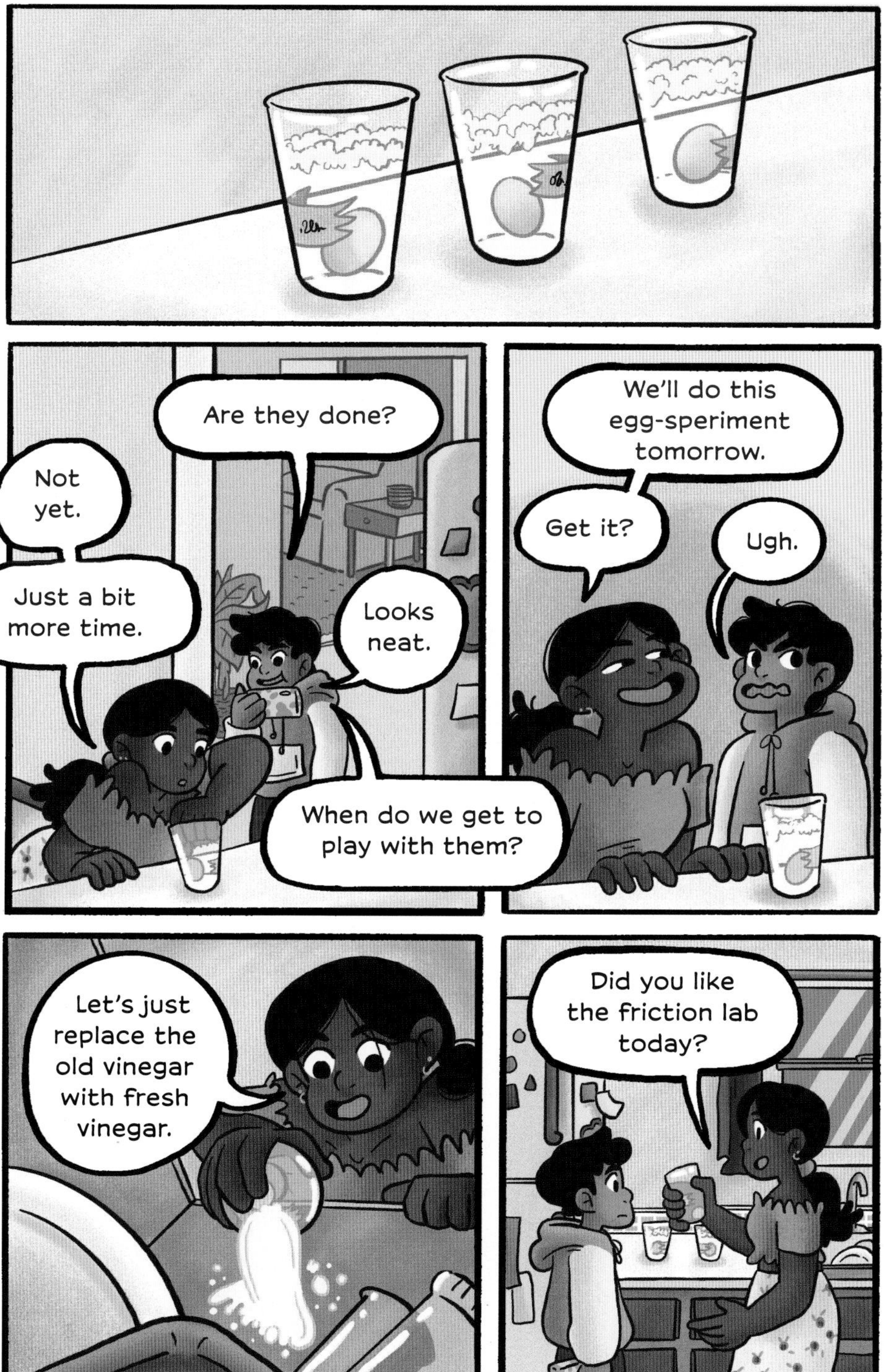
Are they done?
Not yet.
Just a bit more time.
Looks neat.
When do we get to play with them?
We'll do this egg-speriment tomorrow.
Get it?
Ugh.
Let's just replace the old vinegar with fresh vinegar.
Did you like the friction lab today?

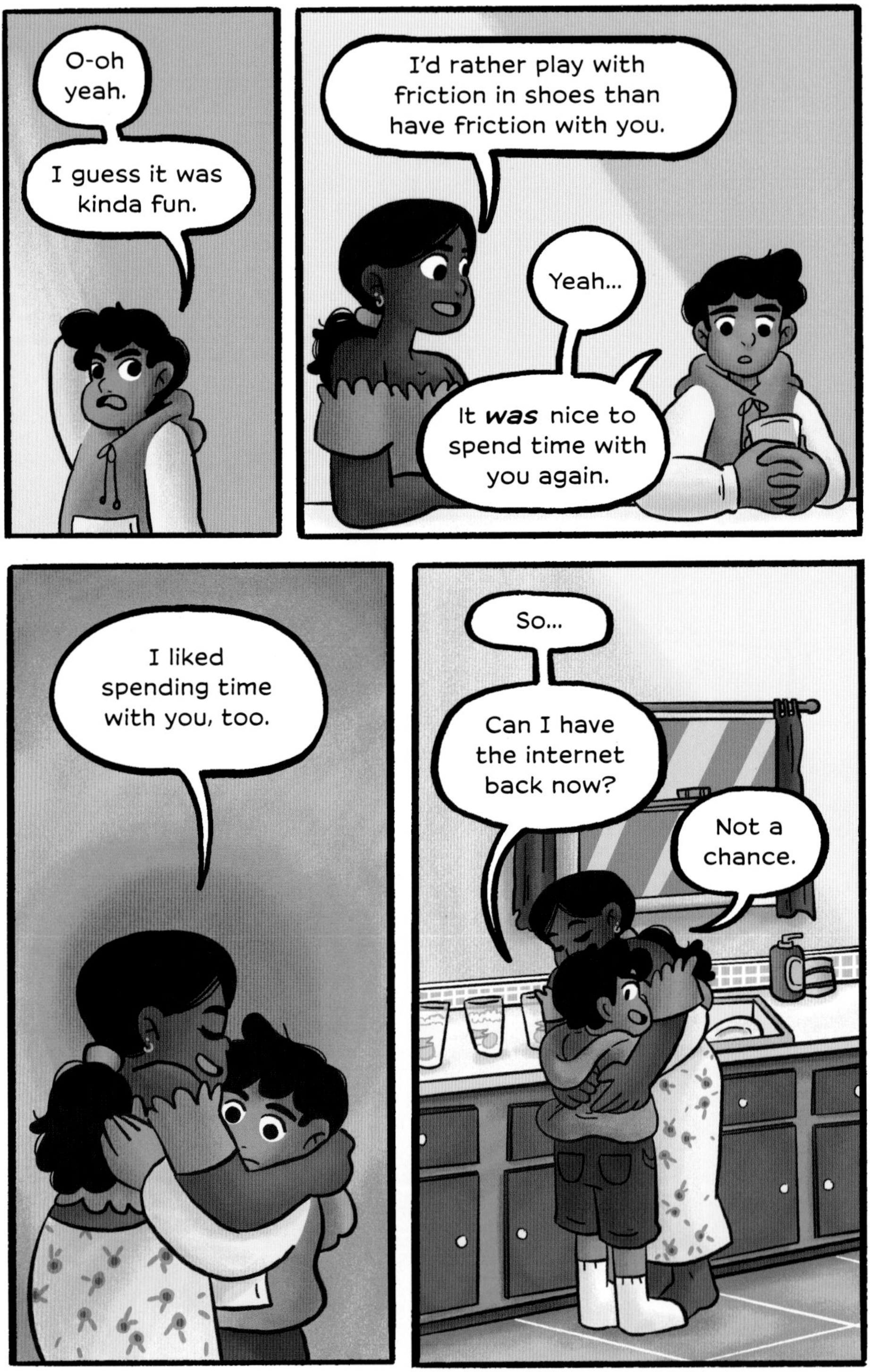
O-oh yeah.
I guess it was kinda fun.
I'd rather play with friction in shoes than have friction with you.
Yeah...
It ***was*** nice to spend time with you again.
I liked spending time with you, too.
So...
Can I have the internet back now?
Not a chance.

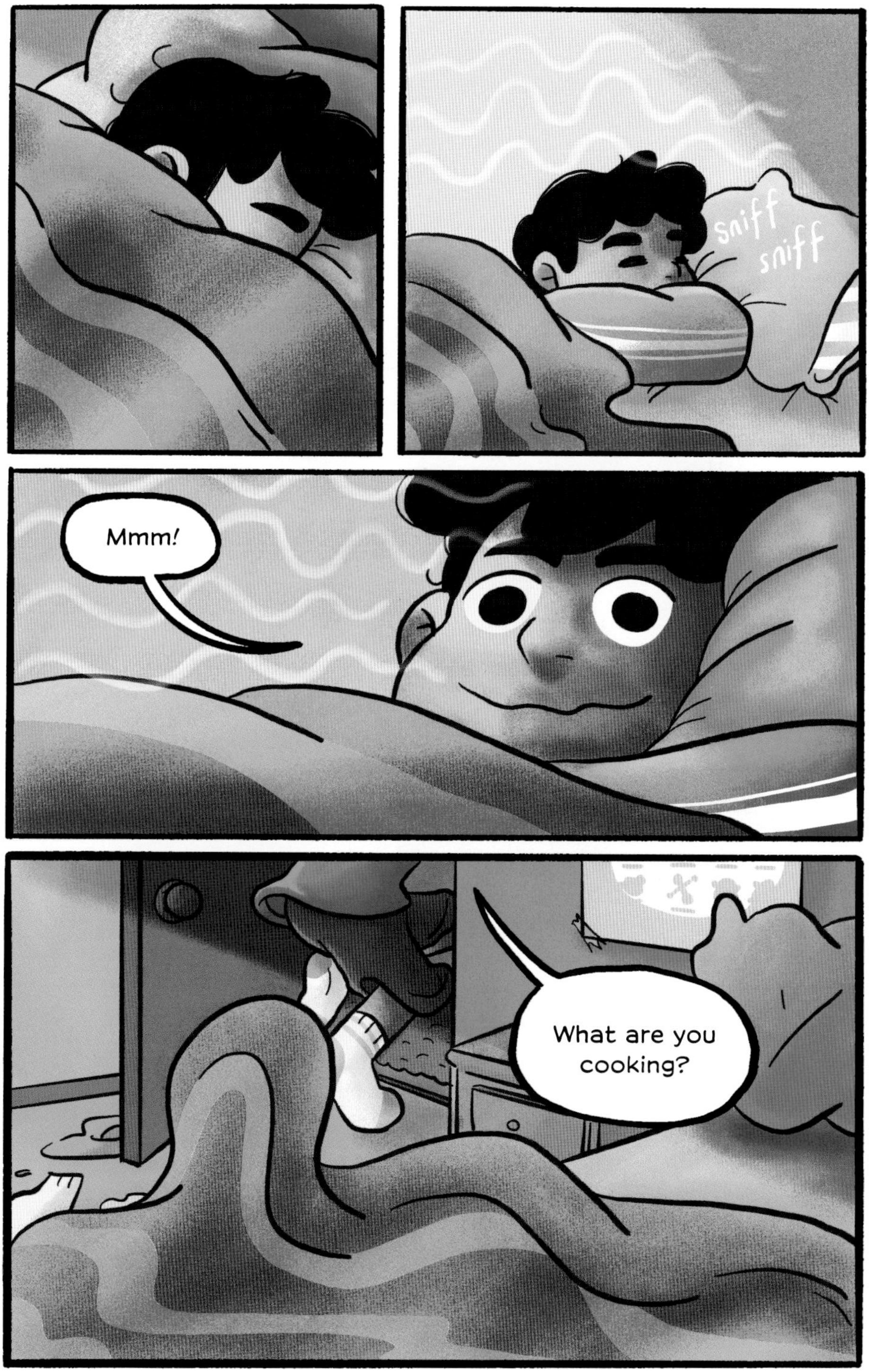
sniff
sniff
Mmm!
What are you cooking?

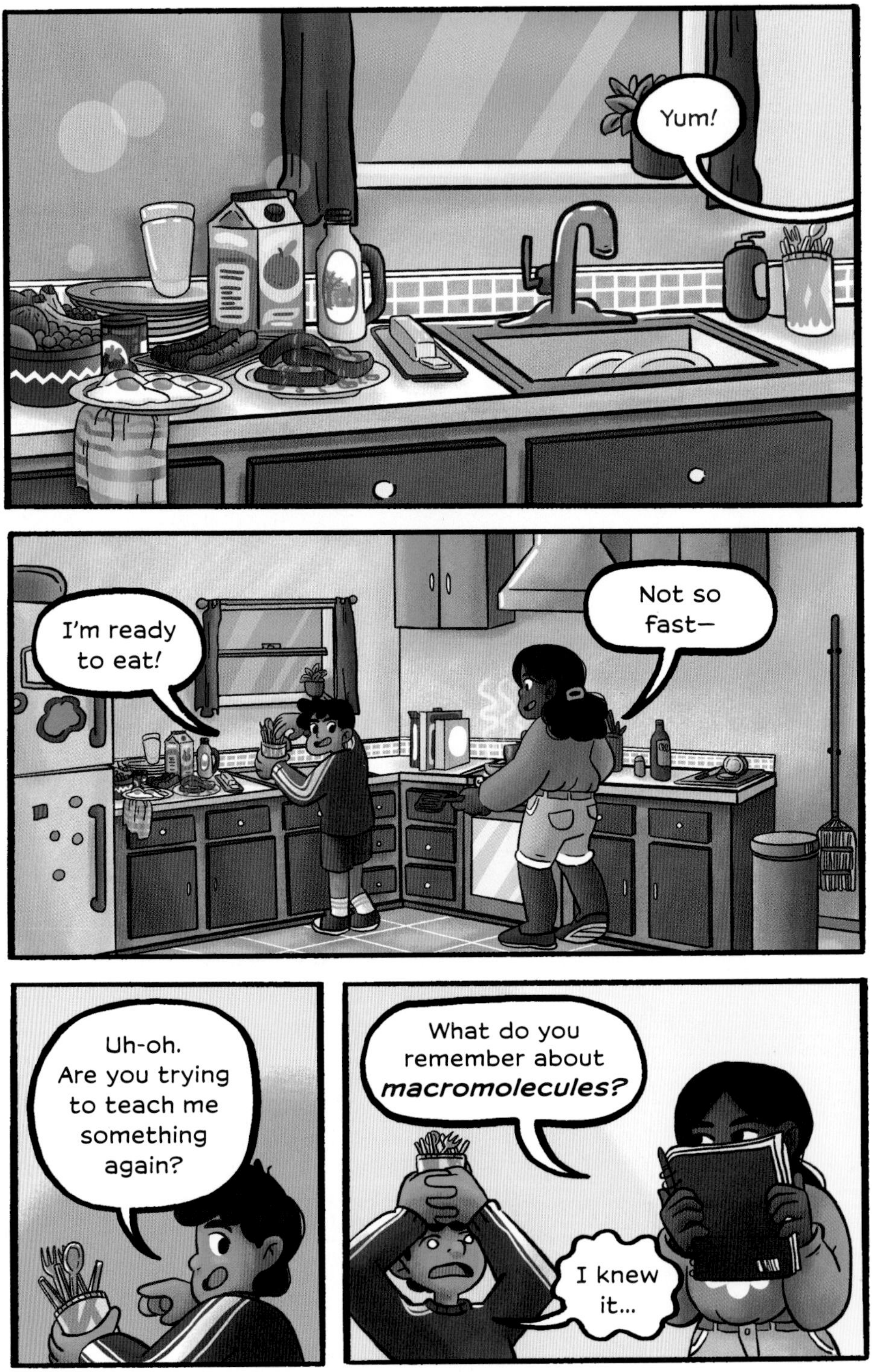
Yum!
I'm ready to eat!
Not so fast—
Uh-oh. Are you trying to teach me something again?
What do you remember about *macromolecules?*
I knew it...

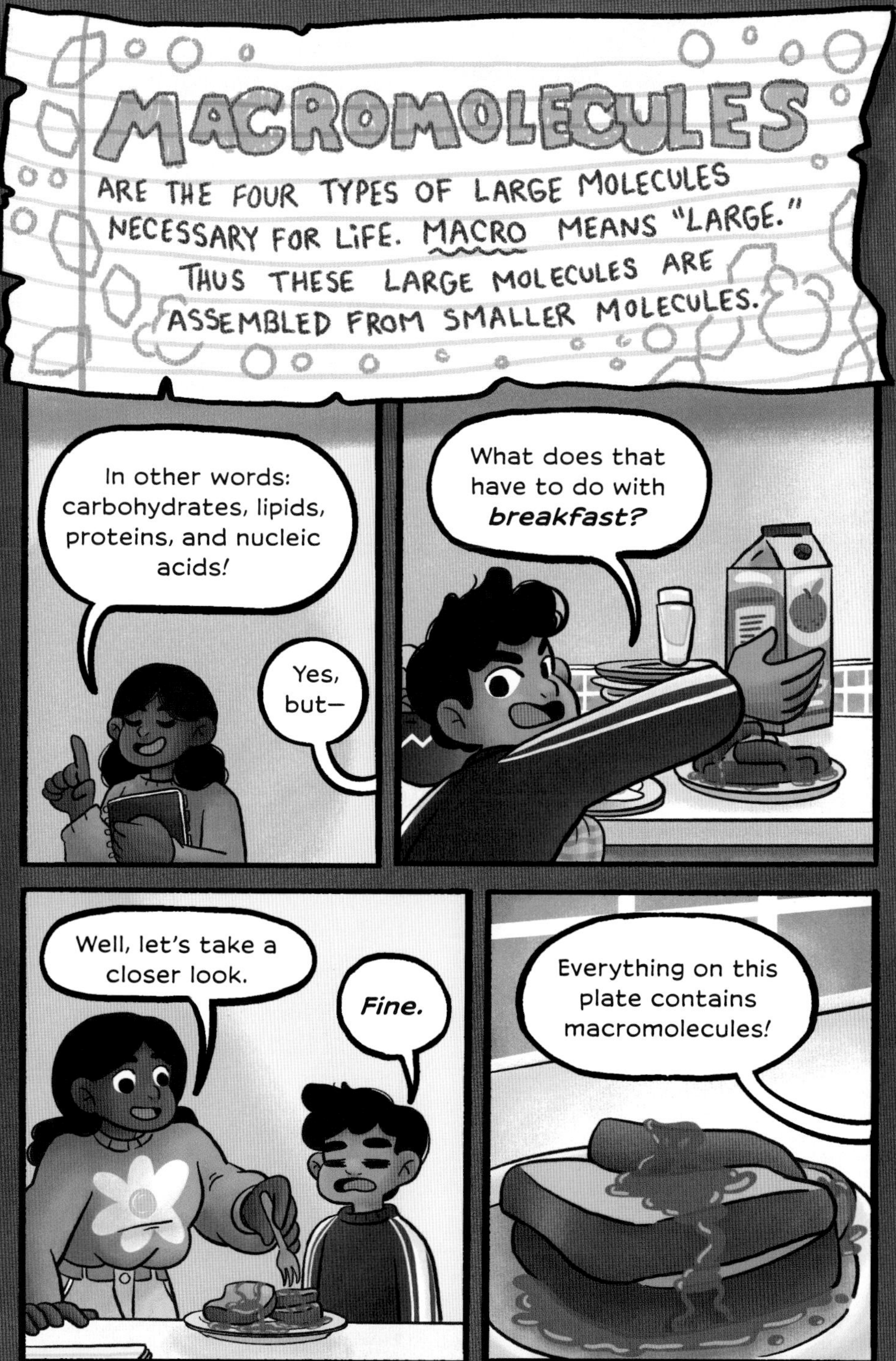
MACROMOLECULES
ARE THE FOUR TYPES OF LARGE MOLECULES NECESSARY FOR LIFE. MACRO MEANS "LARGE." THUS THESE LARGE MOLECULES ARE ASSEMBLED FROM SMALLER MOLECULES.
In other words: carbohydrates, lipids, proteins, and nucleic acids!
Yes, but—
What does that have to do with *breakfast?*
Well, let's take a closer look.
Fine.
Everything on this plate contains macromolecules!

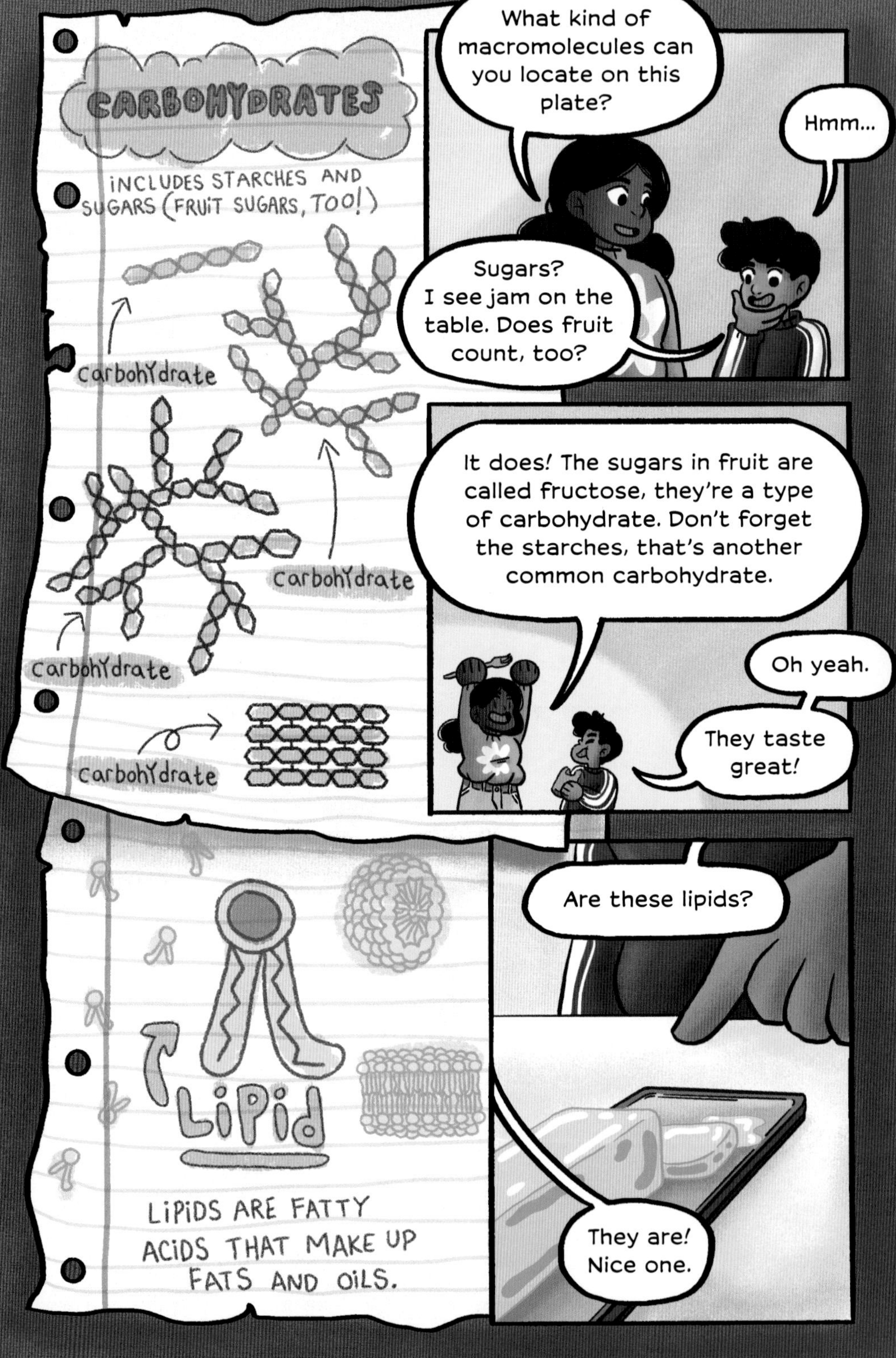
CARBOHYDRATES
INCLUDES STARCHES AND SUGARS (FRUIT SUGARS, TOO!)
carbohydrate
carbohydrate
carbohydrate
carbohydrate
What kind of macromolecules can you locate on this plate?
Hmm...
Sugars? I see jam on the table. Does fruit count, too?
It does! The sugars in fruit are called fructose, they're a type of carbohydrate. Don't forget the starches, that's another common carbohydrate.
Oh yeah.
They taste great!
LIPID
LIPIDS ARE FATTY ACIDS THAT MAKE UP FATS AND OILS.
Are these lipids?
They are! Nice one.

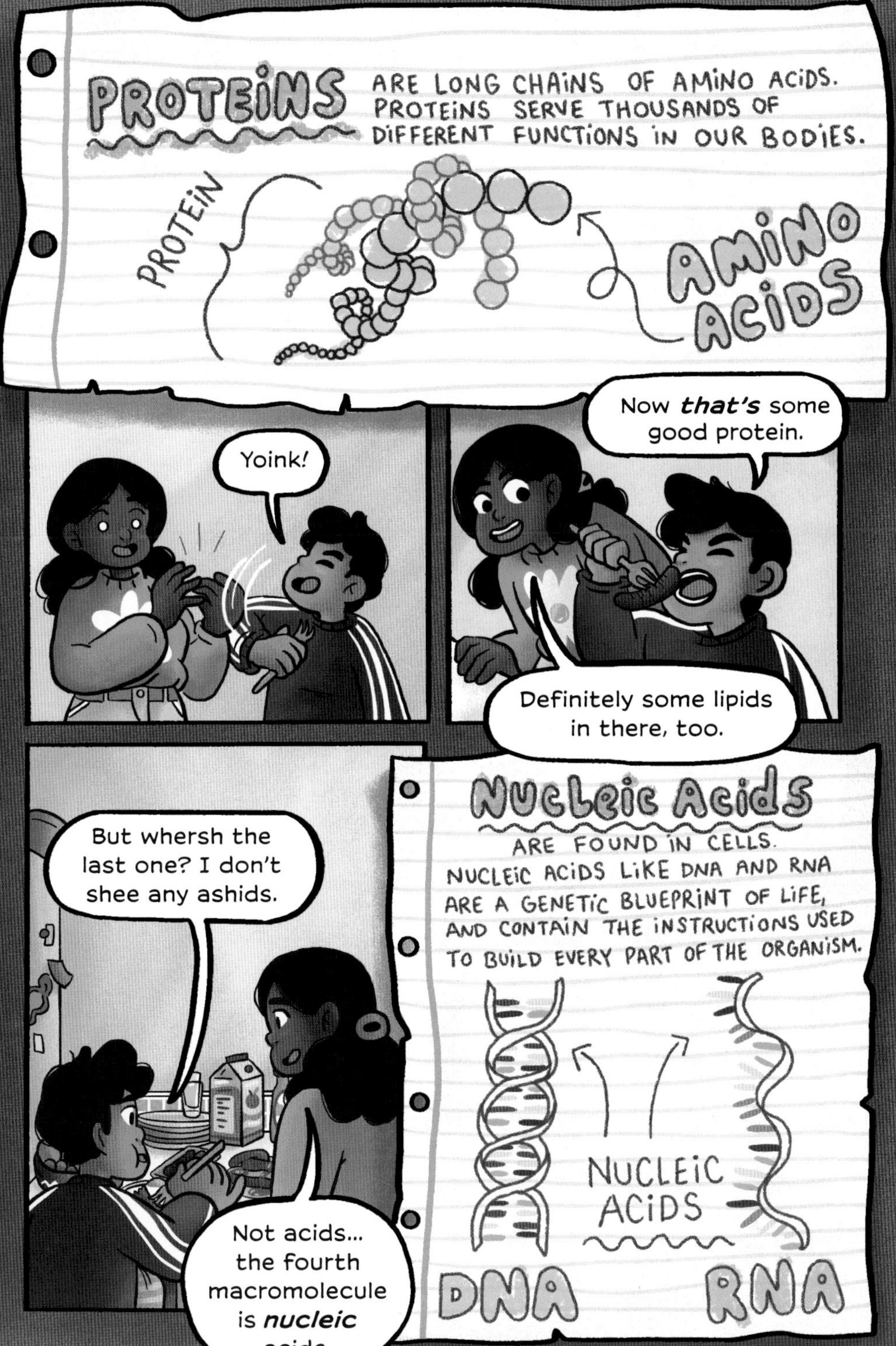
PROTEINS ARE LONG CHAINS OF AMINO ACIDS. PROTEINS SERVE THOUSANDS OF DIFFERENT FUNCTIONS IN OUR BODIES.
PROTEIN
AMINO ACIDS
Yoink!
Now *that's* some good protein.
Definitely some lipids in there, too.
But whersh the last one? I don't shee any ashids.
Not acids... the fourth macromolecule is *nucleic* acids.
NUCLEIC ACIDS ARE FOUND IN CELLS. NUCLEIC ACIDS LIKE DNA AND RNA ARE A GENETIC BLUEPRINT OF LIFE, AND CONTAIN THE INSTRUCTIONS USED TO BUILD EVERY PART OF THE ORGANISM.
NUCLEIC ACIDS
DNA
RNA

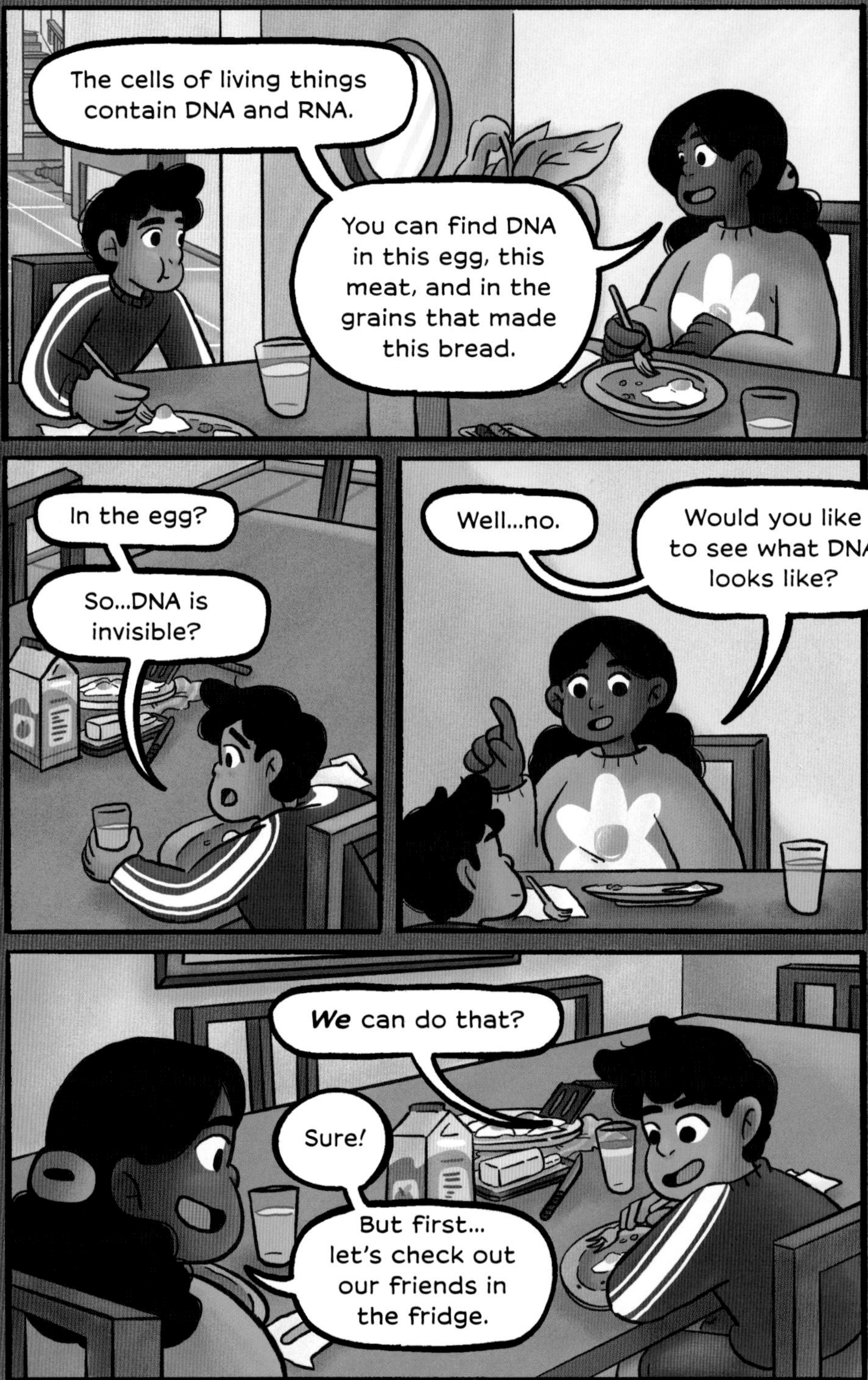
The cells of living things contain DNA and RNA.
You can find DNA in this egg, this meat, and in the grains that made this bread.
In the egg?
So...DNA is invisible?
Well...no.
Would you like to see what DNA looks like?
We can do that?
Sure!
But first... let's check out our friends in the fridge.

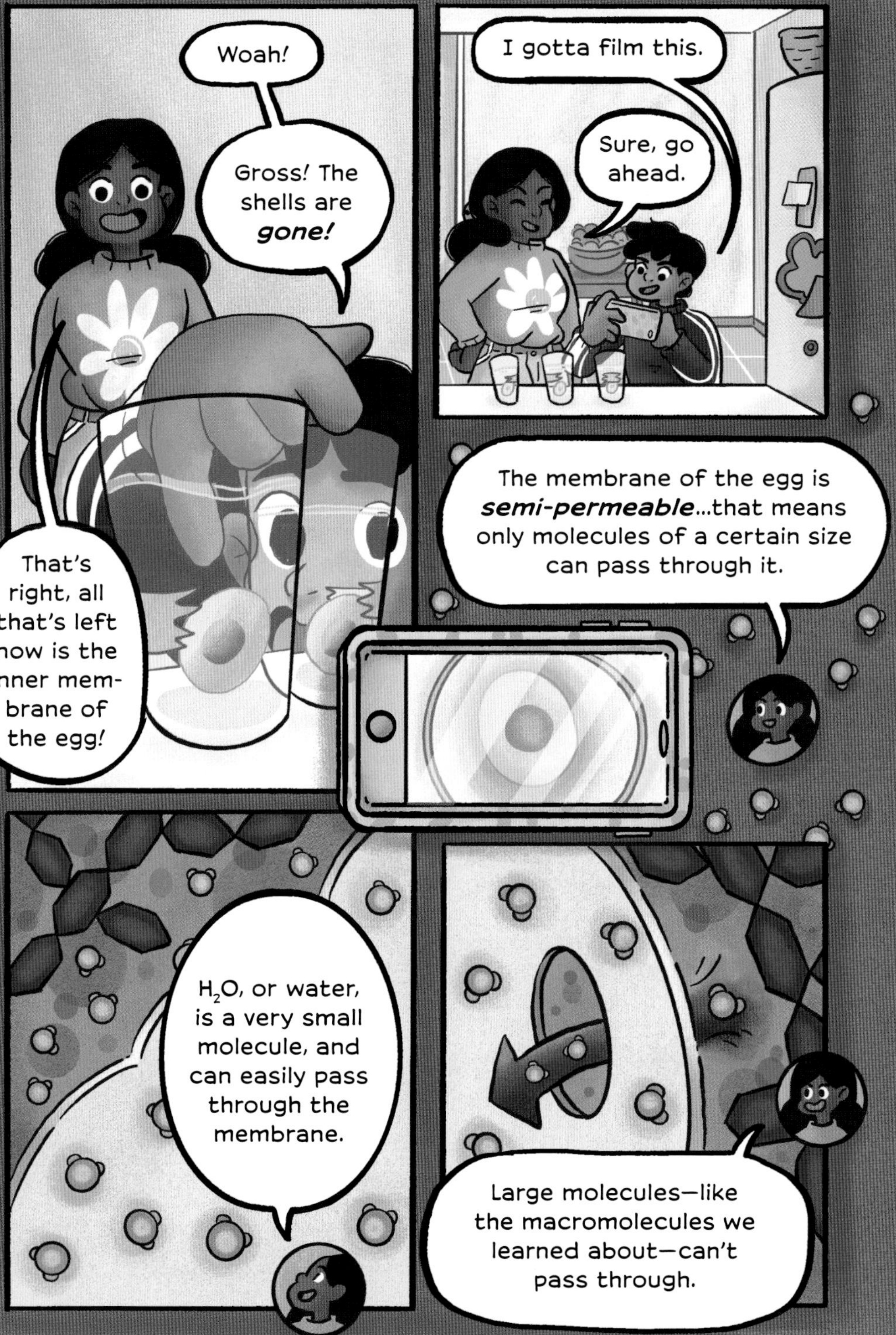

Woah!
Gross! The shells are *gone!*
That's right, all that's left now is the inner membrane of the egg!
I gotta film this.
Sure, go ahead.
The membrane of the egg is *semi-permeable*...that means only molecules of a certain size can pass through it.
H_2O, or water, is a very small molecule, and can easily pass through the membrane.
Large molecules—like the macromolecules we learned about—can't pass through.

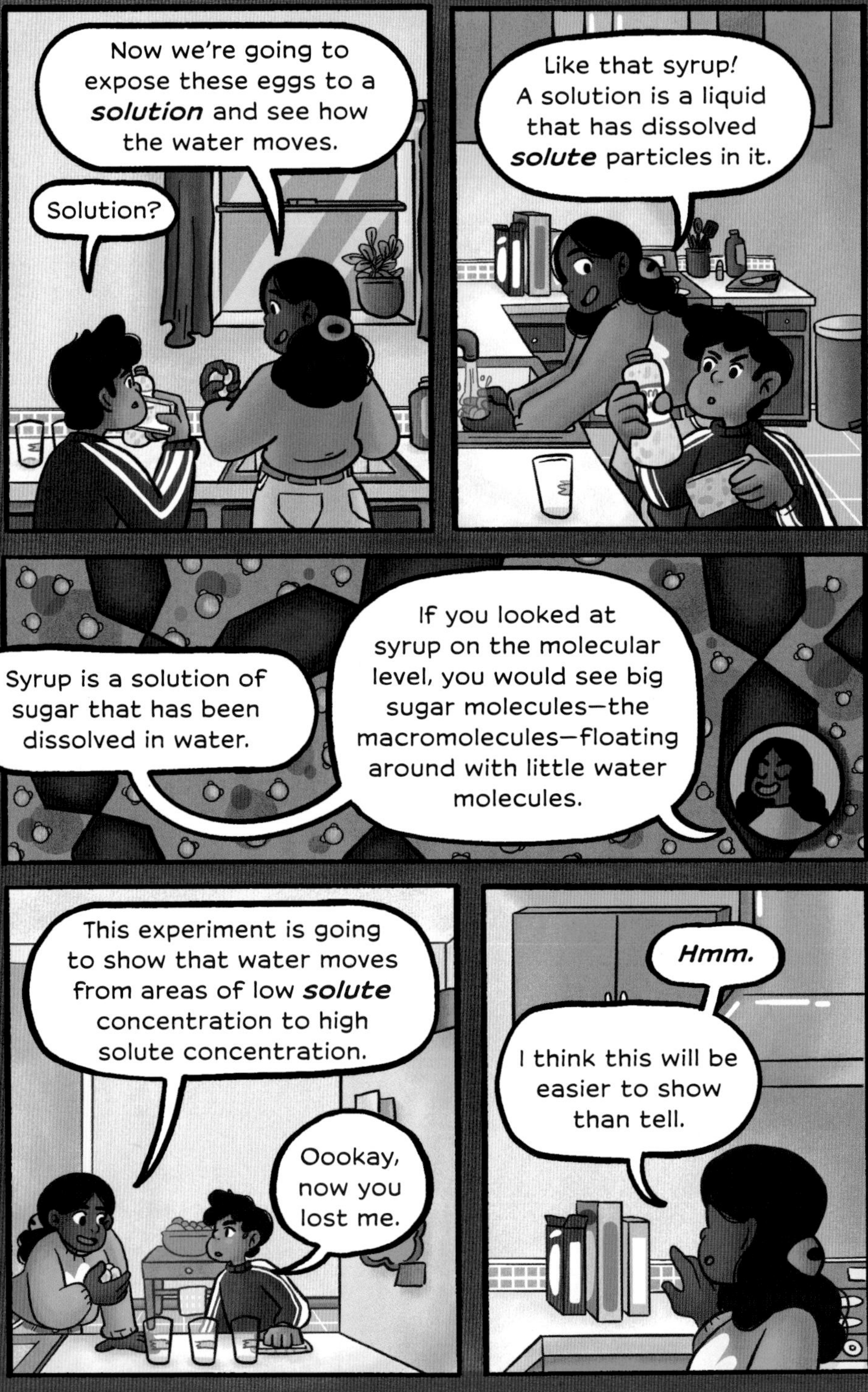
Now we're going to expose these eggs to a ***solution*** and see how the water moves.
Solution?
Like that syrup! A solution is a liquid that has dissolved ***solute*** particles in it.
Syrup is a solution of sugar that has been dissolved in water.
If you looked at syrup on the molecular level, you would see big sugar molecules—the macromolecules—floating around with little water molecules.
This experiment is going to show that water moves from areas of low ***solute*** concentration to high solute concentration.
Oookay, now you lost me.
Hmm.
I think this will be easier to show than tell.

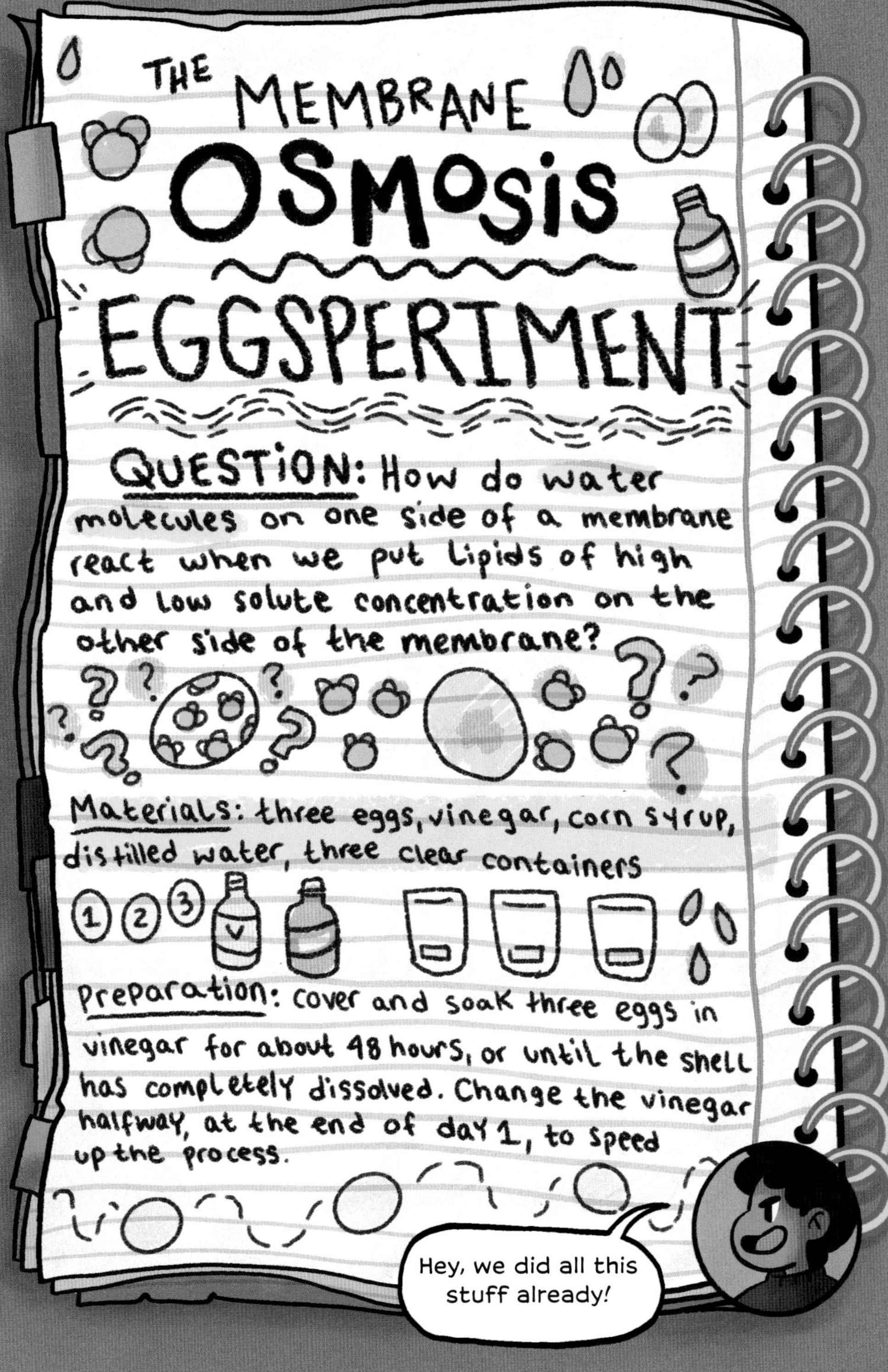
THE MEMBRANE
OSMOSIS
EGGSPERIMENT
QUESTION: How do water molecules on one side of a membrane react when we put lipids of high and low solute concentration on the other side of the membrane?
Materials: three eggs, vinegar, corn syrup, distilled water, three clear containers
1
2
3
V
Preparation: cover and soak three eggs in vinegar for about 48 hours, or until the shell has completely dissolved. Change the vinegar halfway, at the end of day 1, to speed up the process.
Hey, we did all this stuff already!

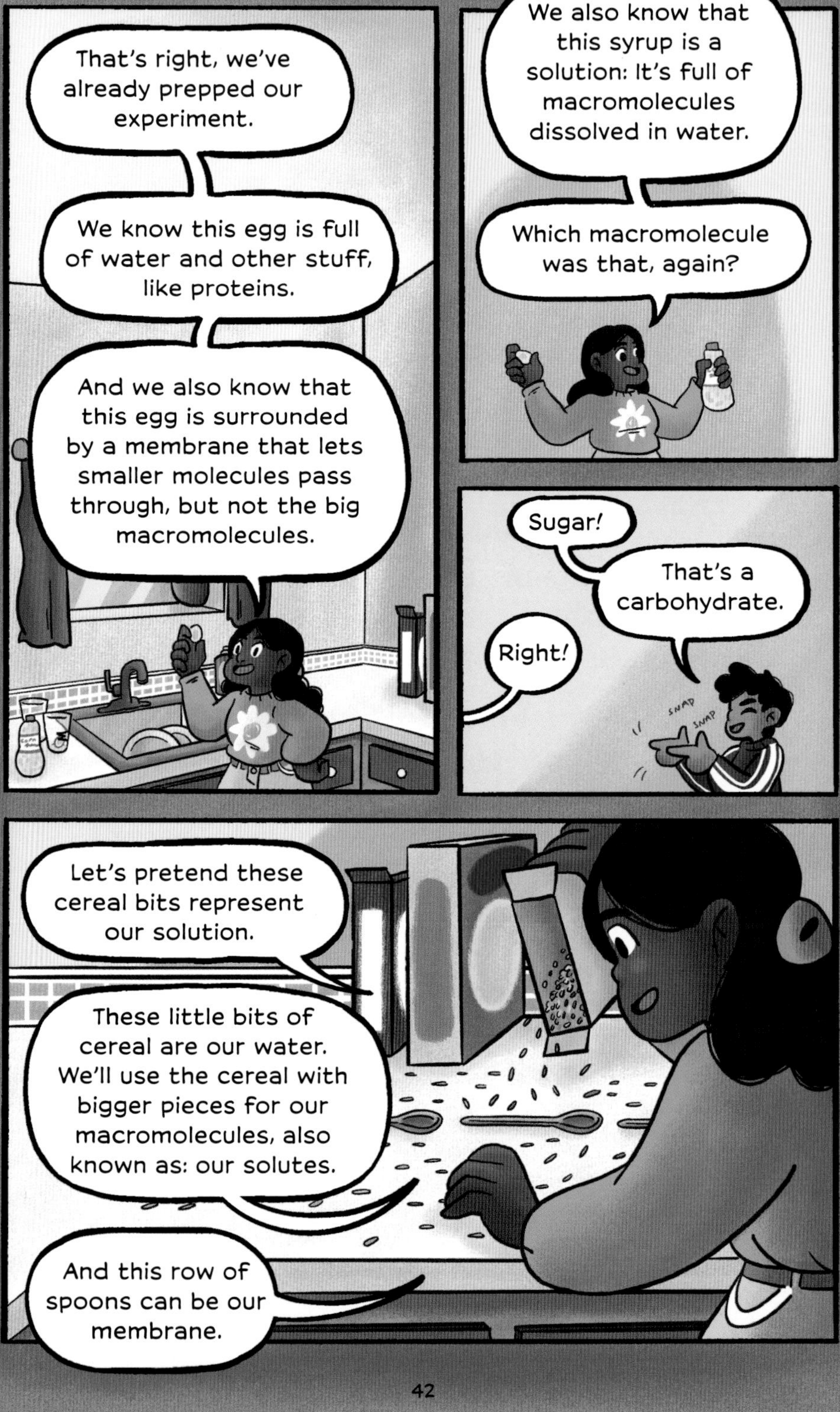
That's right, we've already prepped our experiment.
We know this egg is full of water and other stuff, like proteins.
And we also know that this egg is surrounded by a membrane that lets smaller molecules pass through, but not the big macromolecules.
We also know that this syrup is a solution: It's full of macromolecules dissolved in water.
Which macromolecule was that, again?
Sugar!
That's a carbohydrate.
Right!
SNAP
SNAP
Let's pretend these cereal bits represent our solution.
These little bits of cereal are our water. We'll use the cereal with bigger pieces for our macromolecules, also known as: our solutes.
And this row of spoons can be our membrane.

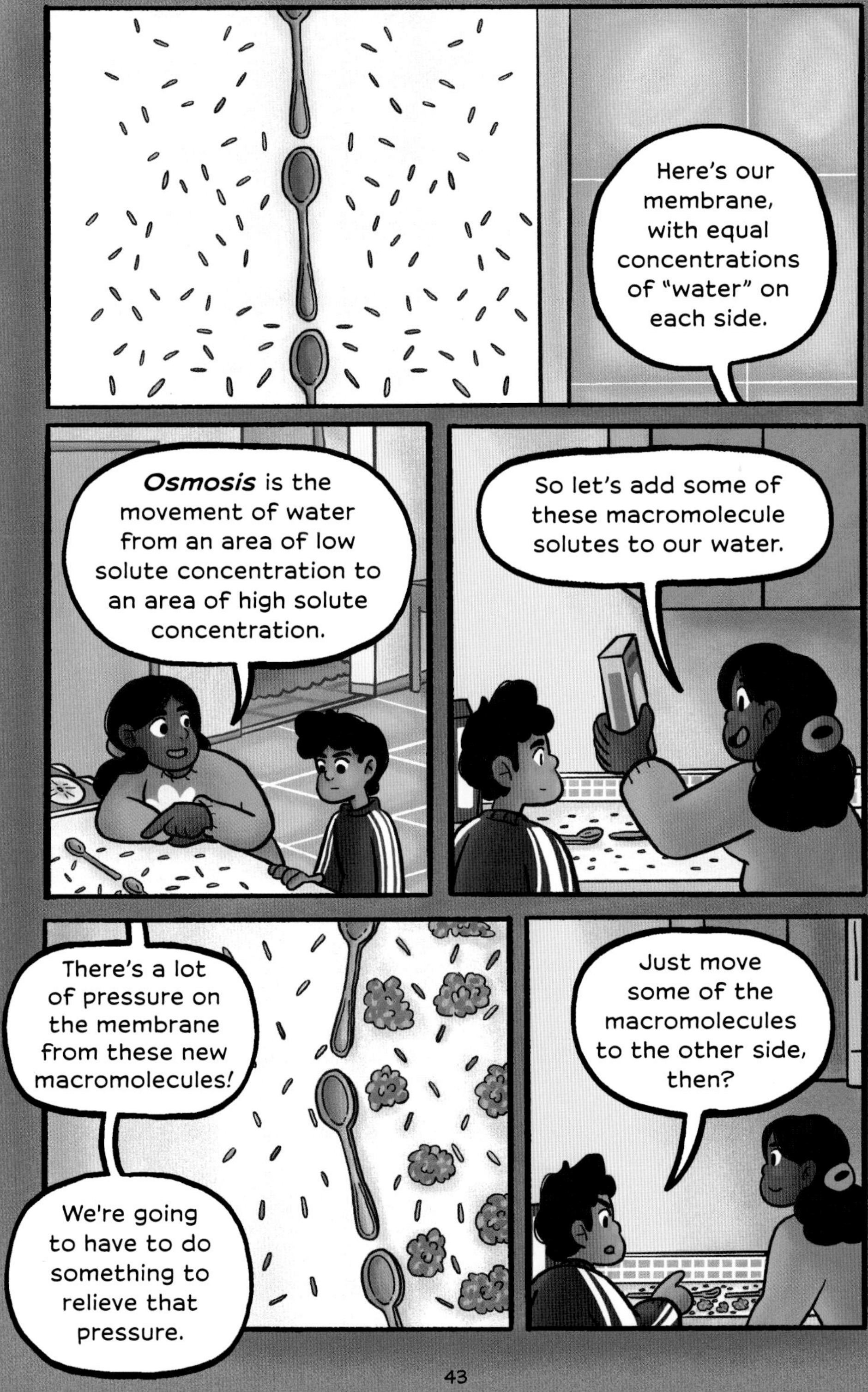
Here's our membrane, with equal concentrations of "water" on each side.
Osmosis is the movement of water from an area of low solute concentration to an area of high solute concentration.
So let's add some of these macromolecule solutes to our water.
There's a lot of pressure on the membrane from these new macromolecules!
We're going to have to do something to relieve that pressure.
Just move some of the macromolecules to the other side, then?

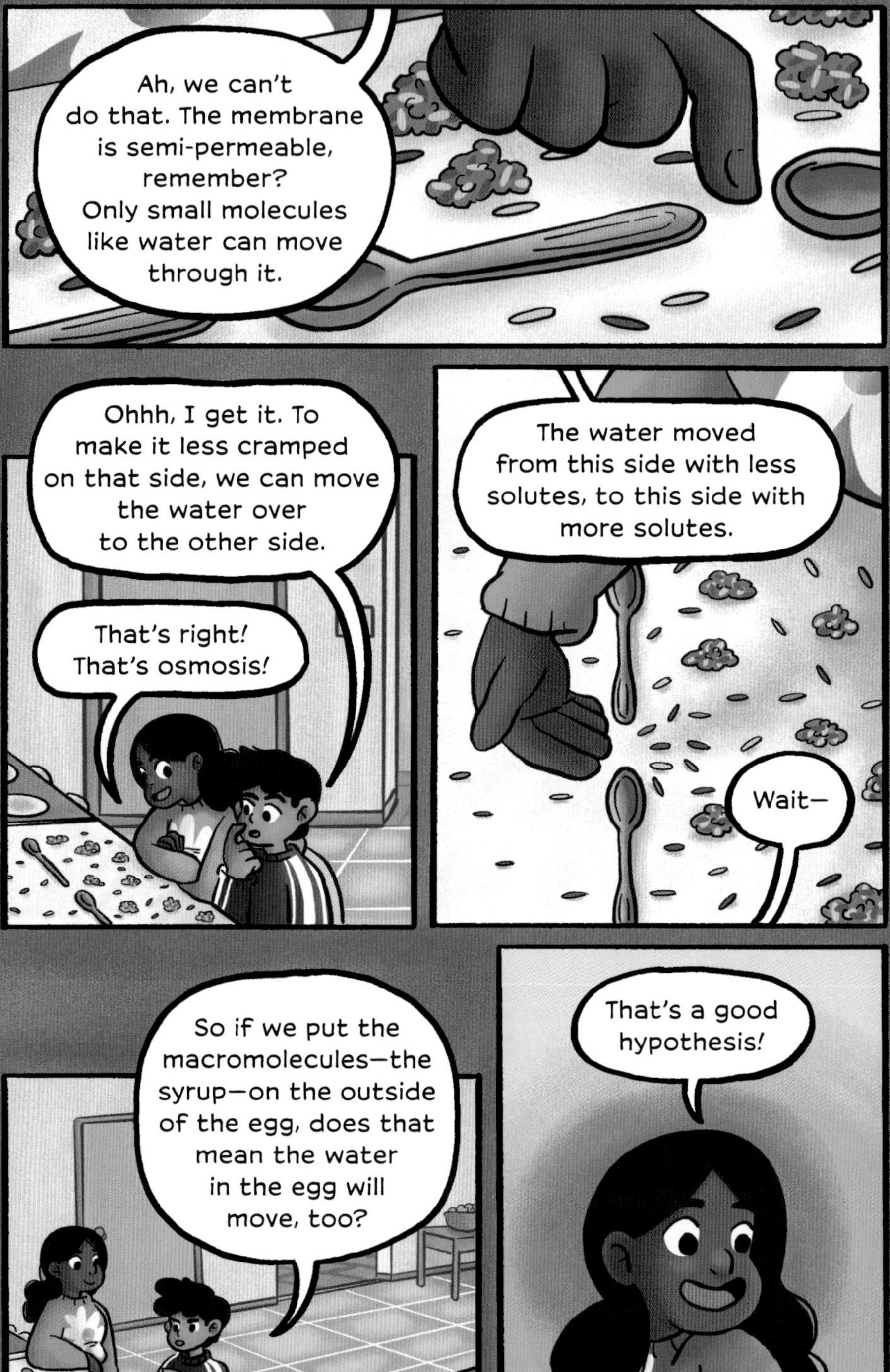
Ah, we can't do that. The membrane is semi-permeable, remember? Only small molecules like water can move through it.
Ohhh, I get it. To make it less cramped on that side, we can move the water over to the other side.
That's right! That's osmosis!
The water moved from this side with less solutes, to this side with more solutes.
Wait—
So if we put the macromolecules—the syrup—on the outside of the egg, does that mean the water in the egg will move, too?
That's a good hypothesis!

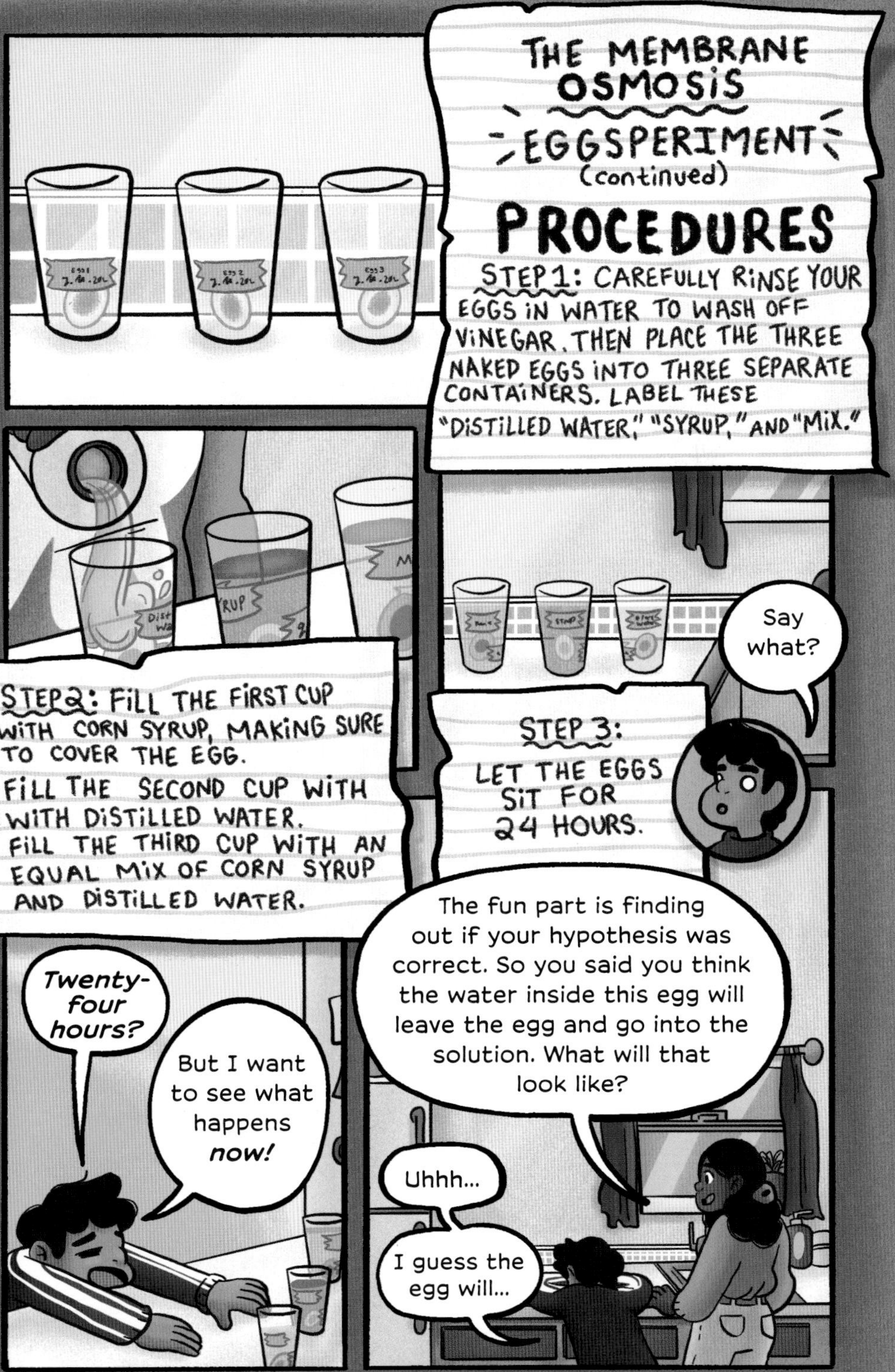
THE MEMBRANE OSMOSIS EGGSPERIMENT (continued)
PROCEDURES
STEP 1: CAREFULLY RINSE YOUR EGGS IN WATER TO WASH OFF VINEGAR. THEN PLACE THE THREE NAKED EGGS INTO THREE SEPARATE CONTAINERS. LABEL THESE "DISTILLED WATER," "SYRUP," AND "MIX."
Say what?
STEP 2: FILL THE FIRST CUP WITH CORN SYRUP, MAKING SURE TO COVER THE EGG.
FILL THE SECOND CUP WITH WITH DISTILLED WATER.
FILL THE THIRD CUP WITH AN EQUAL MIX OF CORN SYRUP AND DISTILLED WATER.
STEP 3:
LET THE EGGS SIT FOR 24 HOURS.
Twenty-four hours?
But I want to see what happens *now!*
The fun part is finding out if your hypothesis was correct. So you said you think the water inside this egg will leave the egg and go into the solution. What will that look like?
Uhhh...
I guess the egg will...

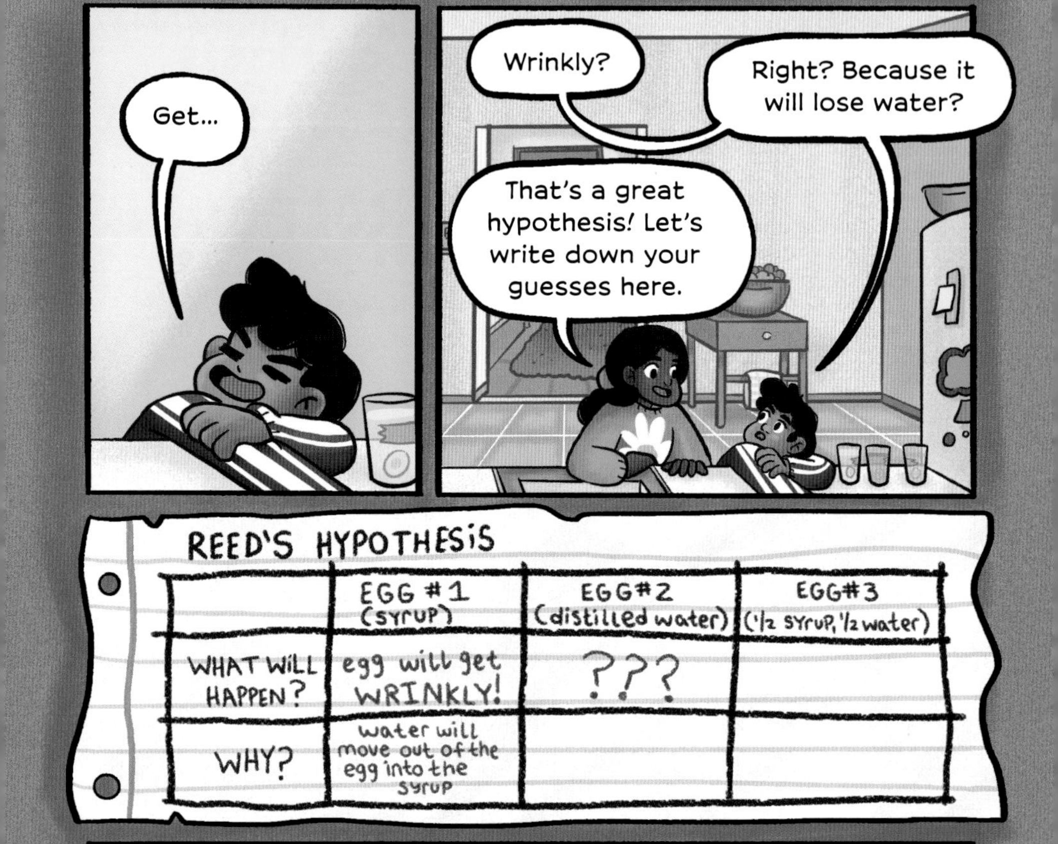
Get...
Wrinkly?
Right? Because it will lose water?
That's a great hypothesis! Let's write down your guesses here.

REED'S HYPOTHESIS

	EGG #1 (SYRUP)	EGG #2 (distilled water)	EGG #3 (½ SYRUP, ½ water)
WHAT WILL HAPPEN?	egg will get WRINKLY!	???	
WHY?	water will move out of the egg into the syrup		

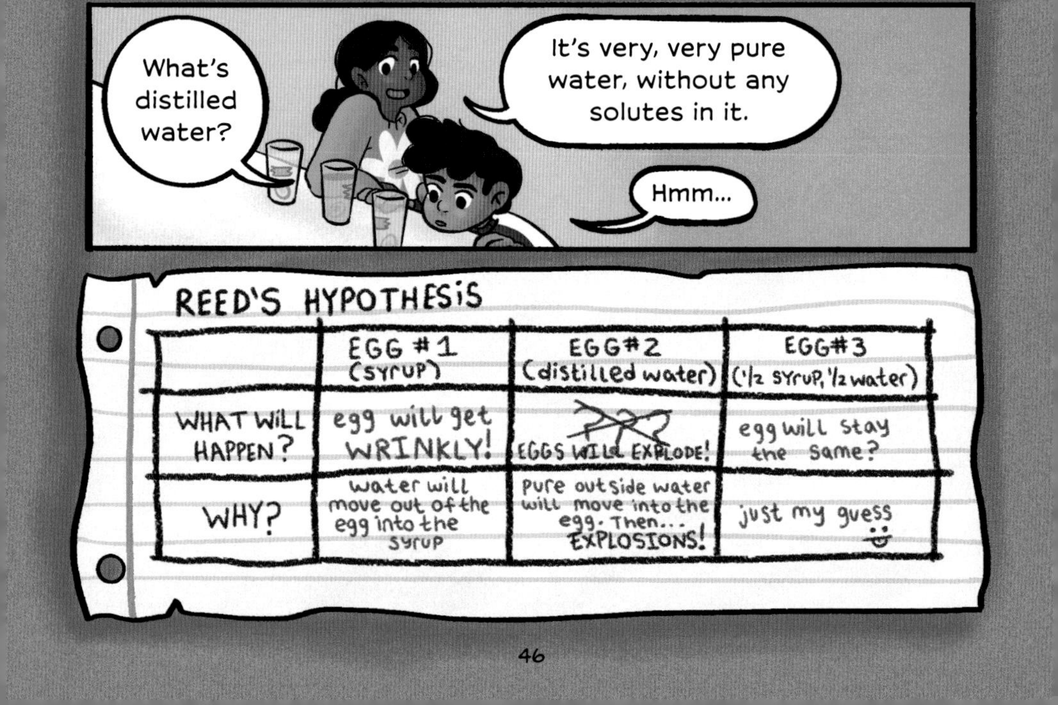
What's distilled water?
It's very, very pure water, without any solutes in it.
Hmm...

REED'S HYPOTHESIS

	EGG #1 (SYRUP)	EGG #2 (distilled water)	EGG #3 (½ SYRUP, ½ water)
WHAT WILL HAPPEN?	egg will get WRINKLY!	~~???~~ EGGS WILL EXPLODE!	egg will stay the same?
WHY?	water will move out of the egg into the syrup	Pure outside water will move into the egg. Then... EXPLOSIONS!	just my guess

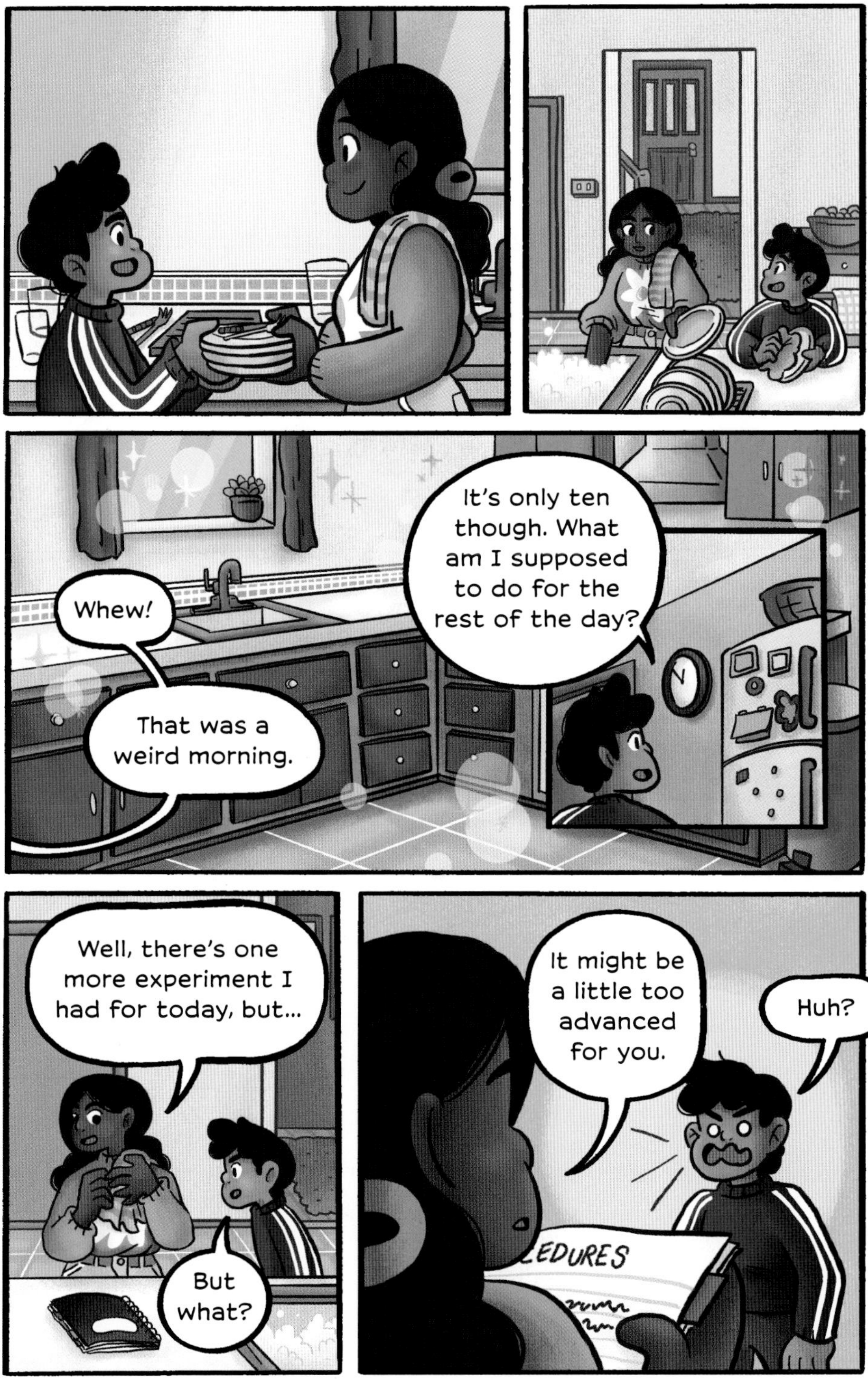
Whew!
That was a weird morning.
It's only ten though. What am I supposed to do for the rest of the day?
Well, there's one more experiment I had for today, but...
But what?
It might be a little too advanced for you.
Huh?
EDURES

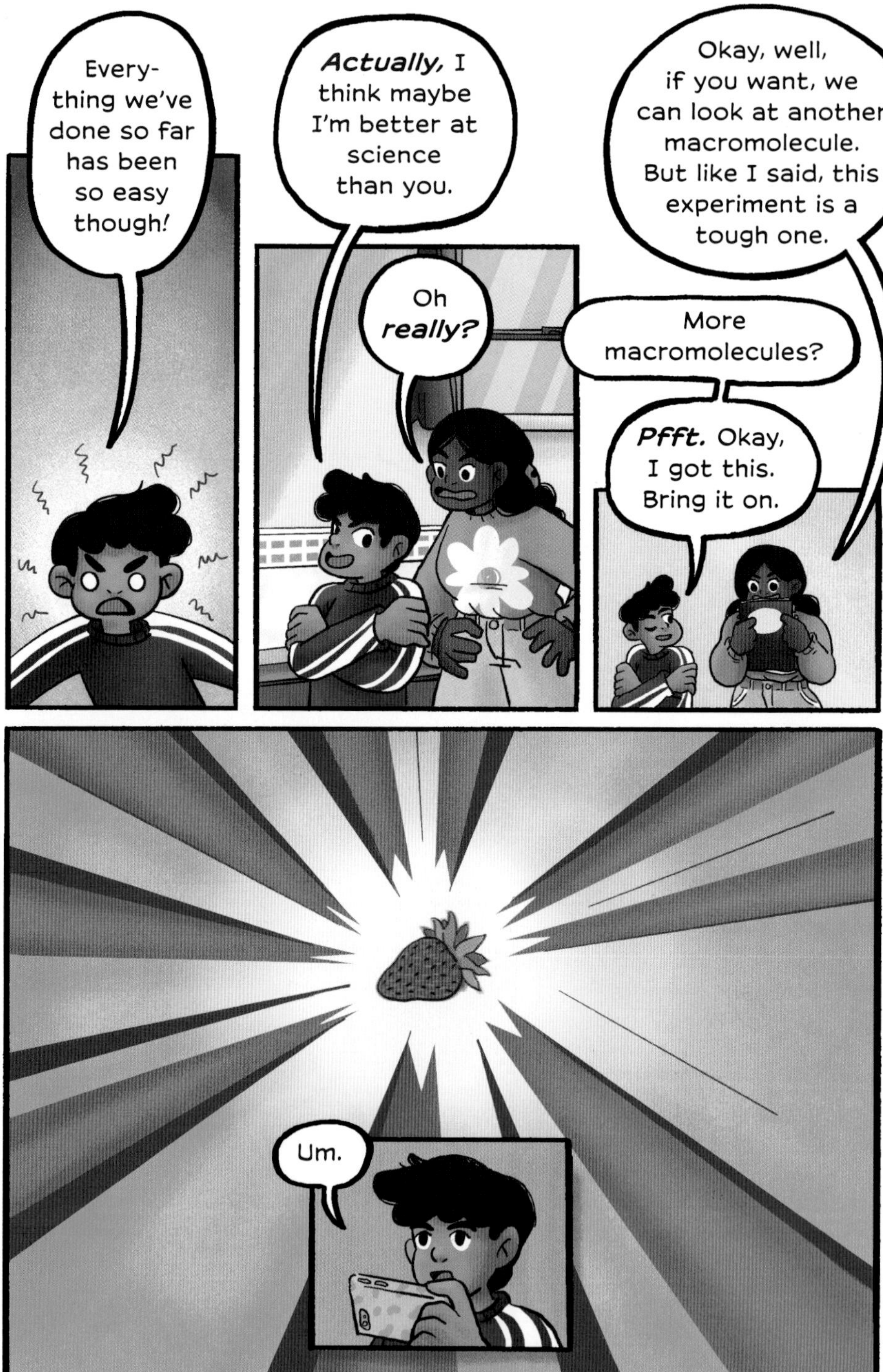
Every-thing we've done so far has been so easy though!
Actually, I think maybe I'm better at science than you.
Oh *really?*
Okay, well, if you want, we can look at another macromolecule. But like I said, this experiment is a tough one.
More macromolecules?
Pfft. Okay, I got this. Bring it on.
Um.

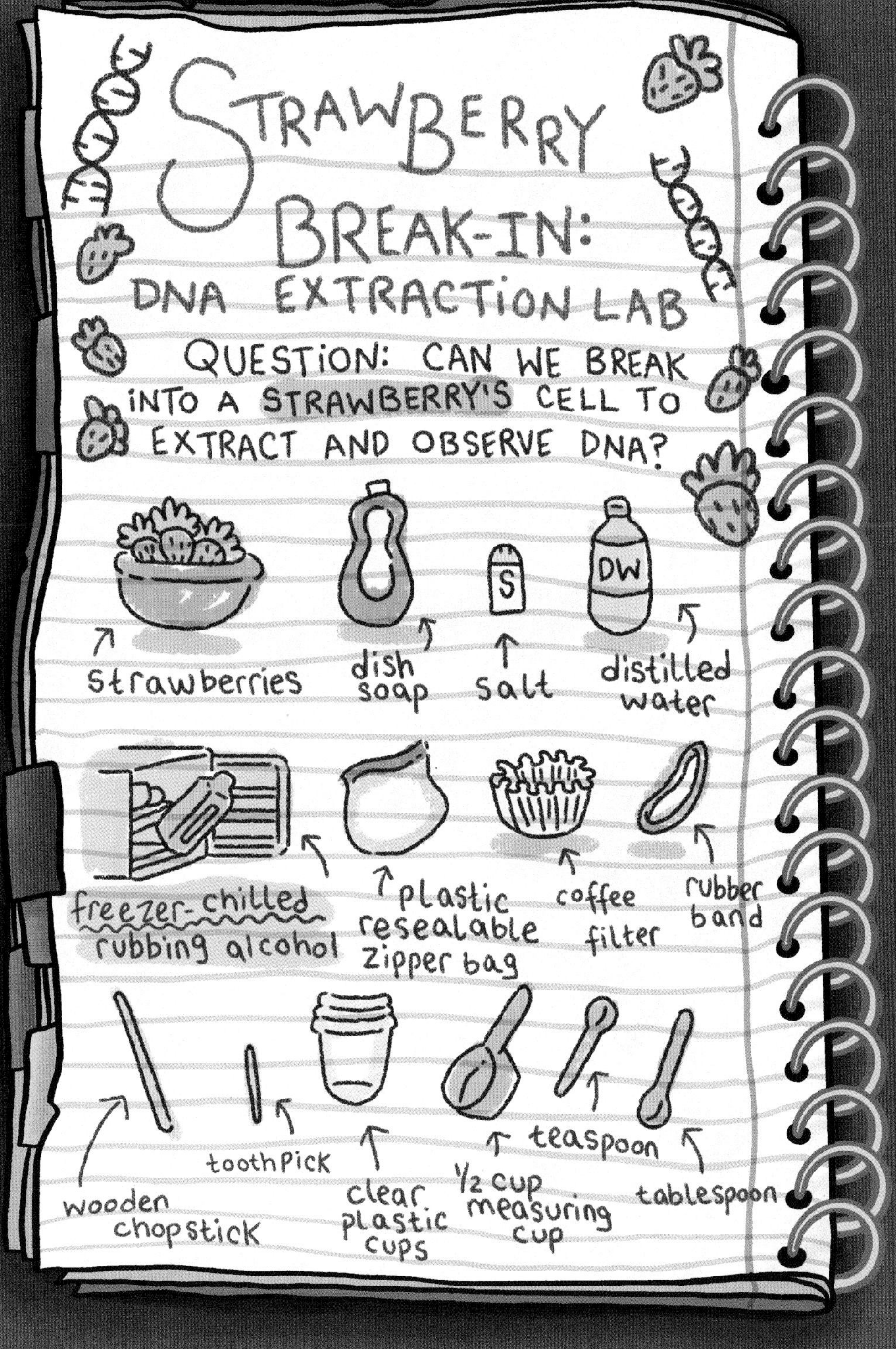
STRAWBERRY BREAK-IN:
DNA EXTRACTION LAB
QUESTION: CAN WE BREAK INTO A STRAWBERRY'S CELL TO EXTRACT AND OBSERVE DNA?
strawberries
dish soap
S
salt
DW
distilled water
freezer-chilled rubbing alcohol
plastic resealable zipper bag
coffee filter
rubber band
wooden chopstick
toothpick
clear plastic cups
1/2 cup measuring cup
teaspoon
tablespoon

PROCEDURES

STEP 1: TAKE A PLASTIC CUP AND ADD 2 tsp OF DISH SOAP. THEN MIX IN 1 tsp OF SALT. THEN MIX IN ½ CUP OF DISTILLED WATER. THIS MIX WILL BE OUR DNA EXTRACTION LIQUID.

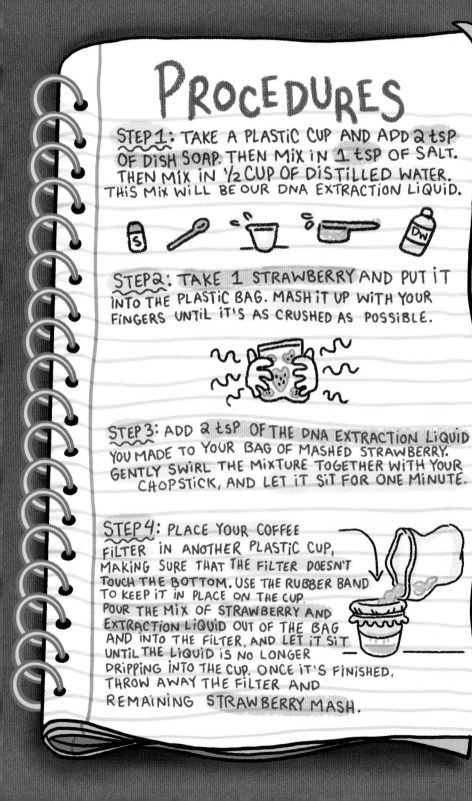

STEP 2: TAKE 1 STRAWBERRY AND PUT IT INTO THE PLASTIC BAG. MASH IT UP WITH YOUR FINGERS UNTIL IT'S AS CRUSHED AS POSSIBLE.

STEP 3: ADD 2 tsp OF THE DNA EXTRACTION LIQUID YOU MADE TO YOUR BAG OF MASHED STRAWBERRY. GENTLY SWIRL THE MIXTURE TOGETHER WITH YOUR CHOPSTICK, AND LET IT SIT FOR ONE MINUTE.

STEP 4: PLACE YOUR COFFEE FILTER IN ANOTHER PLASTIC CUP, MAKING SURE THAT THE FILTER DOESN'T TOUCH THE BOTTOM. USE THE RUBBER BAND TO KEEP IT IN PLACE ON THE CUP. POUR THE MIX OF STRAWBERRY AND EXTRACTION LIQUID OUT OF THE BAG AND INTO THE FILTER, AND LET IT SIT UNTIL THE LIQUID IS NO LONGER DRIPPING INTO THE CUP. ONCE IT'S FINISHED, THROW AWAY THE FILTER AND REMAINING STRAWBERRY MASH.

PROCEDURES
(continued)

Step 5: Take your rubbing alcohol out of the freezer, and pour it into a new cup until it looks equal to the amount of strawberry liquid.

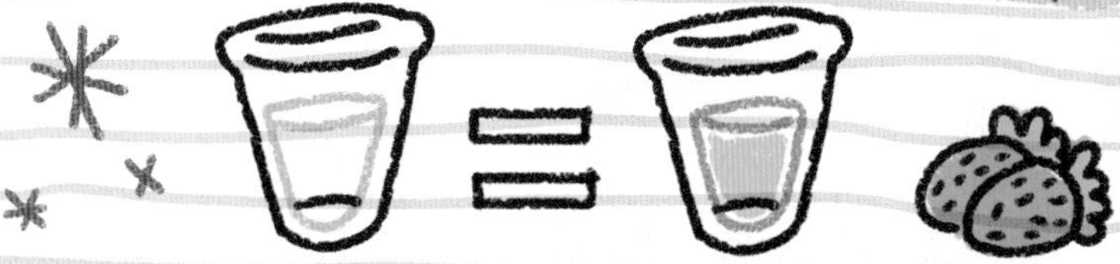

Step 6: Slightly tilt your cup of strawberry liquid. Carefully pour the cold rubbing alcohol down the side of the cup onto the strawberry liquid, but be careful not to mix the two liquids together. Soon you should see a cloudy Substance forming on the top of the Strawberry liquid. This is the strawberry's DNA!

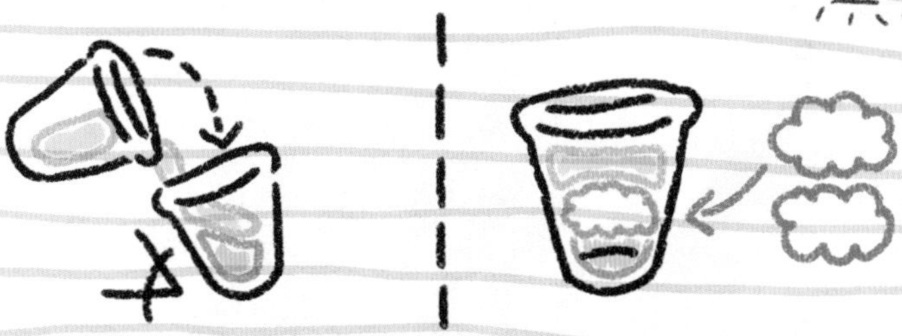

Step 7: Take a toothpick, stick it into the DNA cloud. Twirl the toothpick between your fingers to wind it onto the toothpick.

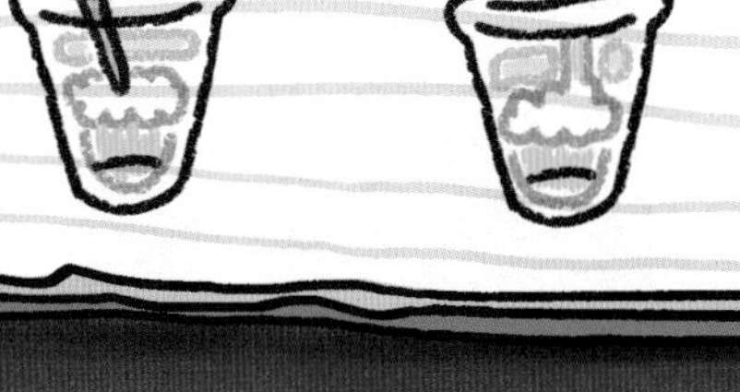

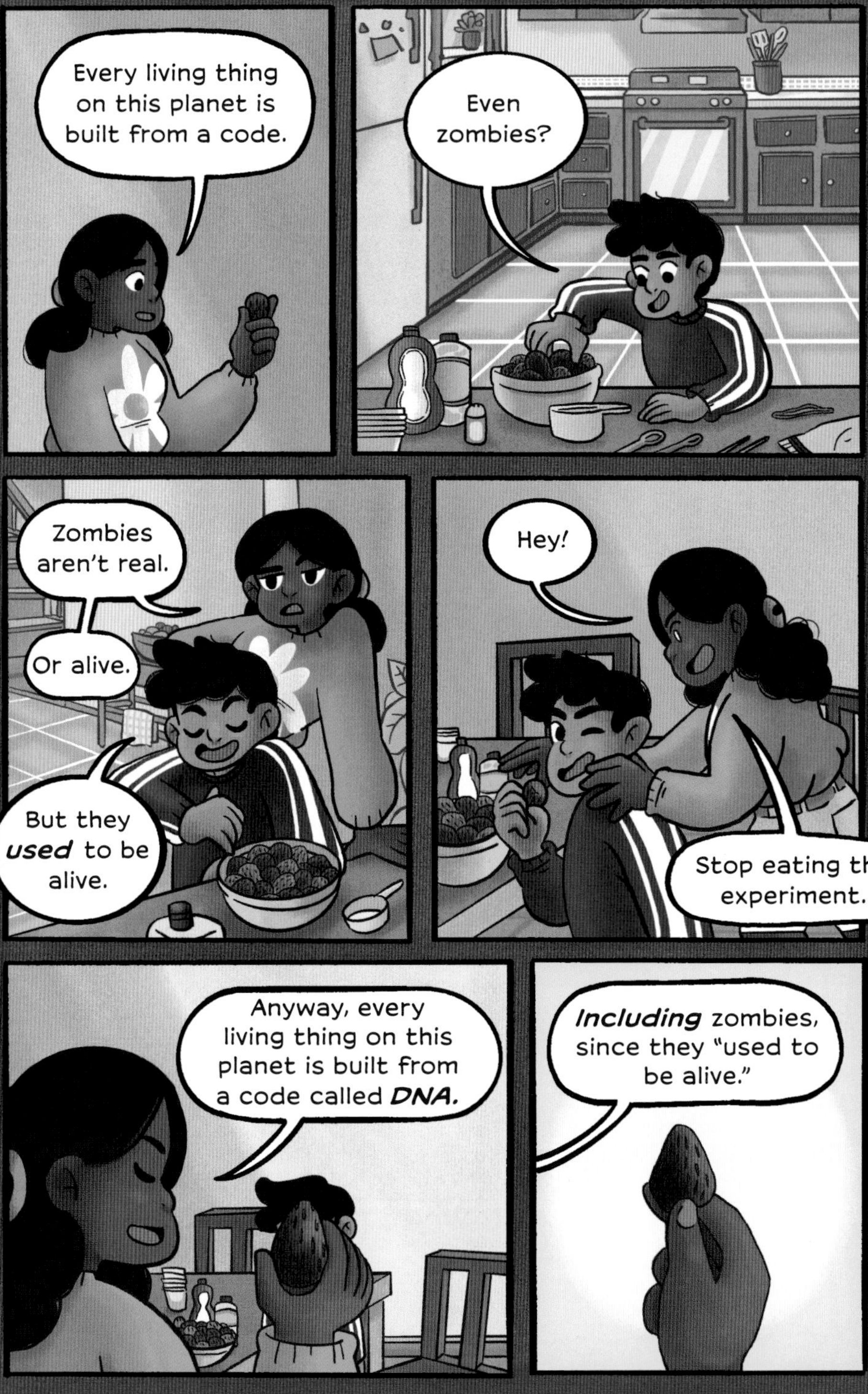
Every living thing on this planet is built from a code.
Even zombies?
Zombies aren't real.
Or alive.
But they *used* to be alive.
Hey!
Stop eating the experiment.
Anyway, every living thing on this planet is built from a code called ***DNA.***
Including zombies, since they "used to be alive."

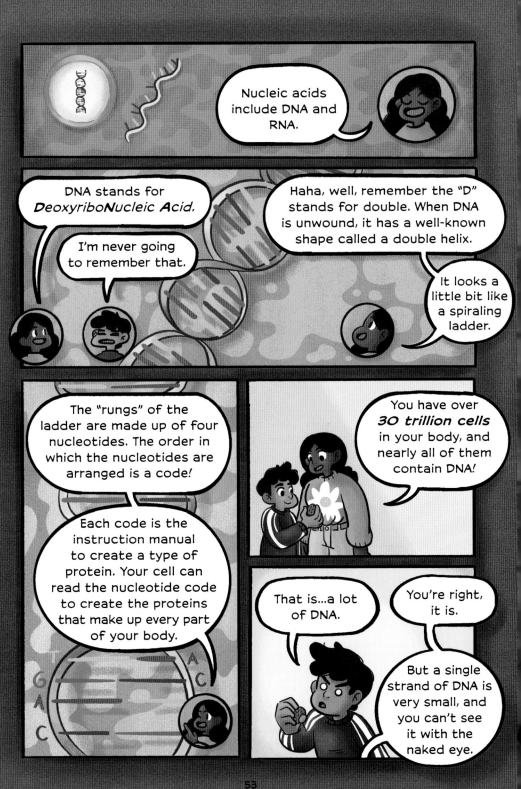

Nucleic acids include DNA and RNA.

DNA stands for *DeoxyriboNucleic Acid.*

I'm never going to remember that.

Haha, well, remember the "D" stands for double. When DNA is unwound, it has a well-known shape called a double helix.

It looks a little bit like a spiraling ladder.

The "rungs" of the ladder are made up of four nucleotides. The order in which the nucleotides are arranged is a code!

Each code is the instruction manual to create a type of protein. Your cell can read the nucleotide code to create the proteins that make up every part of your body.

You have over **30 trillion cells** in your body, and nearly all of them contain DNA!

That is...a lot of DNA.

You're right, it is.

But a single strand of DNA is very small, and you can't see it with the naked eye.

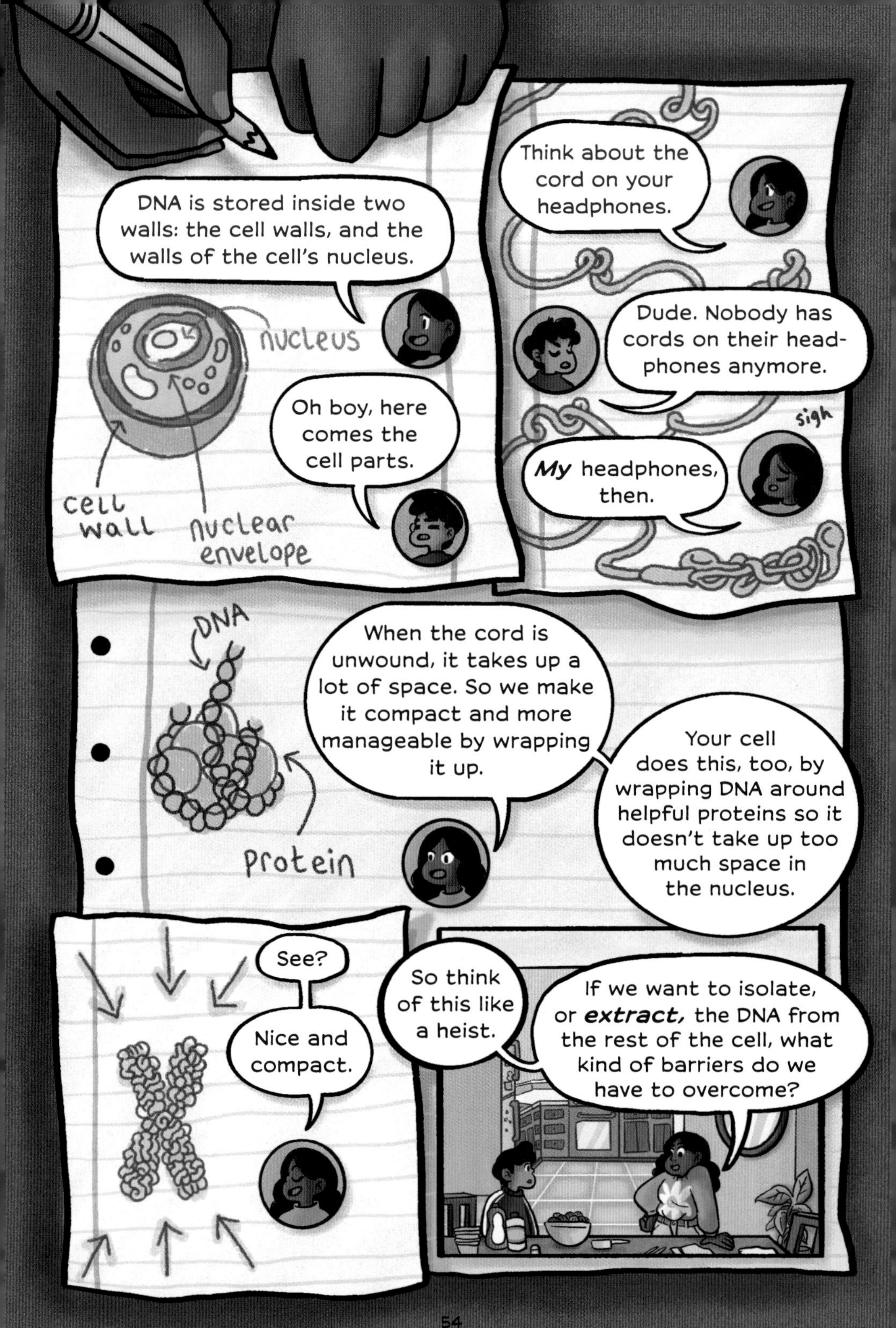
DNA is stored inside two walls: the cell walls, and the walls of the cell's nucleus.
nucleus
cell wall
nuclear envelope
Oh boy, here comes the cell parts.
Think about the cord on your headphones.
Dude. Nobody has cords on their head-phones anymore.
sigh
My headphones, then.
DNA
protein
When the cord is unwound, it takes up a lot of space. So we make it compact and more manageable by wrapping it up.
Your cell does this, too, by wrapping DNA around helpful proteins so it doesn't take up too much space in the nucleus.
See?
Nice and compact.
So think of this like a heist.
If we want to isolate, or ***extract,*** the DNA from the rest of the cell, what kind of barriers do we have to overcome?

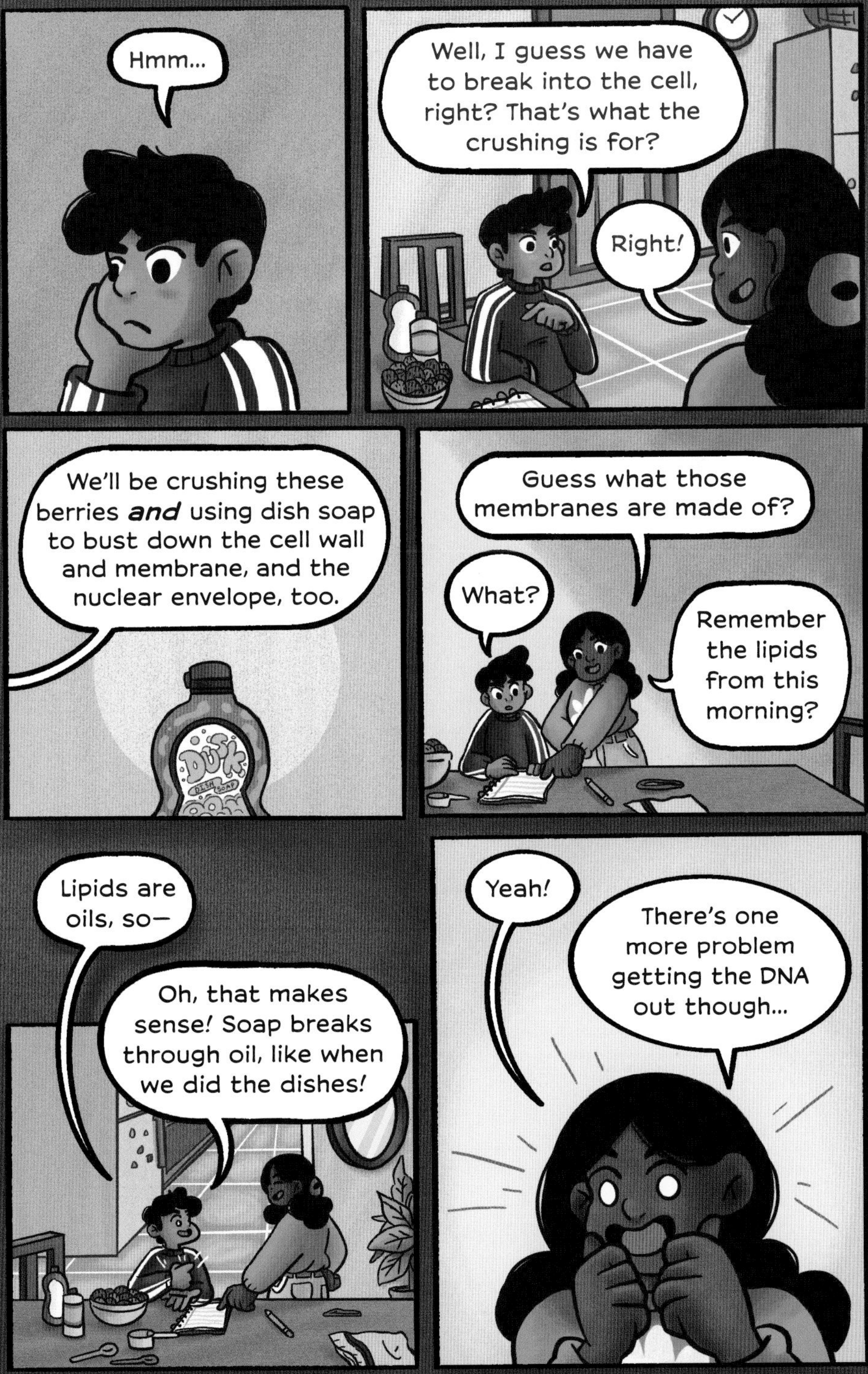
Hmm...
Well, I guess we have to break into the cell, right? That's what the crushing is for?
Right!
We'll be crushing these berries ***and*** using dish soap to bust down the cell wall and membrane, and the nuclear envelope, too.
DUSK DISH SOAP
Guess what those membranes are made of?
What?
Remember the lipids from this morning?
Lipids are oils, so—
Oh, that makes sense! Soap breaks through oil, like when we did the dishes!
Yeah!
There's one more problem getting the DNA out though...

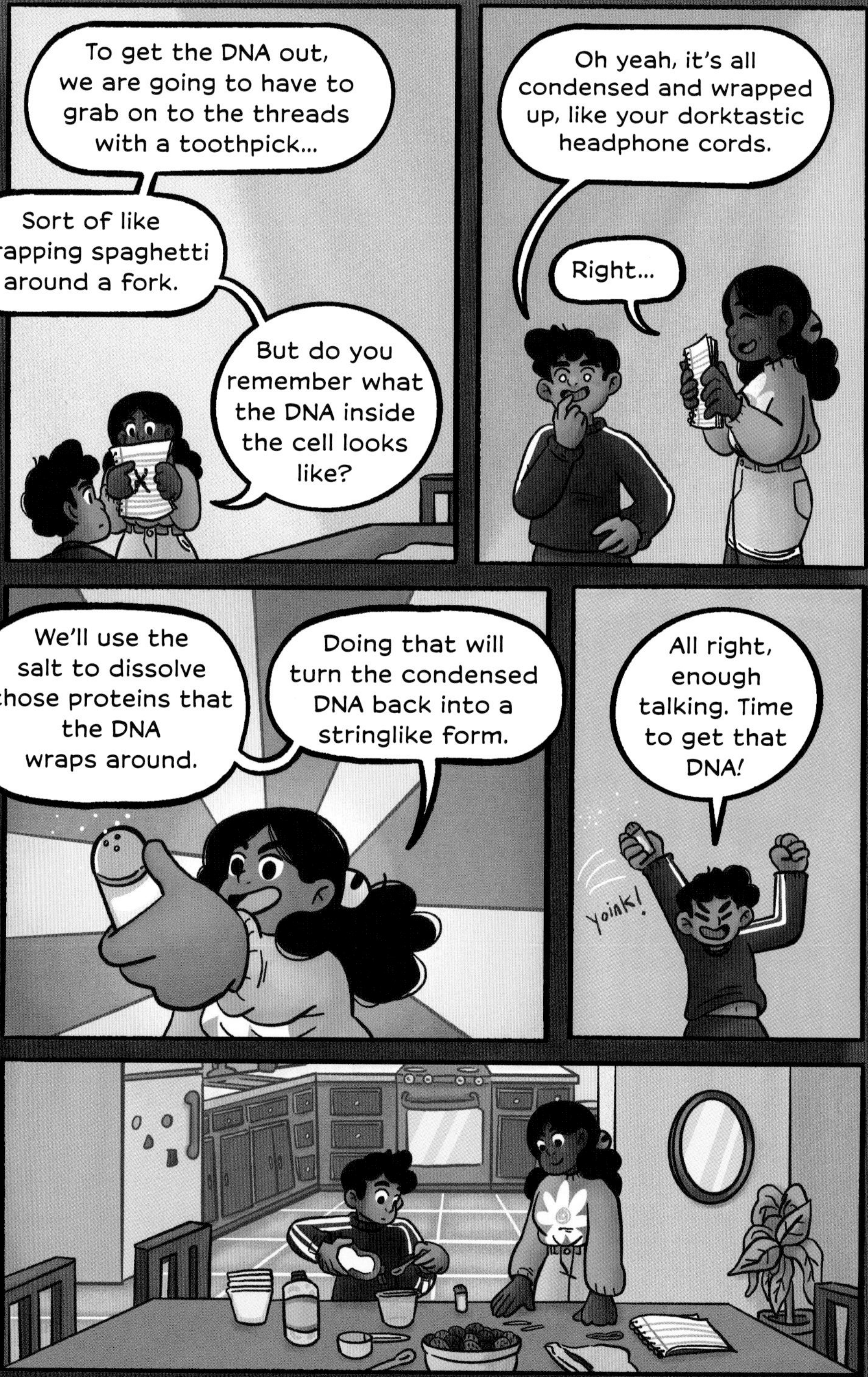
To get the DNA out, we are going to have to grab on to the threads with a toothpick...
Sort of like wrapping spaghetti around a fork.
But do you remember what the DNA inside the cell looks like?
Oh yeah, it's all condensed and wrapped up, like your dorktastic headphone cords.
Right...
We'll use the salt to dissolve those proteins that the DNA wraps around.
Doing that will turn the condensed DNA back into a stringlike form.
All right, enough talking. Time to get that DNA!
yoink!

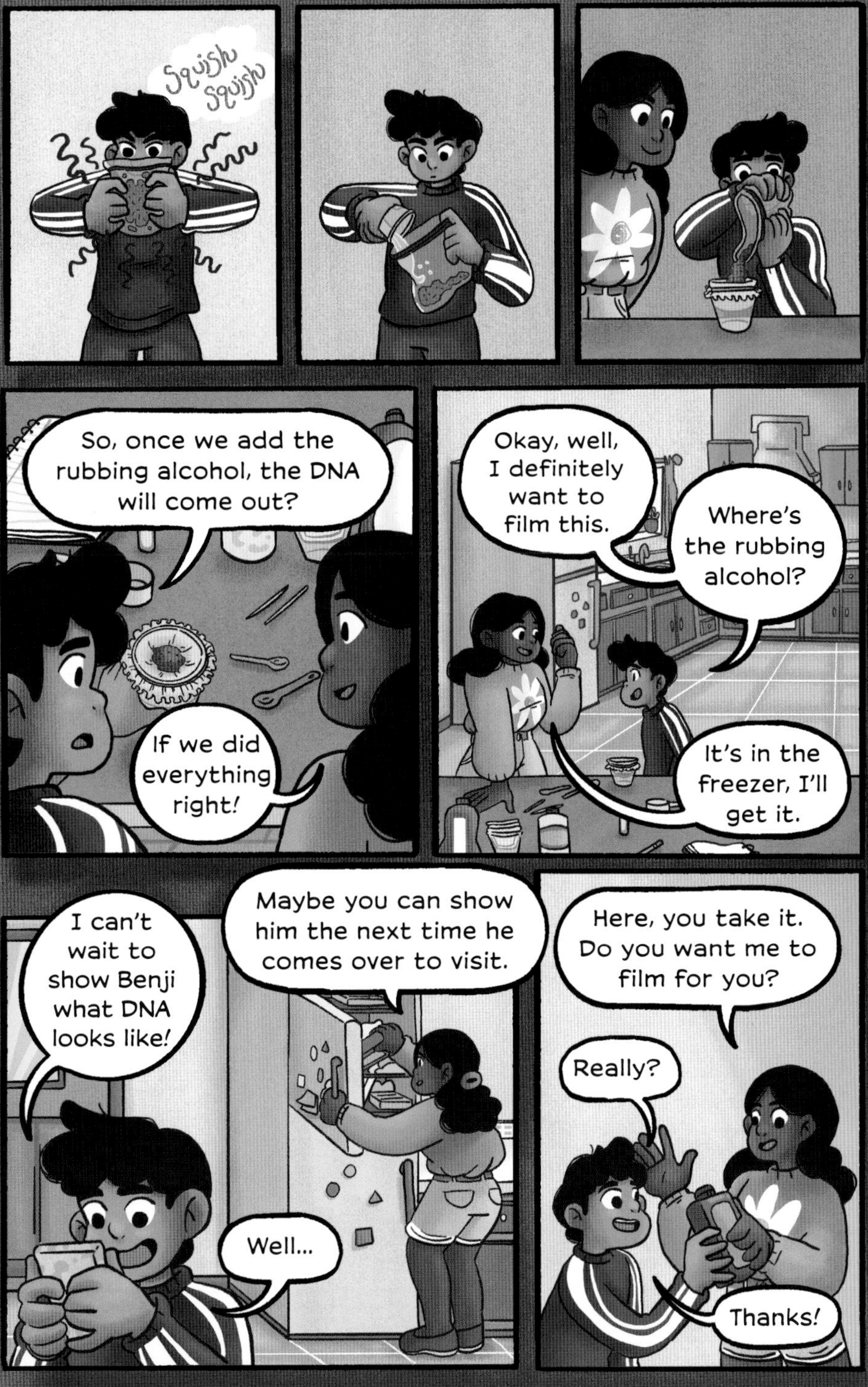
Squish Squish
So, once we add the rubbing alcohol, the DNA will come out?
If we did everything right!
Okay, well, I definitely want to film this.
Where's the rubbing alcohol?
It's in the freezer, I'll get it.
I can't wait to show Benji what DNA looks like!
Maybe you can show him the next time he comes over to visit.
Well...
Here, you take it. Do you want me to film for you?
Really?
Thanks!

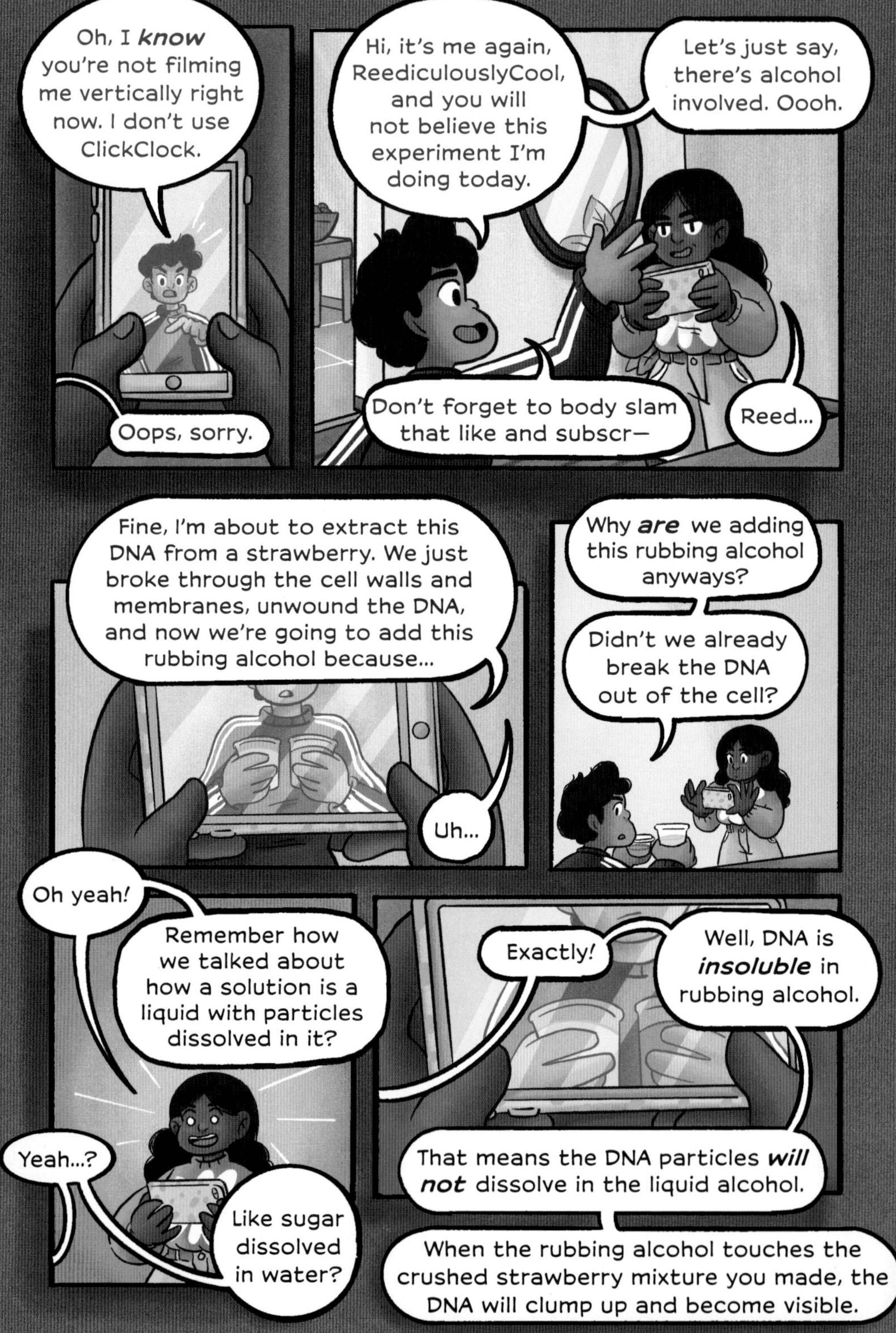

Oh, I *know* you're not filming me vertically right now. I don't use ClickClock.
Oops, sorry.
Hi, it's me again, ReediculouslyCool, and you will not believe this experiment I'm doing today.
Let's just say, there's alcohol involved. Oooh.
Don't forget to body slam that like and subscr—
Reed...
Fine, I'm about to extract this DNA from a strawberry. We just broke through the cell walls and membranes, unwound the DNA, and now we're going to add this rubbing alcohol because...
Uh...
Why *are* we adding this rubbing alcohol anyways?
Didn't we already break the DNA out of the cell?
Oh yeah!
Remember how we talked about how a solution is a liquid with particles dissolved in it?
Yeah...?
Like sugar dissolved in water?
Exactly!
Well, DNA is *insoluble* in rubbing alcohol.
That means the DNA particles *will not* dissolve in the liquid alcohol.
When the rubbing alcohol touches the crushed strawberry mixture you made, the DNA will clump up and become visible.

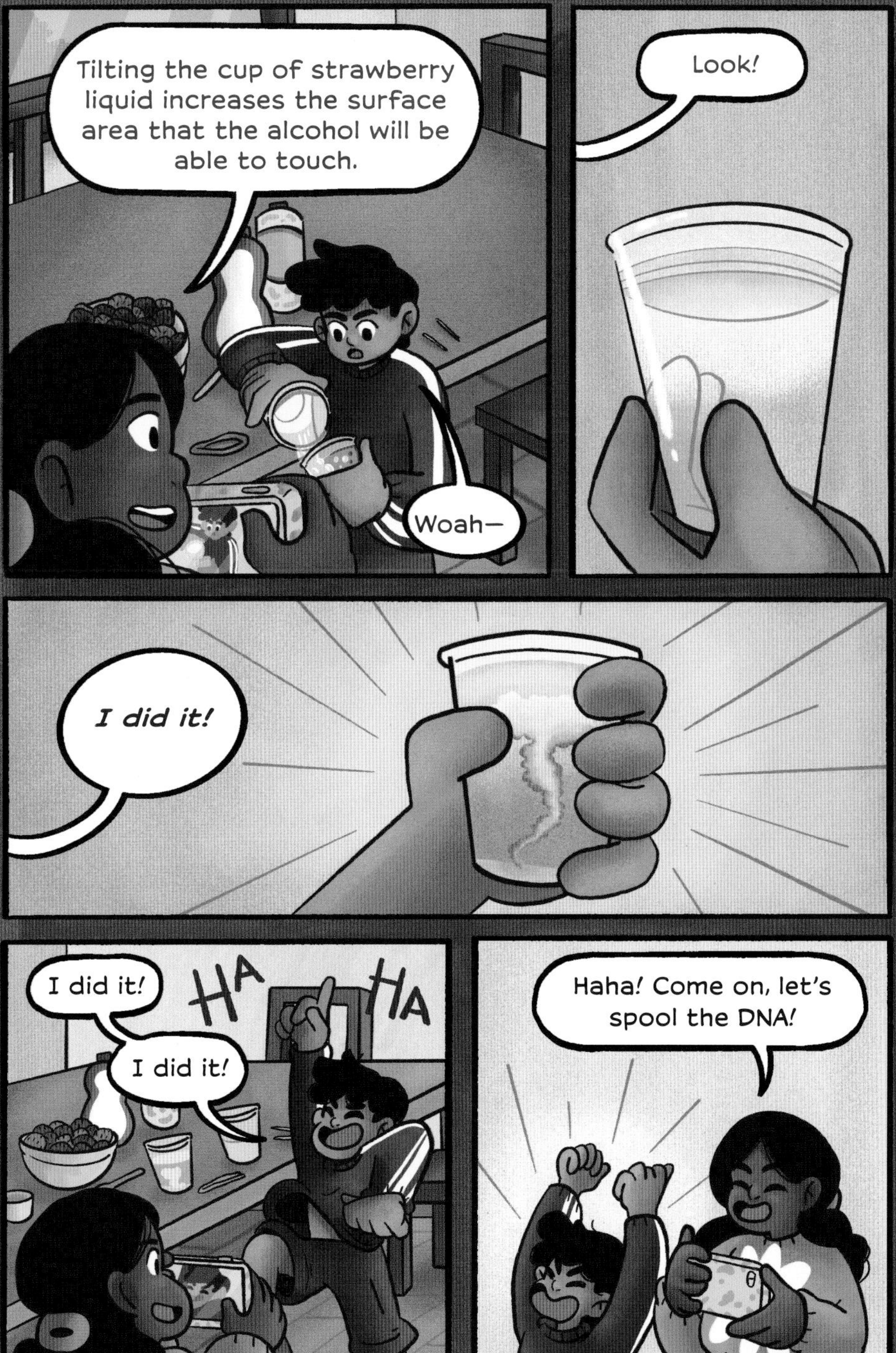
Tilting the cup of strawberry liquid increases the surface area that the alcohol will be able to touch.
Woah—
Look!
I did it!
I did it!
HA HA
I did it!
Haha! Come on, let's spool the DNA!

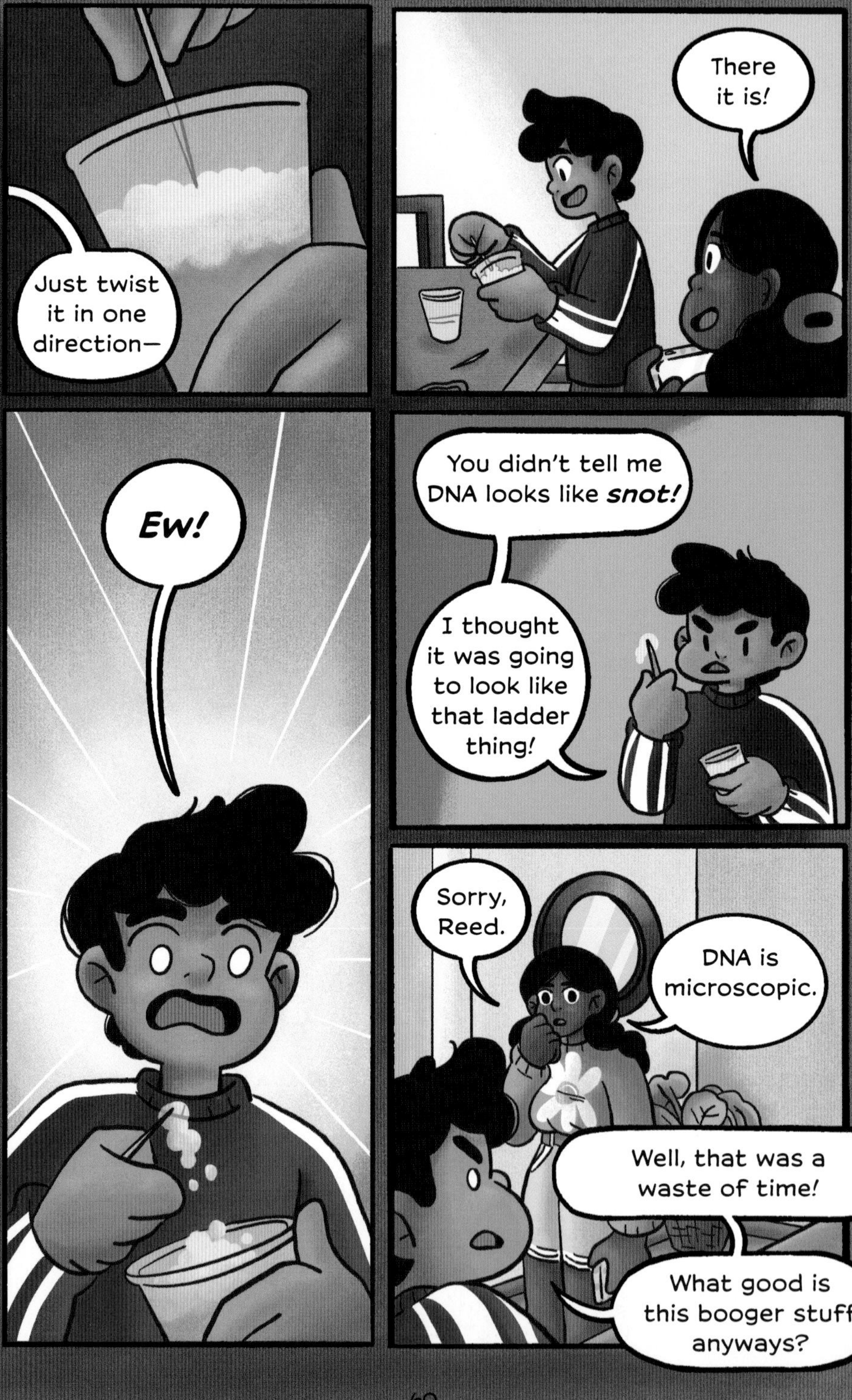
Just twist it in one direction—
There it is!
Ew!
You didn't tell me DNA looks like snot!
I thought it was going to look like that ladder thing!
Sorry, Reed.
DNA is microscopic.
Well, that was a waste of time!
What good is this booger stuff anyways?

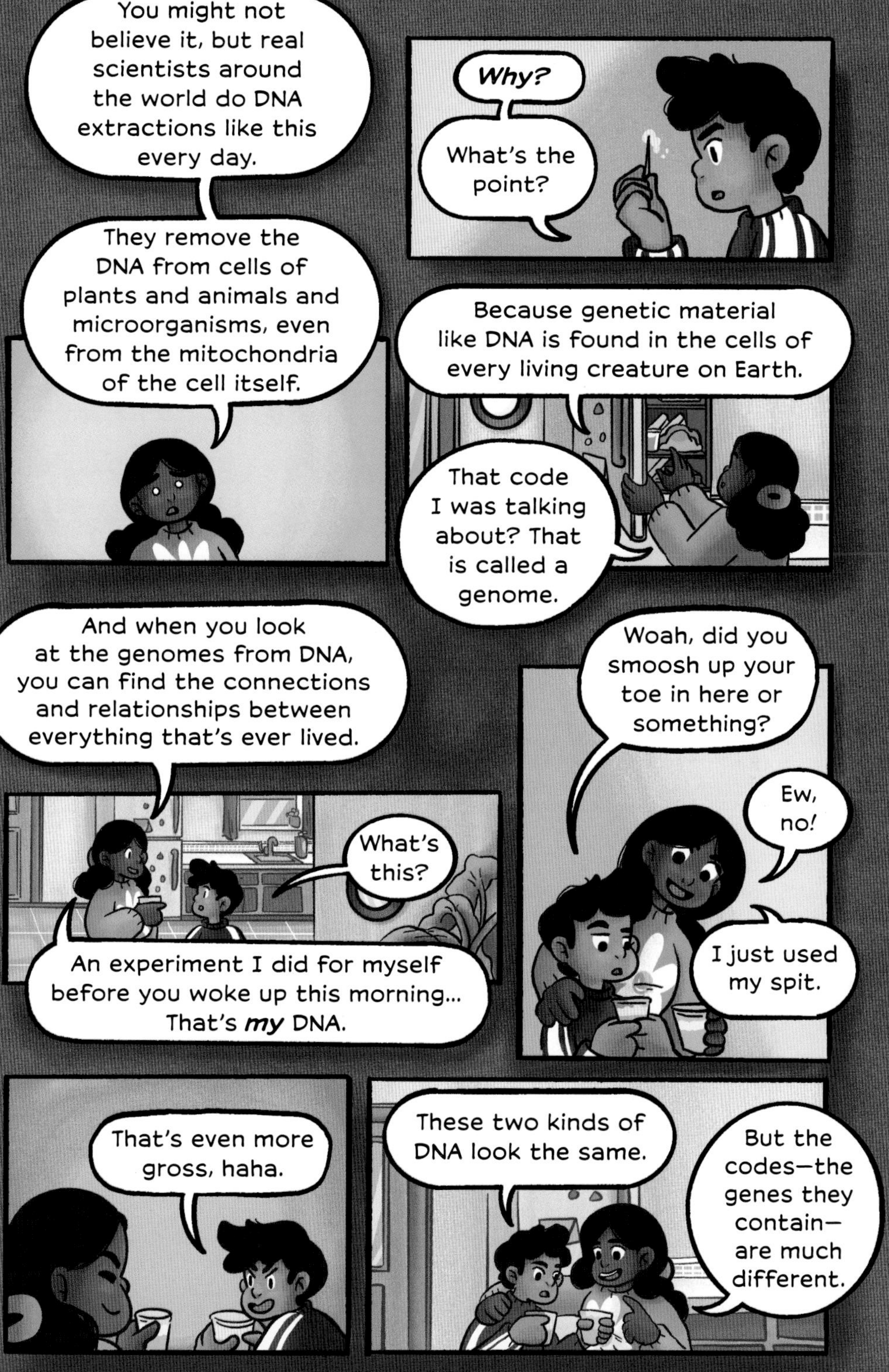
You might not believe it, but real scientists around the world do DNA extractions like this every day.
Why?
What's the point?
They remove the DNA from cells of plants and animals and microorganisms, even from the mitochondria of the cell itself.
Because genetic material like DNA is found in the cells of every living creature on Earth.
That code I was talking about? That is called a genome.
And when you look at the genomes from DNA, you can find the connections and relationships between everything that's ever lived.
What's this?
An experiment I did for myself before you woke up this morning... That's *my* DNA.
Woah, did you smoosh up your toe in here or something?
Ew, no!
I just used my spit.
That's even more gross, haha.
These two kinds of DNA look the same.
But the codes—the genes they contain—are much different.

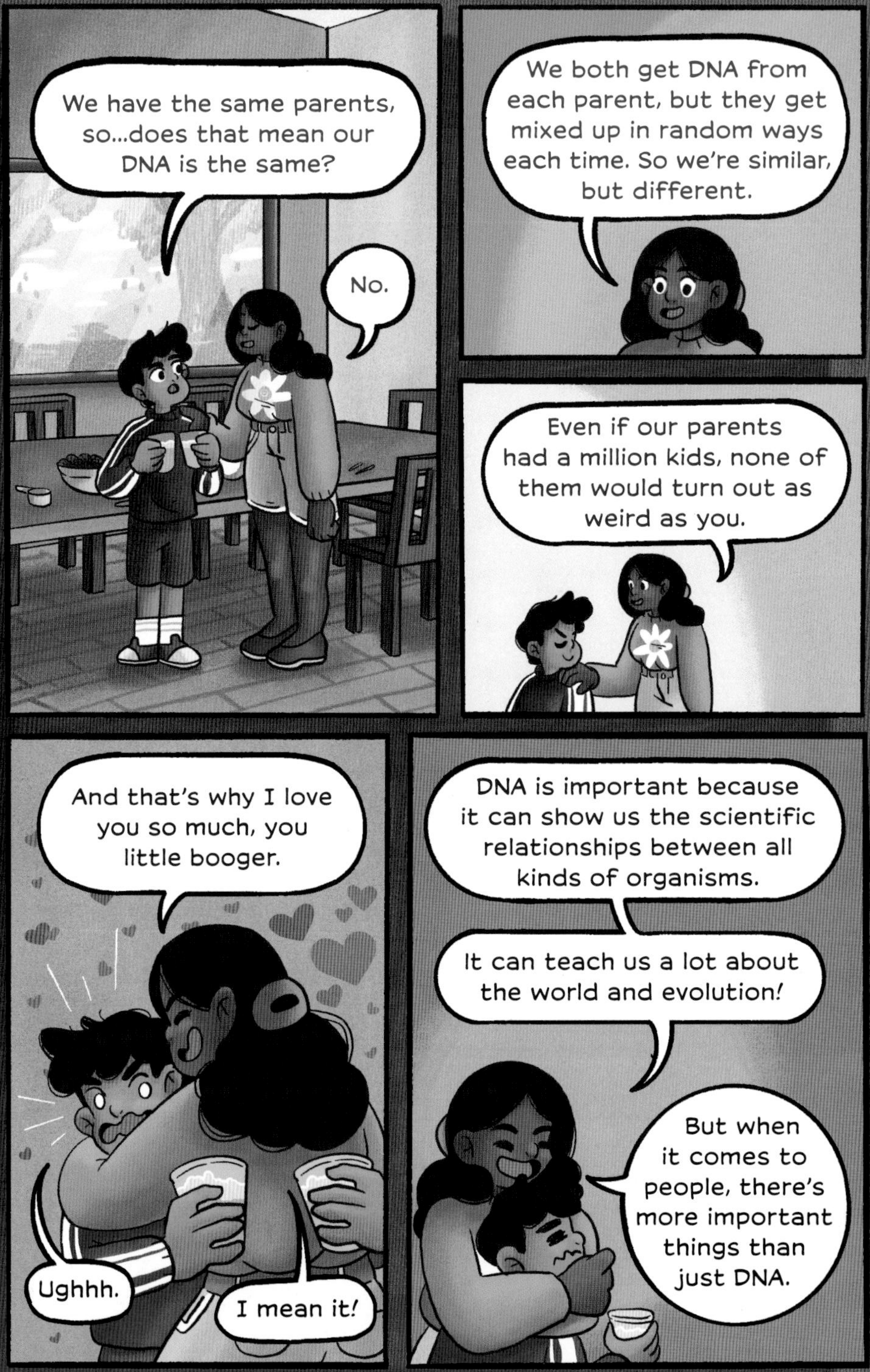
We have the same parents, so...does that mean our DNA is the same?
No.
We both get DNA from each parent, but they get mixed up in random ways each time. So we're similar, but different.
Even if our parents had a million kids, none of them would turn out as weird as you.
And that's why I love you so much, you little booger.
Ughhh.
I mean it!
DNA is important because it can show us the scientific relationships between all kinds of organisms.
It can teach us a lot about the world and evolution!
But when it comes to people, there's more important things than just DNA.

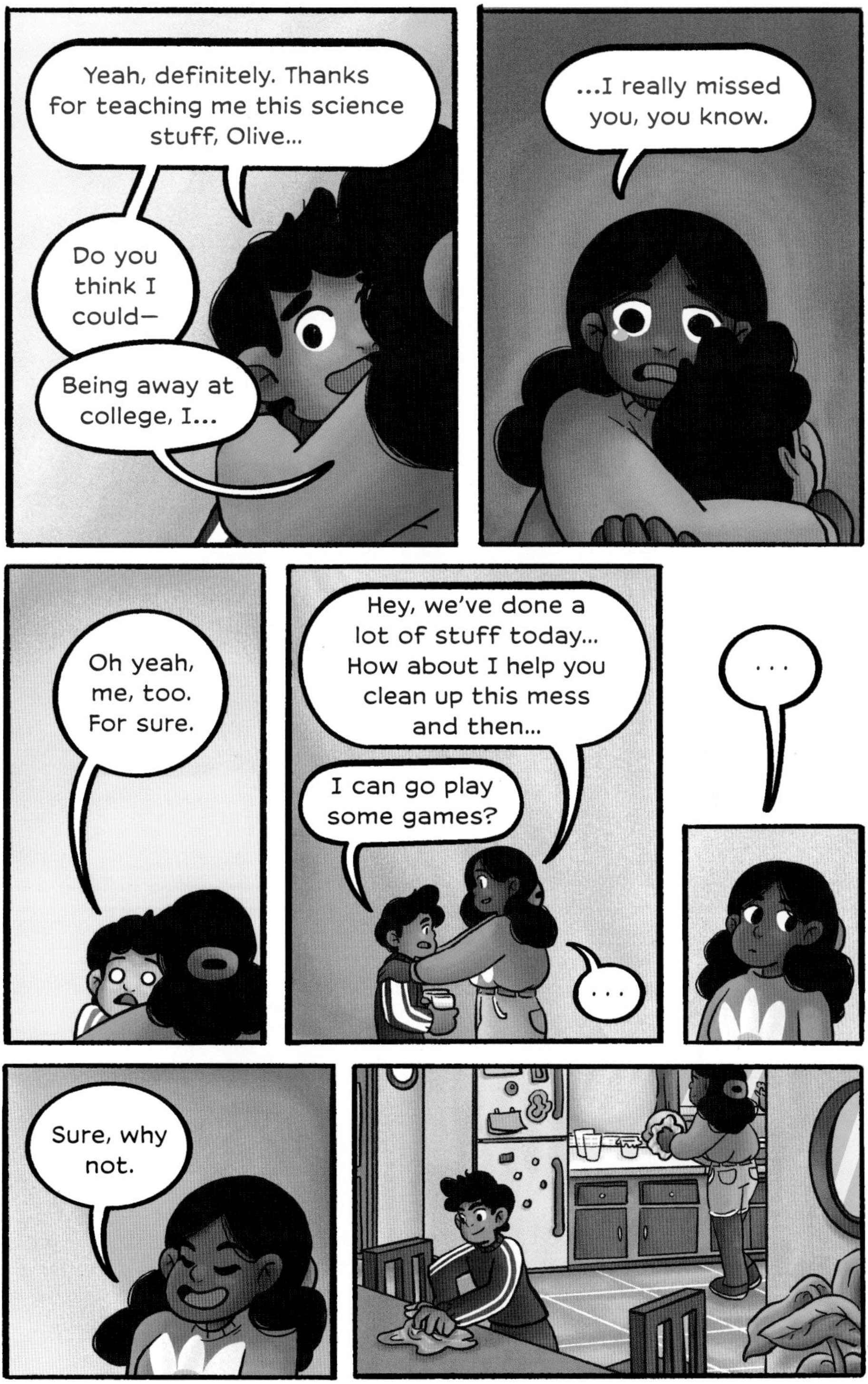
Yeah, definitely. Thanks for teaching me this science stuff, Olive...
Do you think I could—
Being away at college, I...
...I really missed you, you know.
Oh yeah, me, too. For sure.
Hey, we've done a lot of stuff today... How about I help you clean up this mess and then...
I can go play some games?
...
...
Sure, why not.

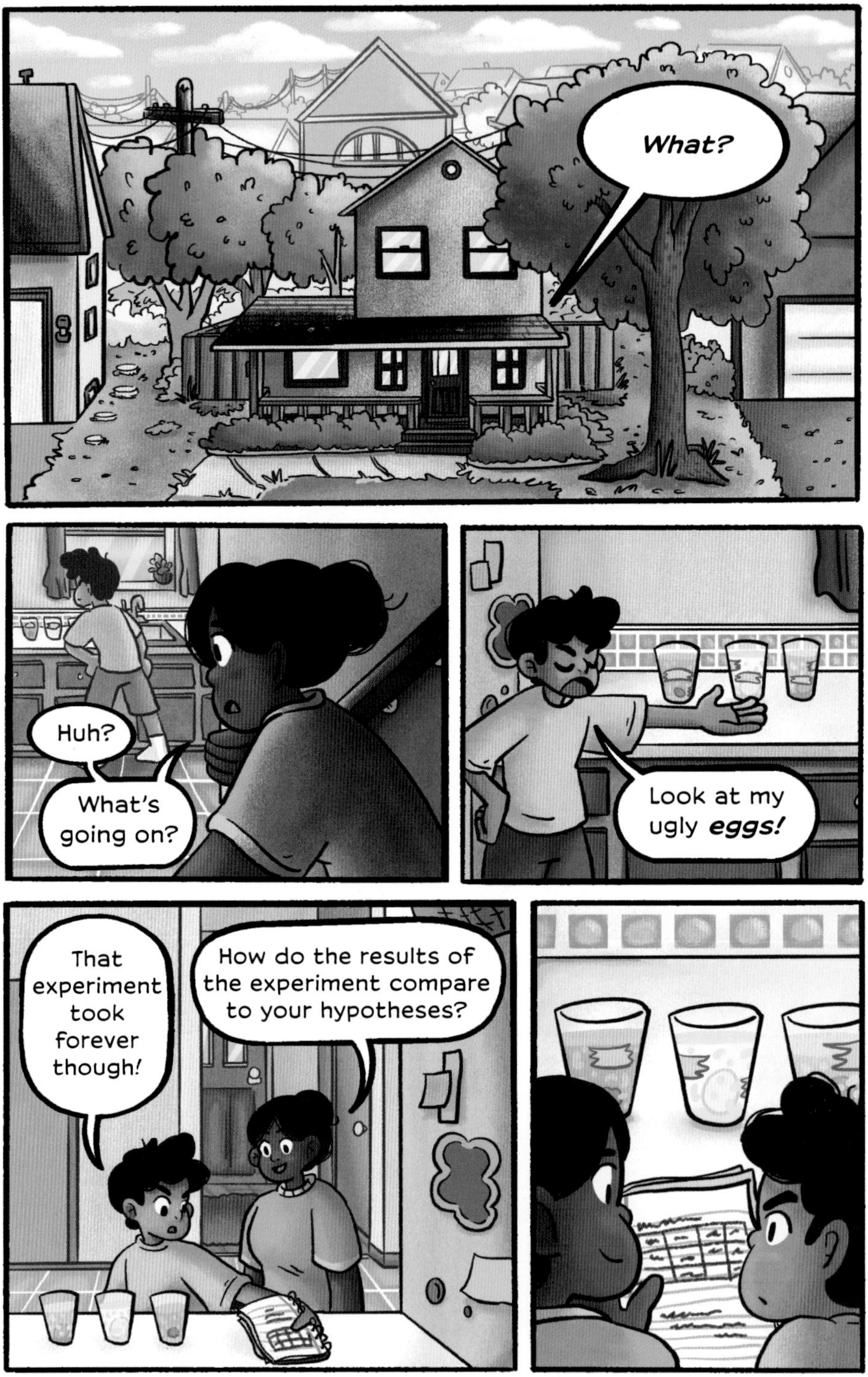

What?
Huh?
What's going on?
Look at my ugly eggs!
That experiment took forever though!
How do the results of the experiment compare to your hypotheses?

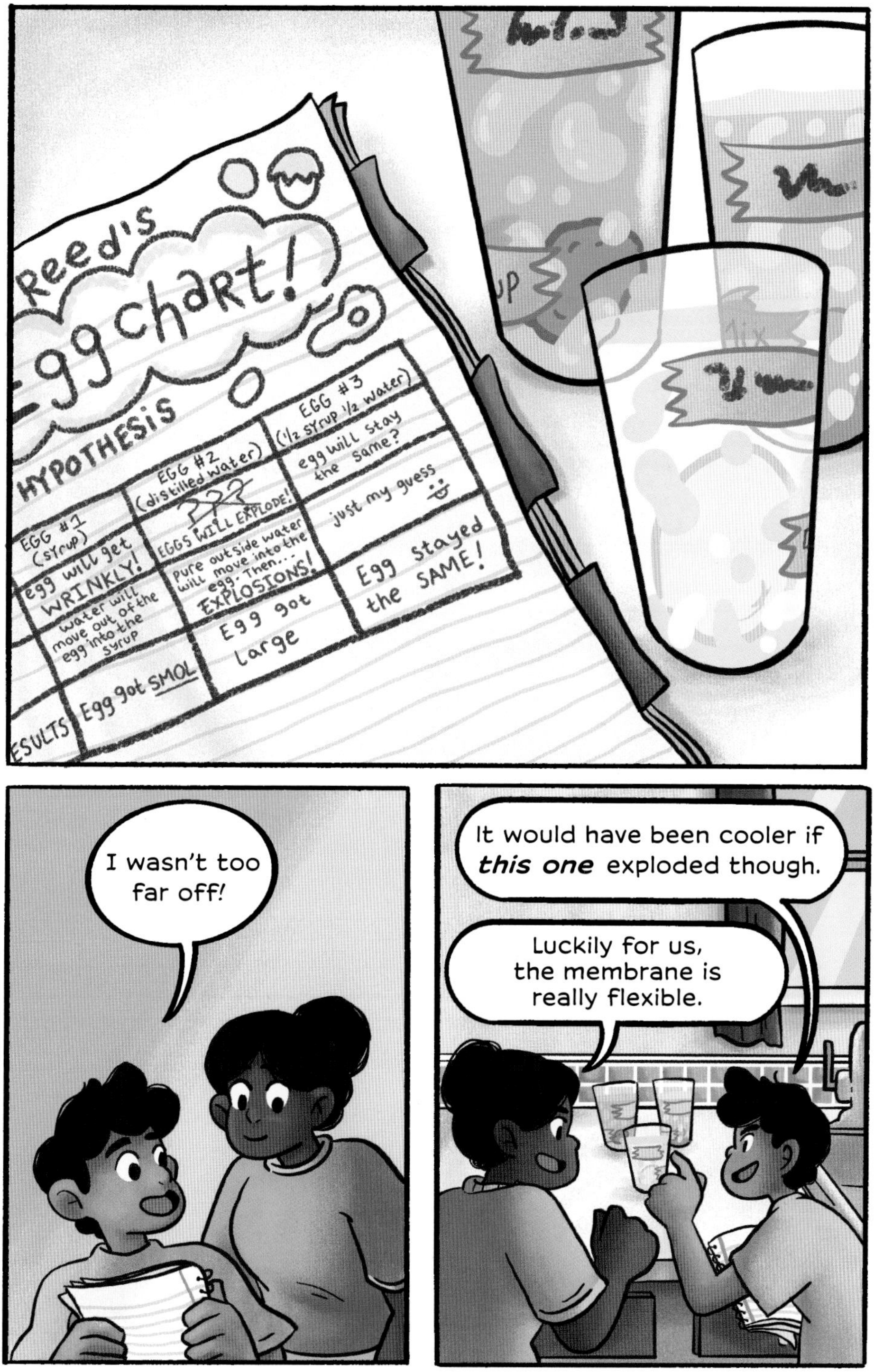

Reed's
Egg chart!
HYPOTHESIS
EGG #1 (syrup)
EGG #2 (distilled water)
EGG #3 (1/2 syrup 1/2 water)
egg will get WRINKLY!
water will move out of the egg into the syrup
EGGS WILL EXPLODE!
Pure outside water will move into the egg. Then... EXPLOSIONS!
egg will stay the same?
just my guess
ESULTS
Egg got SMOL
Egg got large
Egg stayed the SAME!
I wasn't too far off!
It would have been cooler if *this one* exploded though.
Luckily for us, the membrane is really flexible.

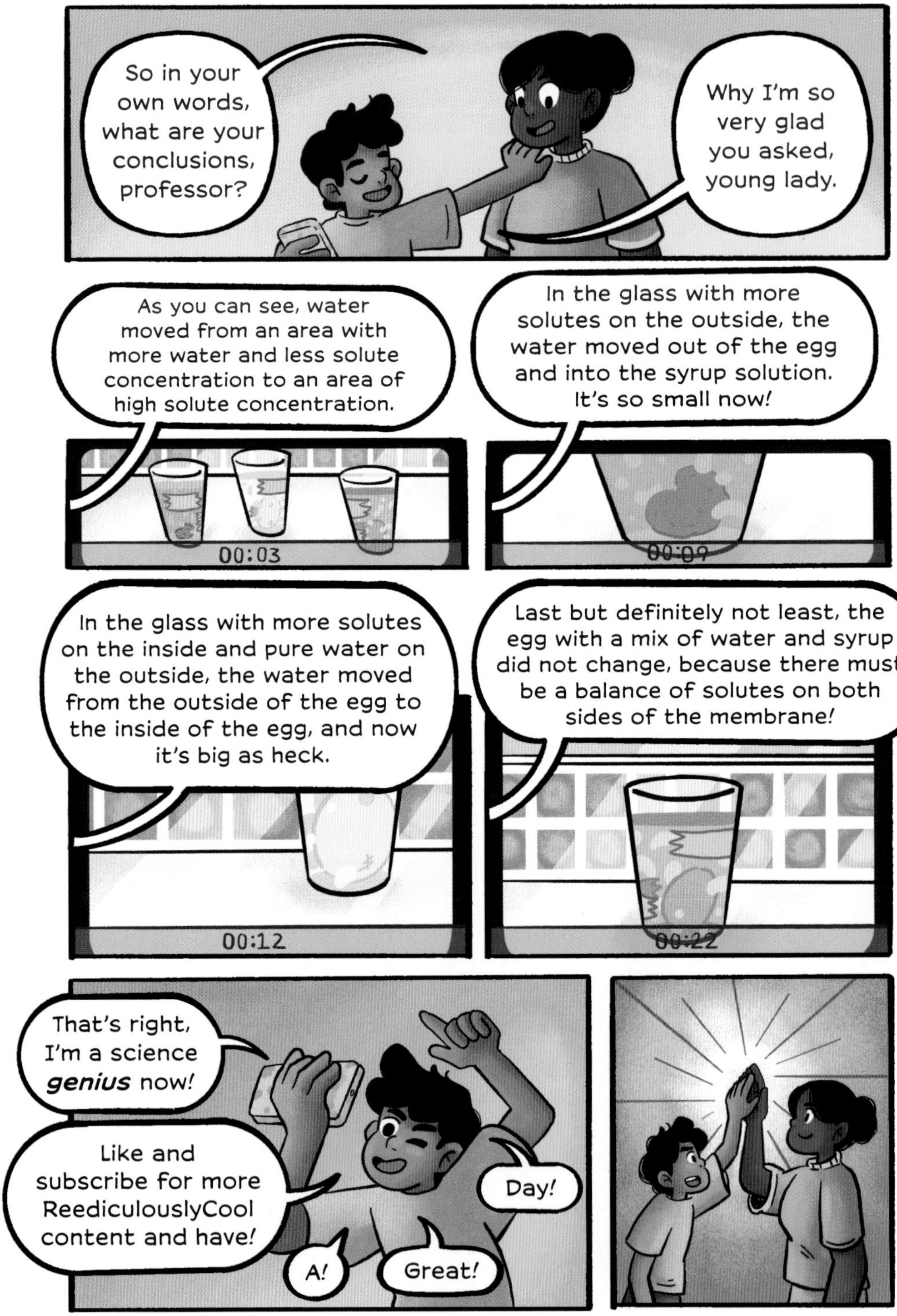
So in your own words, what are your conclusions, professor?
Why I'm so very glad you asked, young lady.
As you can see, water moved from an area with more water and less solute concentration to an area of high solute concentration.
00:03
In the glass with more solutes on the outside, the water moved out of the egg and into the syrup solution. It's so small now!
00:09
In the glass with more solutes on the inside and pure water on the outside, the water moved from the outside of the egg to the inside of the egg, and now it's big as heck.
00:12
Last but definitely not least, the egg with a mix of water and syrup did not change, because there must be a balance of solutes on both sides of the membrane!
00:22
That's right, I'm a science *genius* now!
Like and subscribe for more ReediculouslyCool content and have!
A!
Great!
Day!

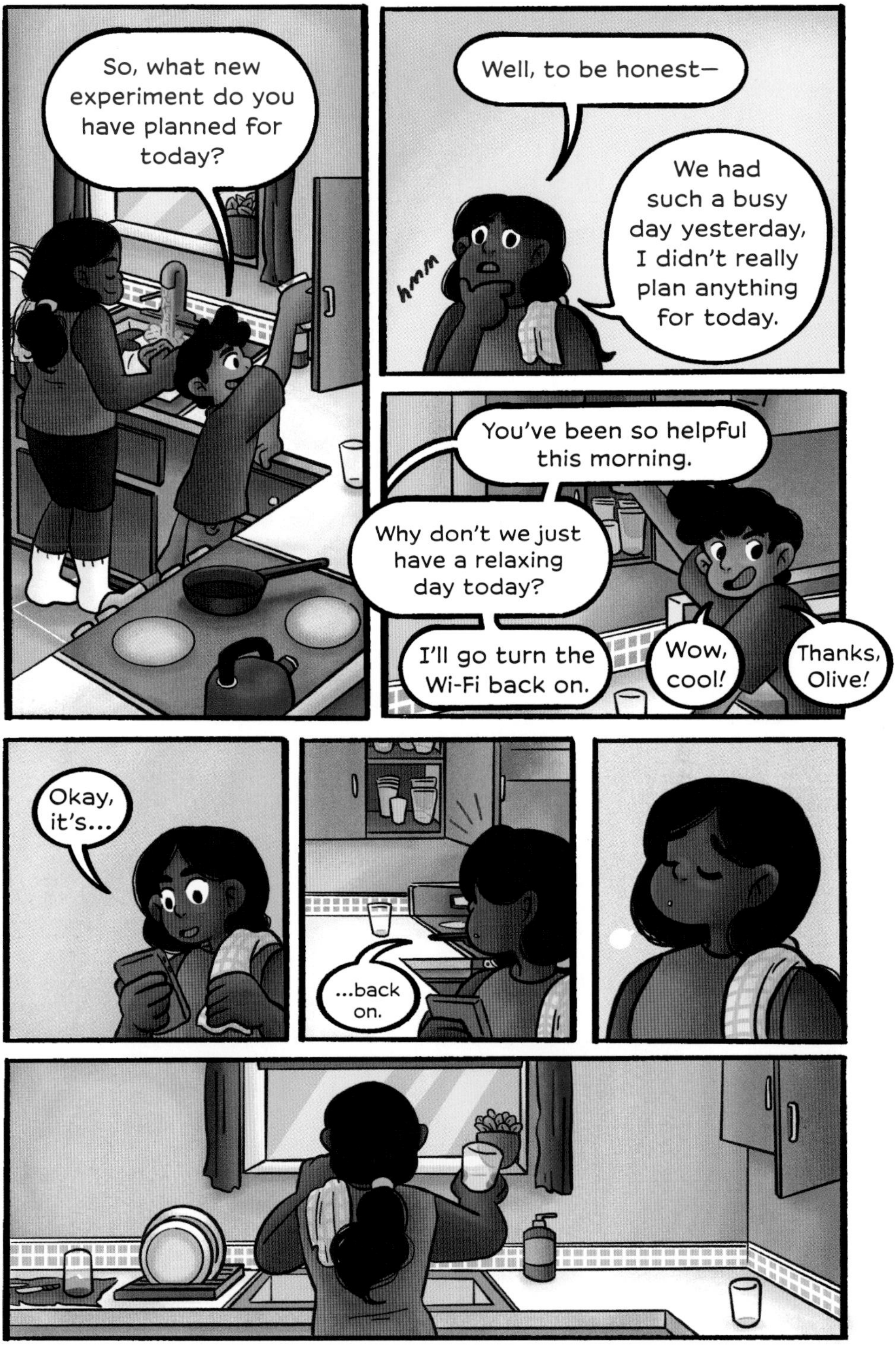
So, what new experiment do you have planned for today?
Well, to be honest—
hmm
We had such a busy day yesterday, I didn't really plan anything for today.
You've been so helpful this morning.
Why don't we just have a relaxing day today?
I'll go turn the Wi-Fi back on.
Wow, cool!
Thanks, Olive!
Okay, it's...
...back on.

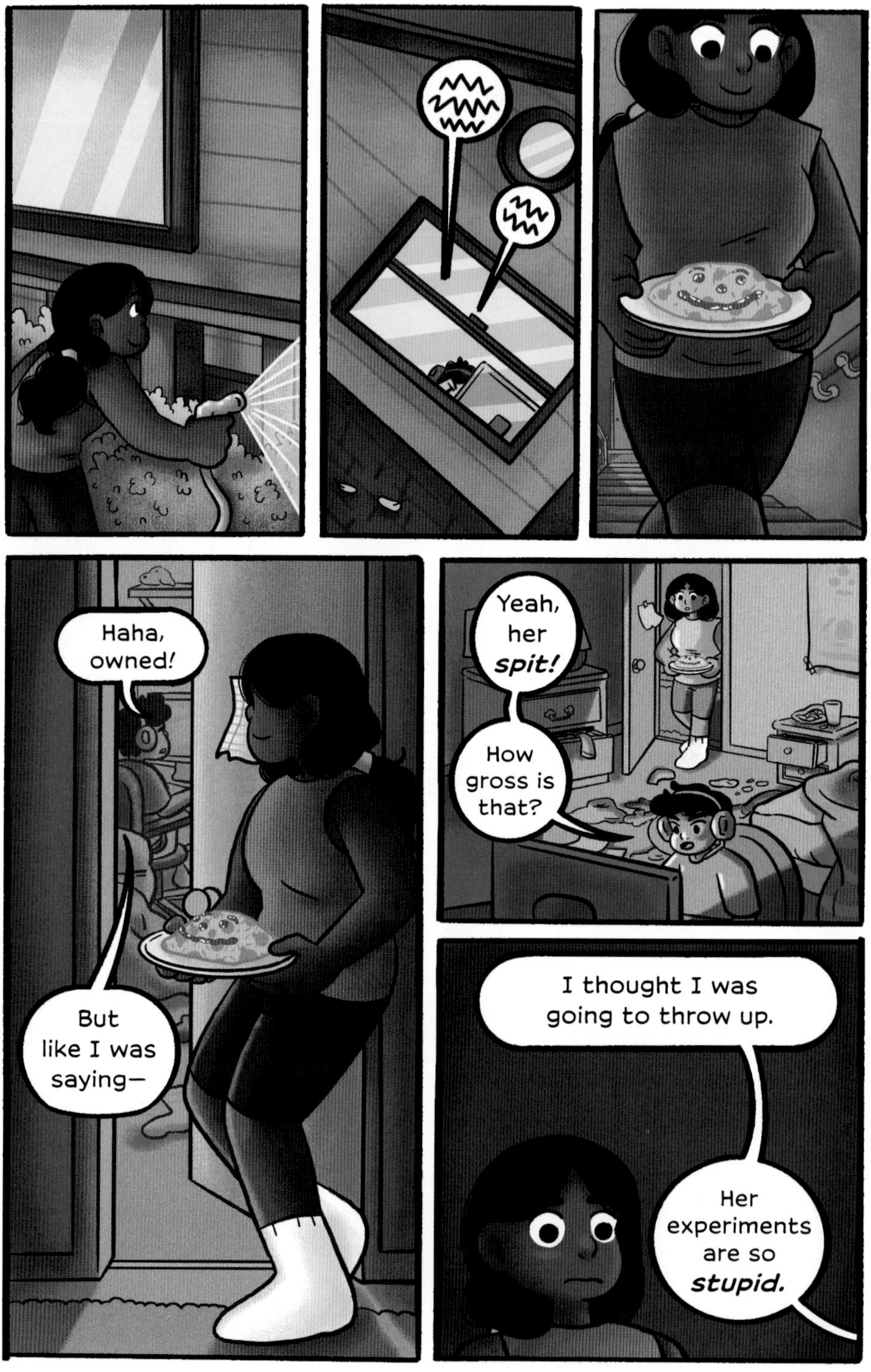
Haha, owned!
But like I was saying—
Yeah, her spit!
How gross is that?
I thought I was going to throw up.
Her experiments are so stupid.

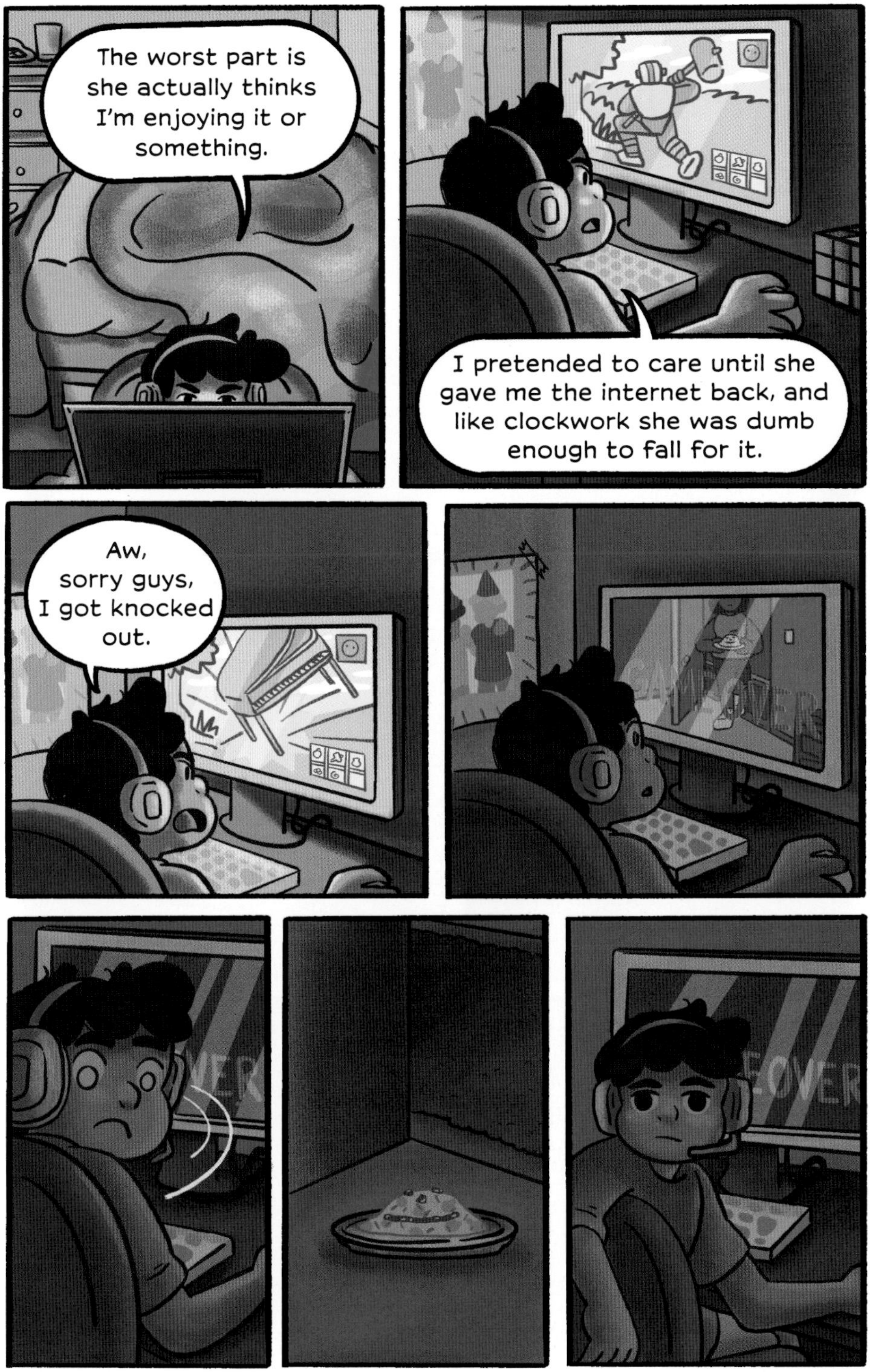
The worst part is she actually thinks I'm enjoying it or something.
I pretended to care until she gave me the internet back, and like clockwork she was dumb enough to fall for it.
Aw, sorry guys, I got knocked out.

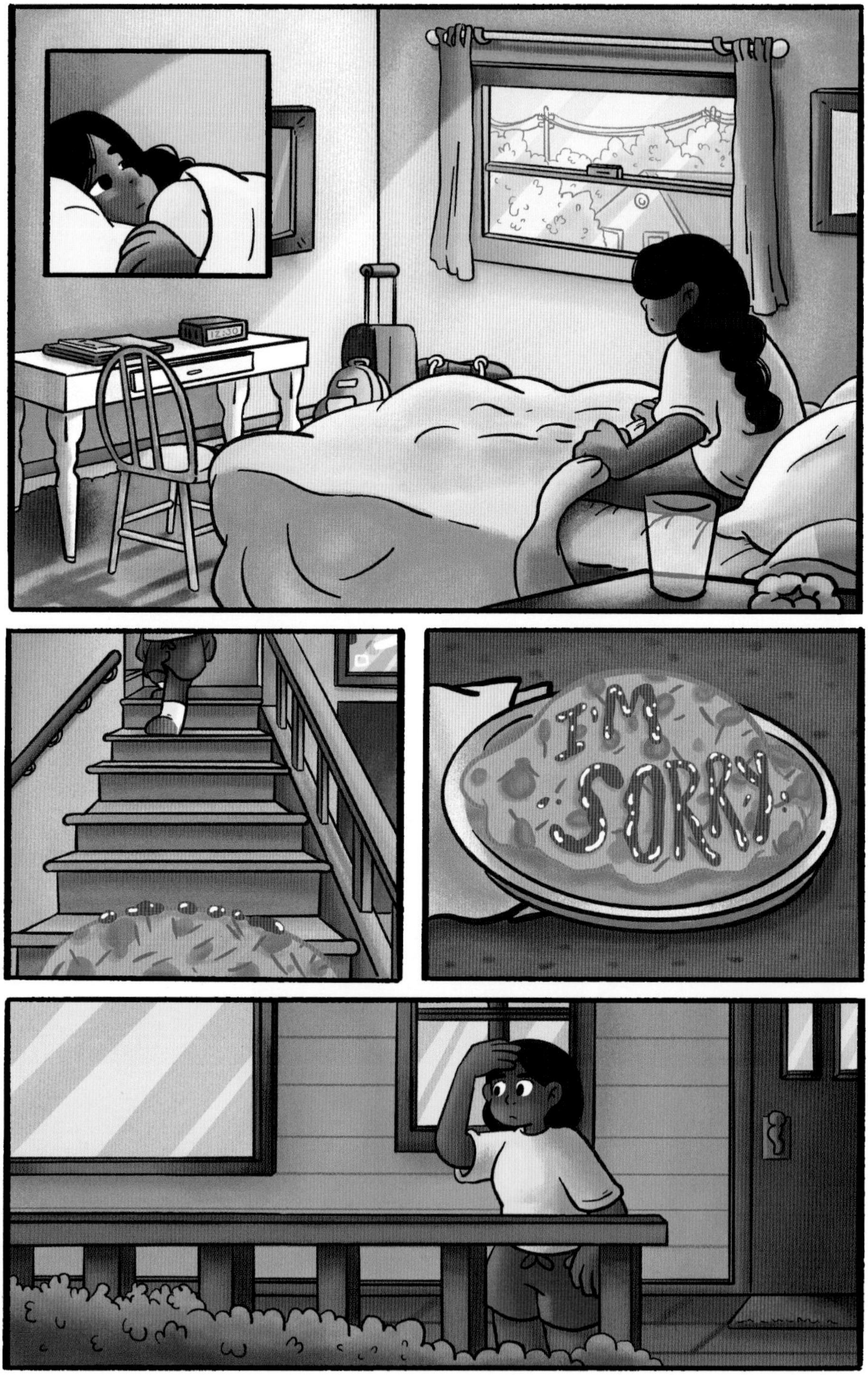
12:30
I'M SORRY

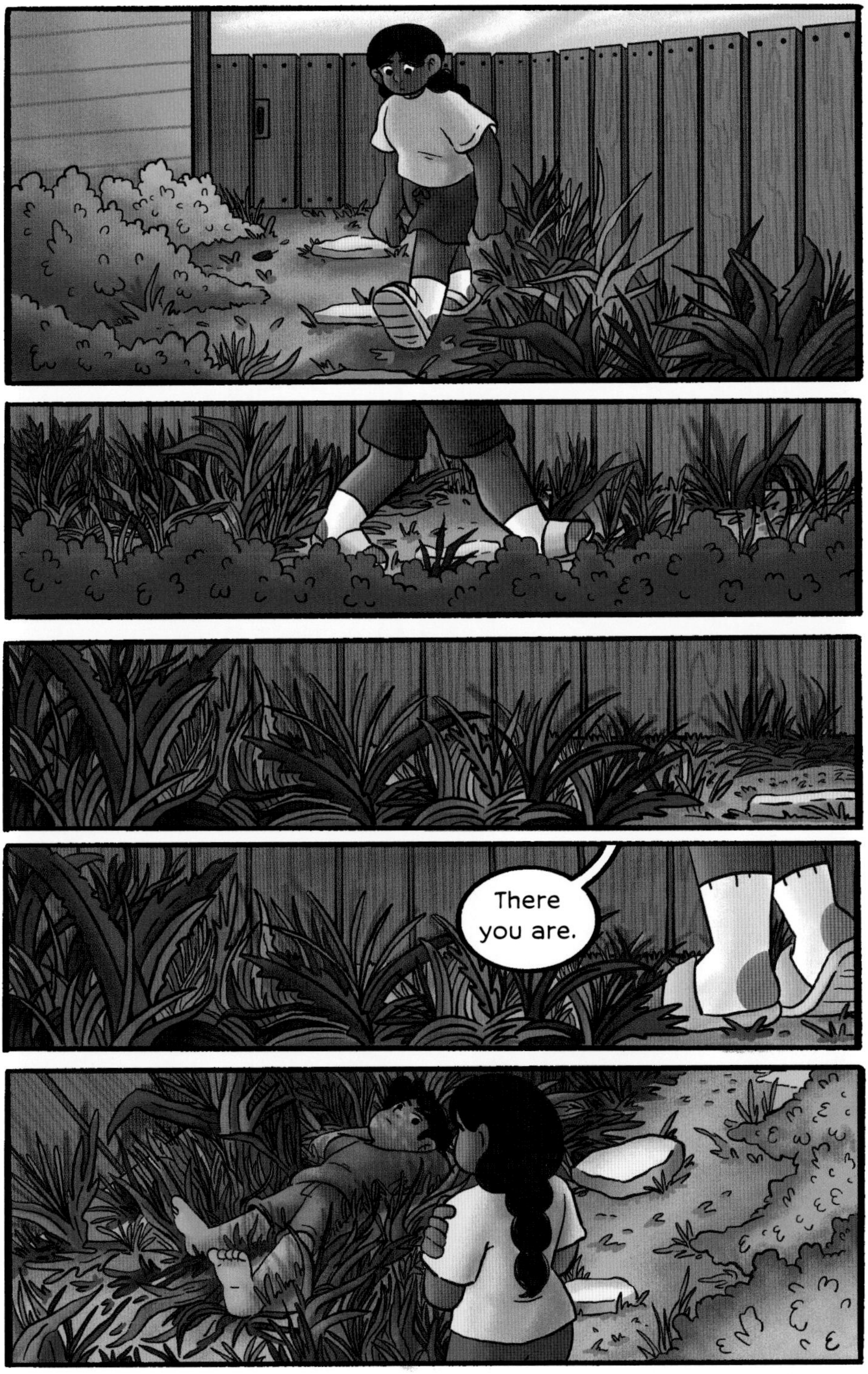
There you are.

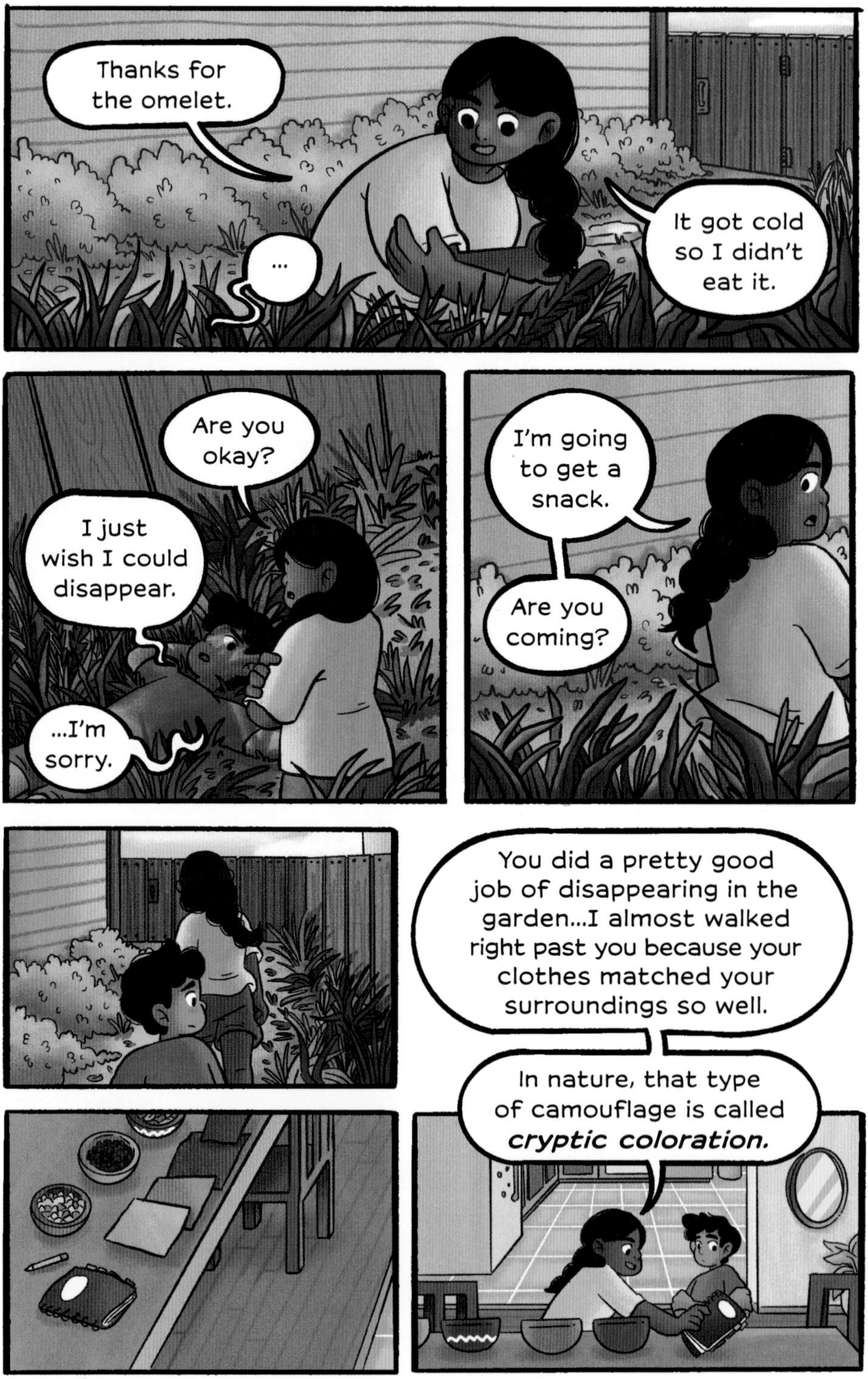
Thanks for the omelet.
...
It got cold so I didn't eat it.
Are you okay?
I just wish I could disappear.
...I'm sorry.
I'm going to get a snack.
Are you coming?
You did a pretty good job of disappearing in the garden...I almost walked right past you because your clothes matched your surroundings so well.
In nature, that type of camouflage is called ***cryptic coloration.***

THE SNEAKY SNACK EXPERIMENT

QUESTION:

HOW DOES CRYPTIC COLORATION WORK? DOES AN "ANIMAL'S" COLORATION GIVE IT AN ADVANTAGE IN DIFFERENT ENVIRONMENTS?

MATERIALS:

- A MULTICOLORED SMALL SNACK*
  ↳ SMALL DRIED FRUIT BITS, CHOCOLATES OR CANDIES, COLORFUL CRACKERS, OR ANOTHER SIMILAR SNACK THAT IS MULTICOLORED AND IS TOO SMALL TO BECOME A CHOKING HAZARD
- ONE SHEET OF WHITE PAPER
- FOUR SHEETS OF CONSTRUCTION PAPER THAT MATCHES THE SNACK BITS
- A TIMER

*IF SNACKING ON THESE TYPES OF FOOD ISN'T YOUR THING, TRY SUBSTITUTING SMALL, COLORFUL NONEDIBLE ITEMS LIKE BUTTONS OR BEADS INSTEAD. COLLECT THEM IN A BOWL TO "CAPTURE" YOUR PREY.

PREPARATION:

PREPARE 4 BOWLS OF COLORFUL SMALL SNACKS, SEPARATED BY COLOR.

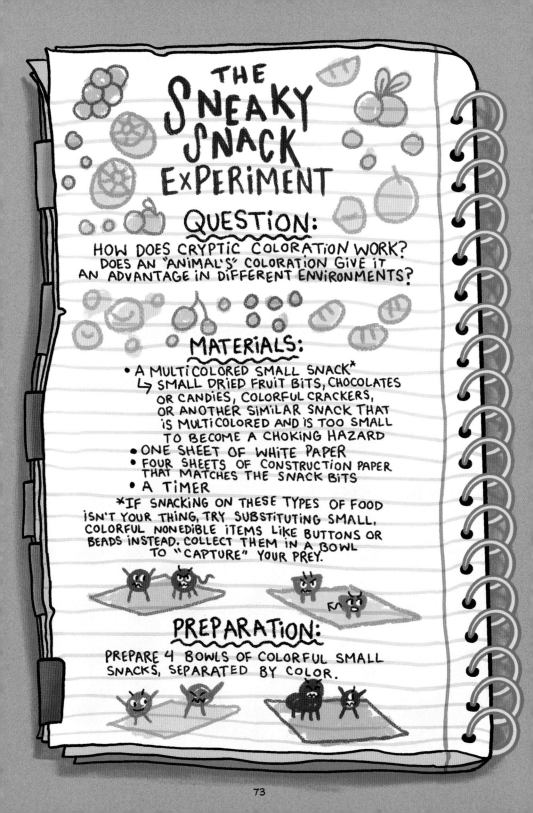

PROCEDURES

STEP 1: LAY DOWN A PIECE OF WHITE PAPER, AND PUT 40 COLORFUL SNACK PIECES (10 OF EACH COLOR) ONTO THE PAPER. THESE WILL BE YOUR "PREY."

STEP 2: SET A TIMER FOR 5 SECONDS.

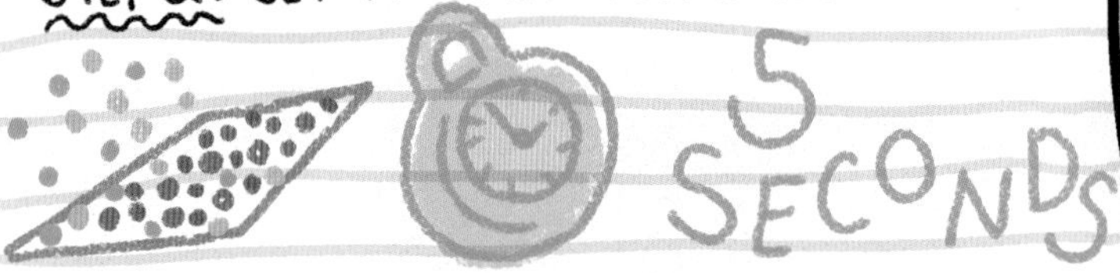
5
SECONDS

STEP 3: YOU'RE THE "PREDATOR!" WITH ONE HAND BEHIND YOU, USE TWO FINGERS ON YOUR OTHER HAND TO EAT AS MANY SNACKS AS YOU CAN BEFORE THE TIMER RINGS.

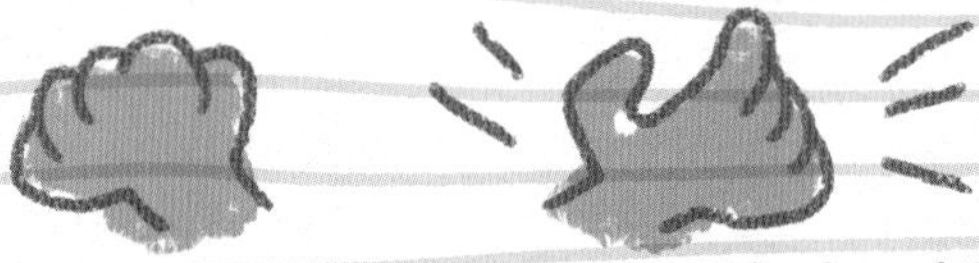

STEP 4: WHEN THE TIMER IS UP, COUNT HOW MANY OF EACH COLOR OF SNACK REMAINS.

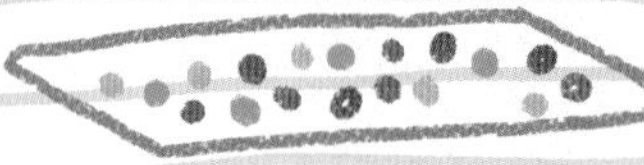

STEP 5: USING THE SAME HAND, REPEAT THE EXPERIMENT 4 MORE TIMES, USING THE OTHER COLORS OF CONSTRUCTION PAPER AND FORM A CONCLUSION ABOUT YOUR RESULTS.

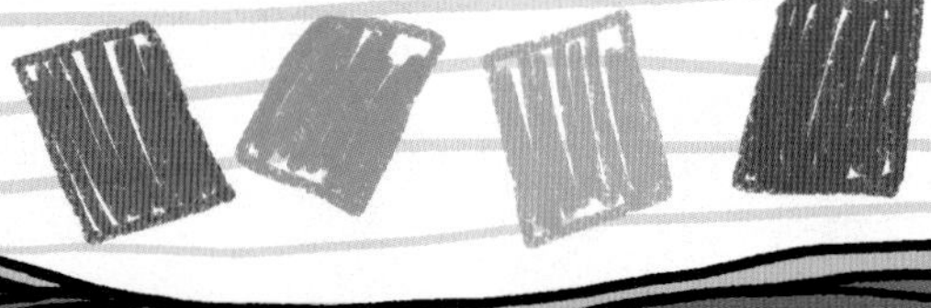

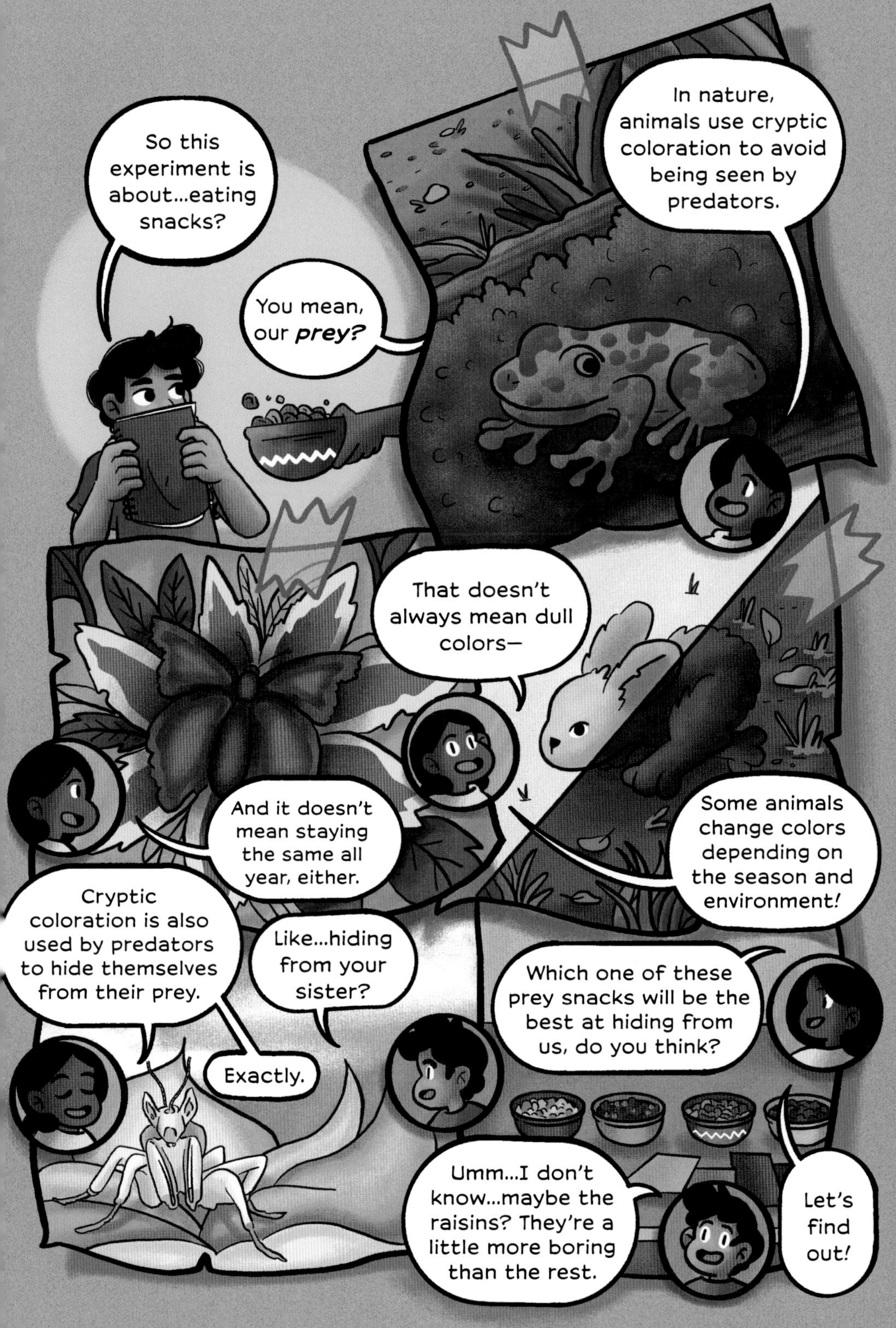
So this experiment is about...eating snacks?
In nature, animals use cryptic coloration to avoid being seen by predators.
You mean, our ***prey?***
That doesn't always mean dull colors—
And it doesn't mean staying the same all year, either.
Some animals change colors depending on the season and environment!
Cryptic coloration is also used by predators to hide themselves from their prey.
Like...hiding from your sister?
Exactly.
Which one of these prey snacks will be the best at hiding from us, do you think?
Umm...I don't know...maybe the raisins? They're a little more boring than the rest.
Let's find out!

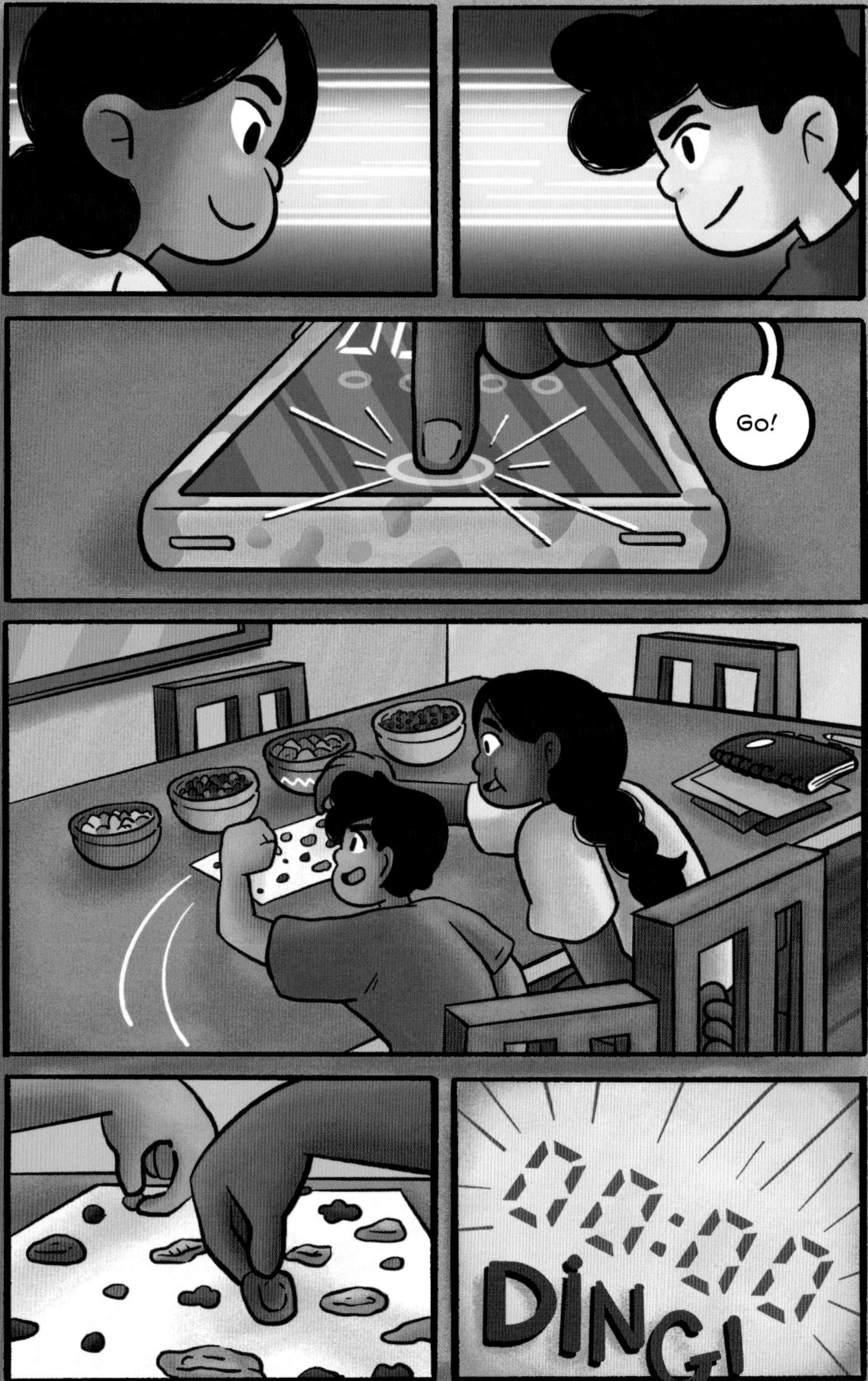
Go!
00:00
DING!

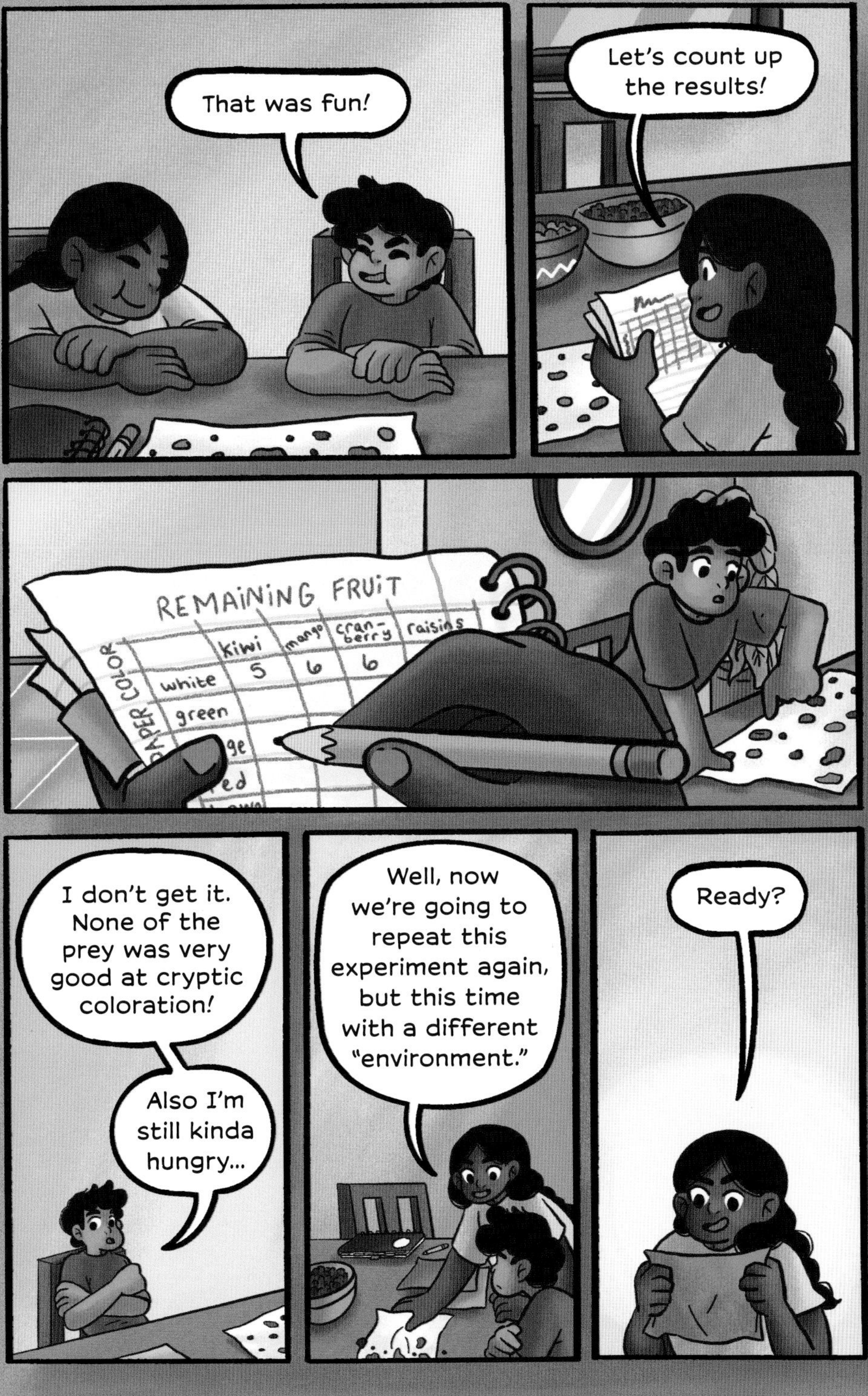
That was fun!
Let's count up the results!
REMAINING FRUIT
PAPER COLOR
kiwi
mango
cran-berry
raisins
white
green
5
6
6
I don't get it. None of the prey was very good at cryptic coloration!
Also I'm still kinda hungry...
Well, now we're going to repeat this experiment again, but this time with a different "environment."
Ready?

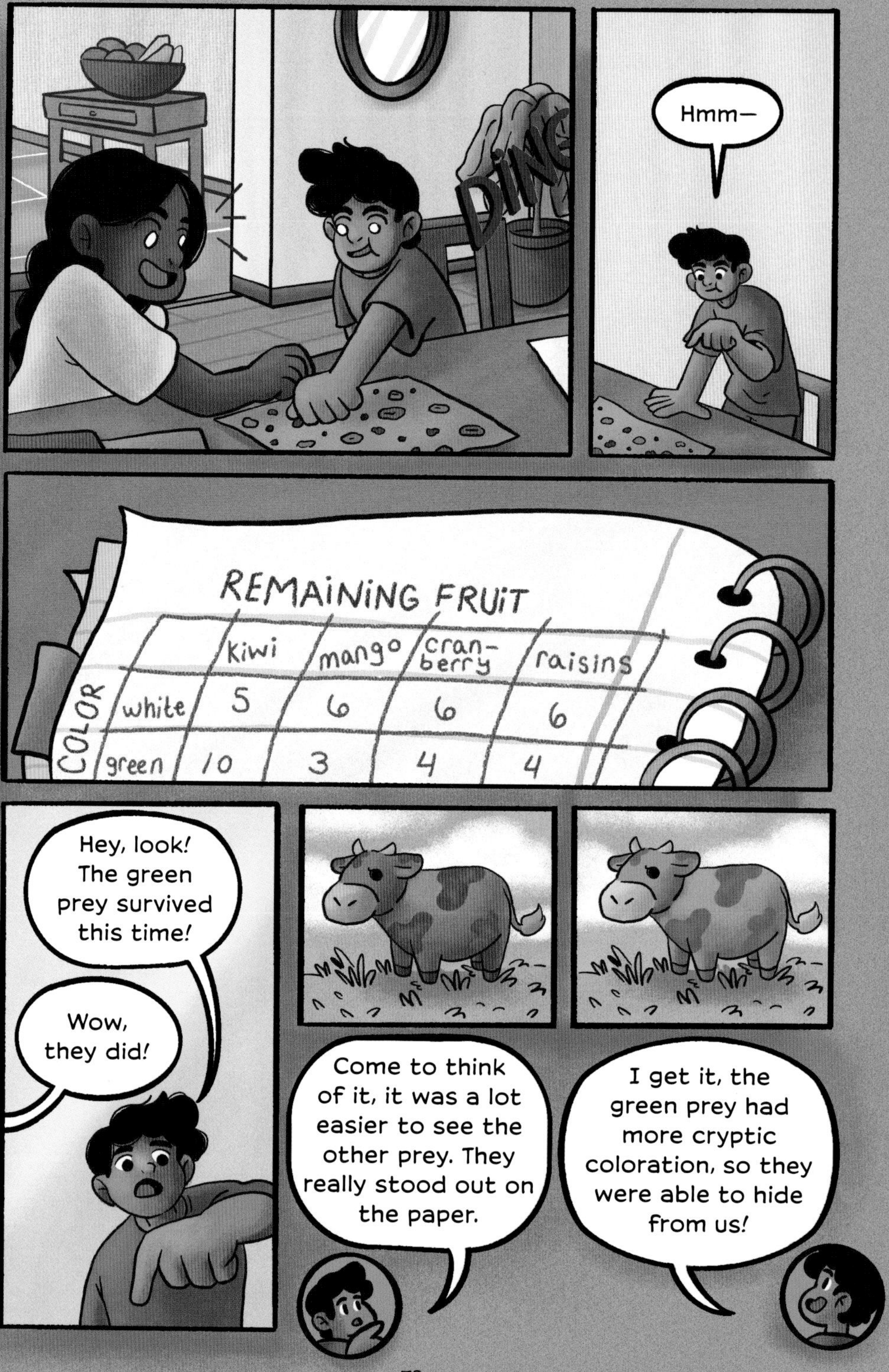
DING
Hmm—
REMAINING FRUIT
kiwi
mango
cran-berry
raisins
COLOR
white
5
6
6
6
green
10
3
4
4
Hey, look! The green prey survived this time!
Wow, they did!
Come to think of it, it was a lot easier to see the other prey. They really stood out on the paper.
I get it, the green prey had more cryptic coloration, so they were able to hide from us!

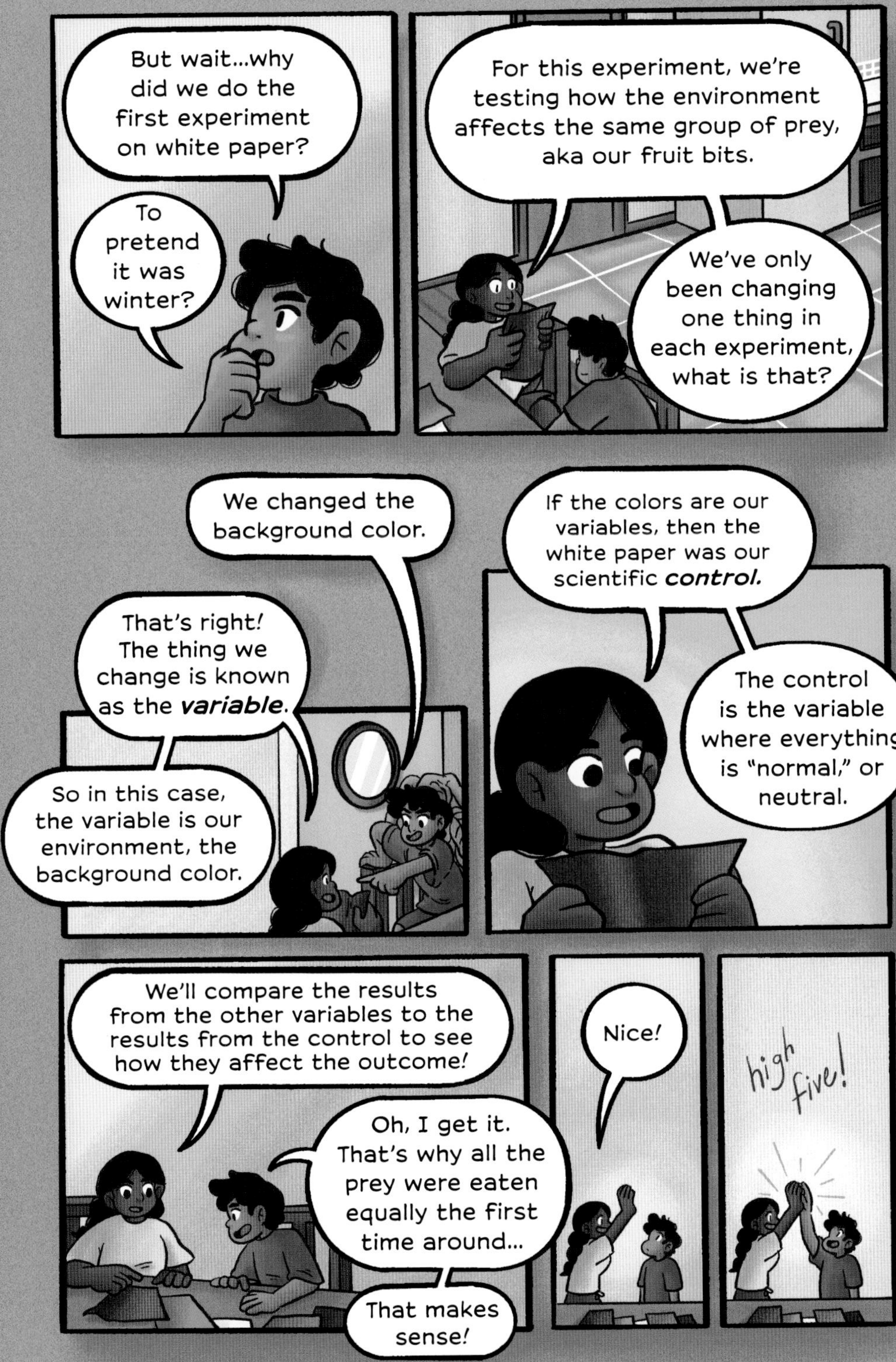

But wait...why did we do the first experiment on white paper?
To pretend it was winter?
For this experiment, we're testing how the environment affects the same group of prey, aka our fruit bits.
We've only been changing one thing in each experiment, what is that?
We changed the background color.
That's right! The thing we change is known as the *variable*.
So in this case, the variable is our environment, the background color.
If the colors are our variables, then the white paper was our scientific *control.*
The control is the variable where everything is "normal," or neutral.
We'll compare the results from the other variables to the results from the control to see how they affect the outcome!
Oh, I get it. That's why all the prey were eaten equally the first time around...
That makes sense!
Nice!
high five!

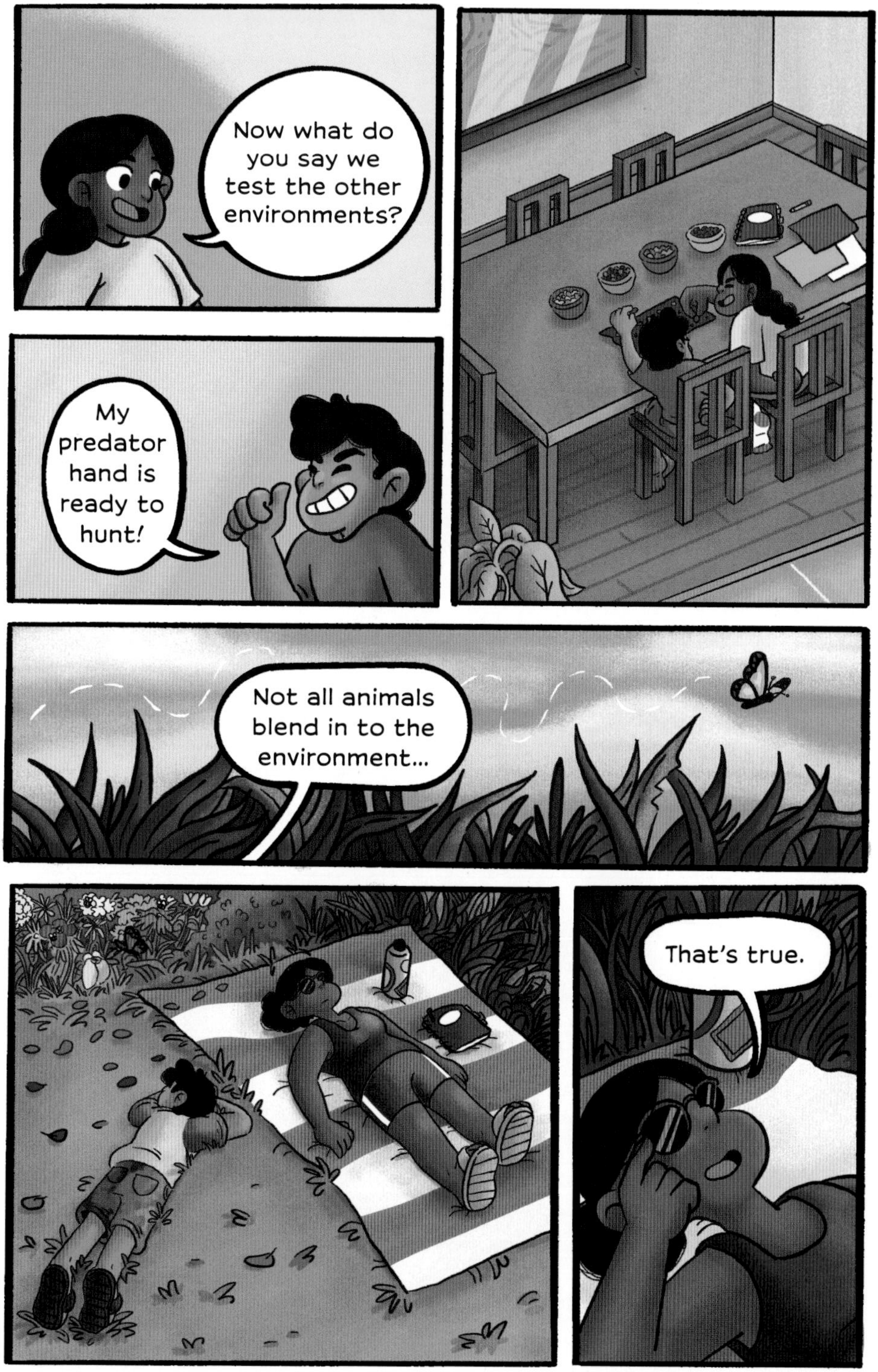
Now what do you say we test the other environments?
My predator hand is ready to hunt!
Not all animals blend in to the environment...
That's true.

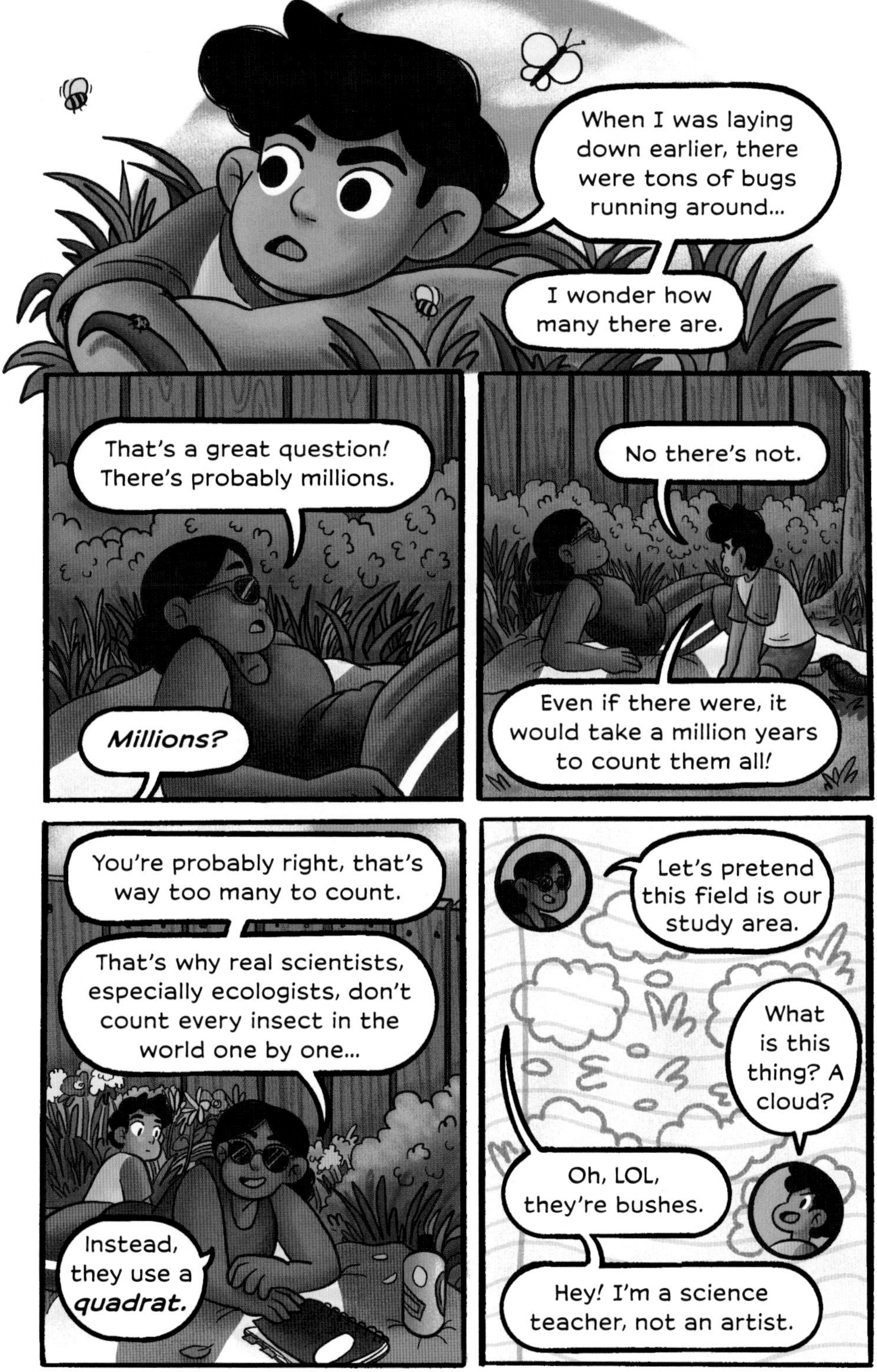
When I was laying down earlier, there were tons of bugs running around...
I wonder how many there are.
That's a great question! There's probably millions.
Millions?
No there's not.
Even if there were, it would take a million years to count them all!
You're probably right, that's way too many to count.
That's why real scientists, especially ecologists, don't count every insect in the world one by one...
Instead, they use a ***quadrat.***
Let's pretend this field is our study area.
What is this thing? A cloud?
Oh, LOL, they're bushes.
Hey! I'm a science teacher, not an artist.

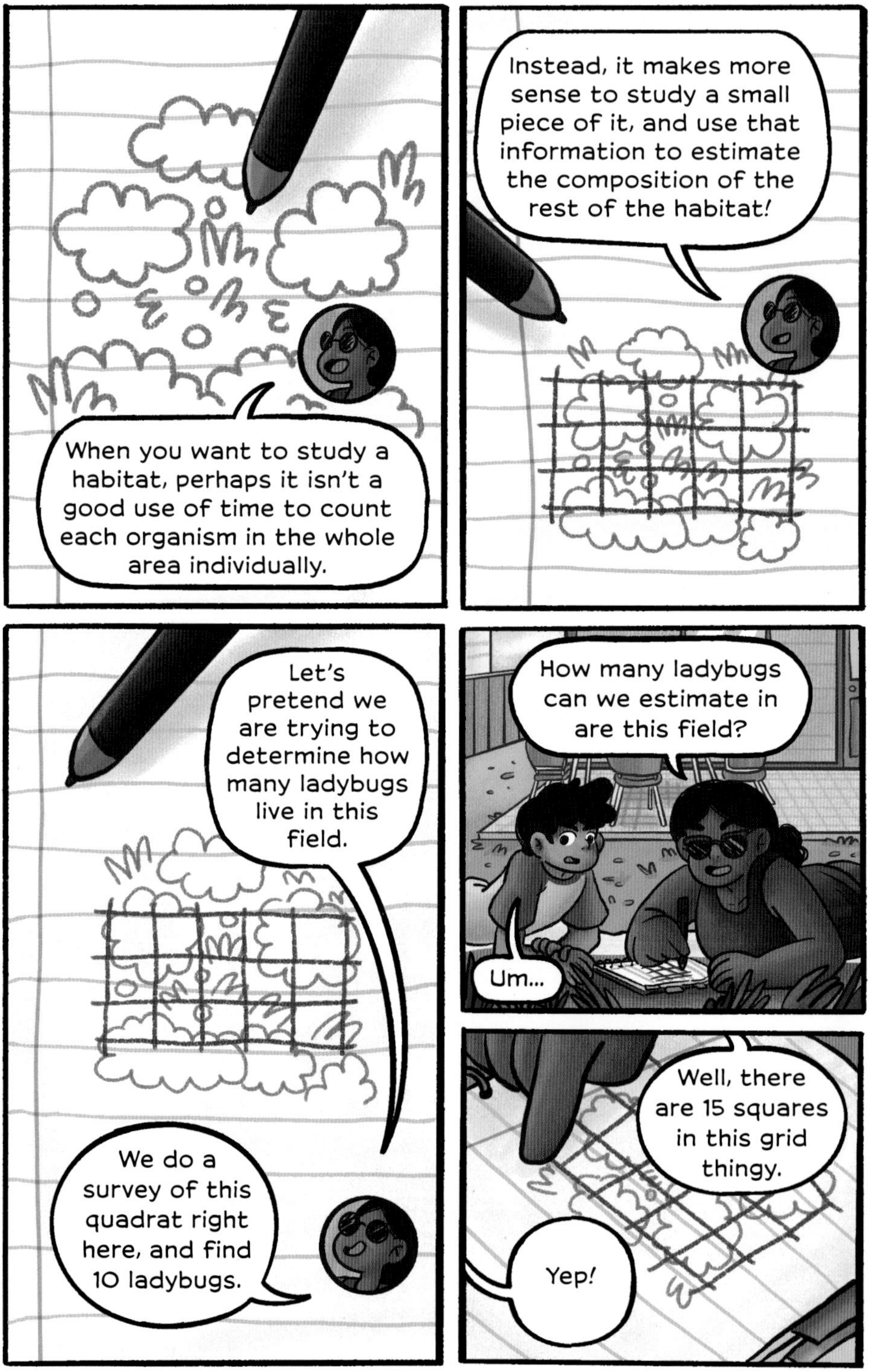
When you want to study a habitat, perhaps it isn't a good use of time to count each organism in the whole area individually.
Instead, it makes more sense to study a small piece of it, and use that information to estimate the composition of the rest of the habitat!
Let's pretend we are trying to determine how many ladybugs live in this field.
We do a survey of this quadrat right here, and find 10 ladybugs.
How many ladybugs can we estimate in are this field?
Um...
Well, there are 15 squares in this grid thingy.
Yep!

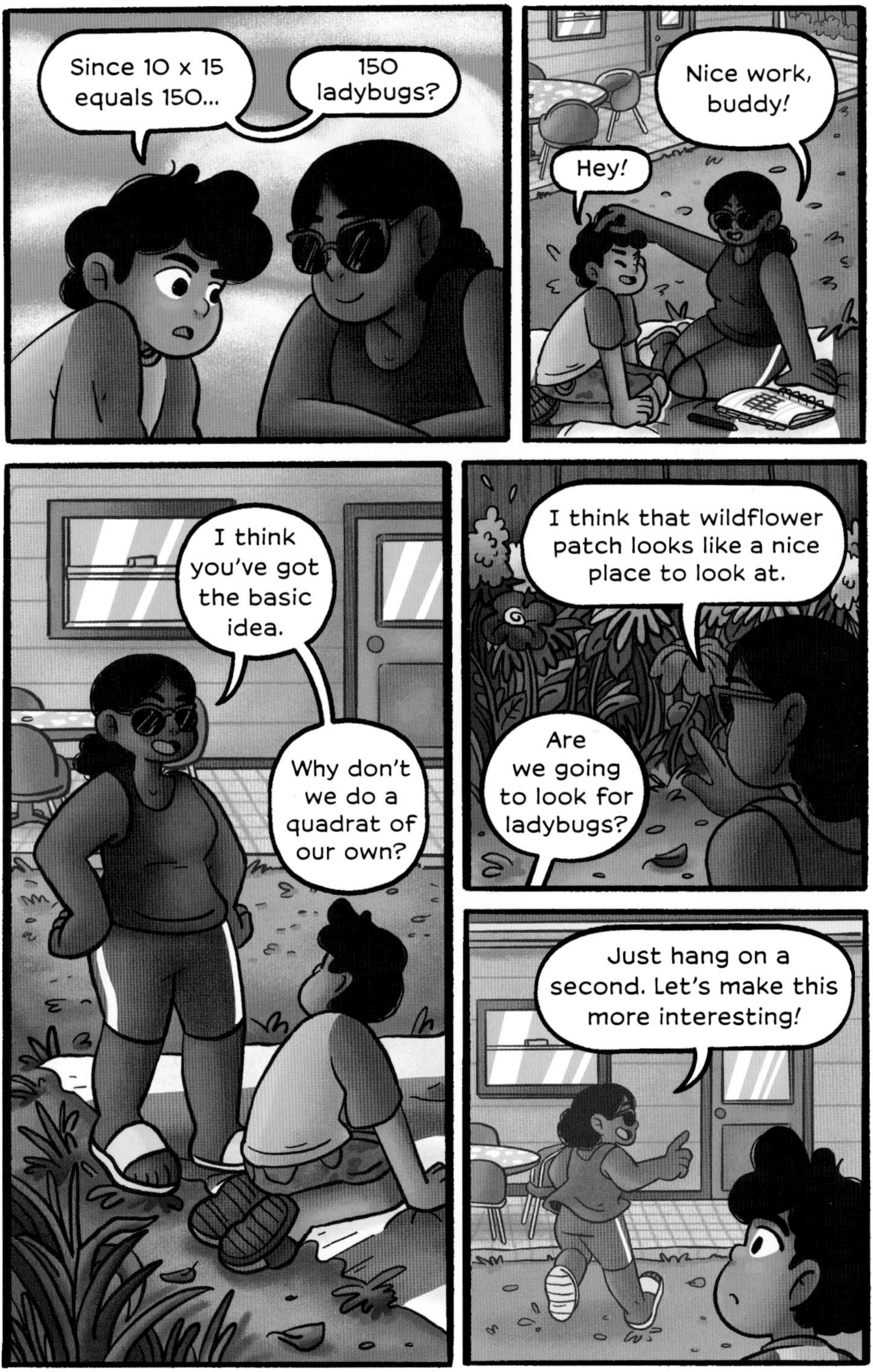
Since 10 x 15 equals 150...
150 ladybugs?
Nice work, buddy!
Hey!
I think you've got the basic idea.
Why don't we do a quadrat of our own?
I think that wildflower patch looks like a nice place to look at.
Are we going to look for ladybugs?
Just hang on a second. Let's make this more interesting!

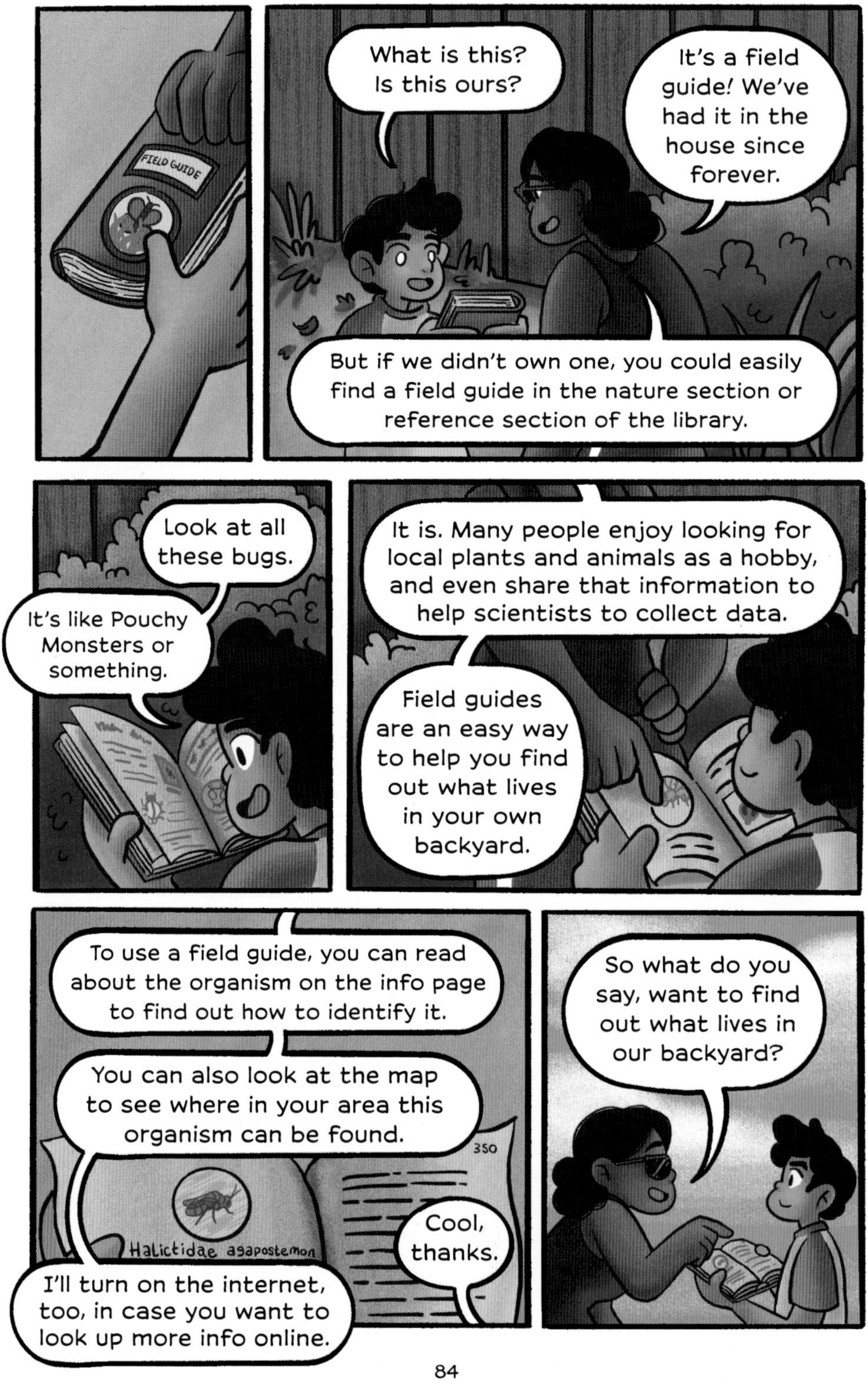
FIELD GUIDE
What is this? Is this ours?
It's a field guide! We've had it in the house since forever.
But if we didn't own one, you could easily find a field guide in the nature section or reference section of the library.
Look at all these bugs.
It's like Pouchy Monsters or something.
It is. Many people enjoy looking for local plants and animals as a hobby, and even share that information to help scientists to collect data.
Field guides are an easy way to help you find out what lives in your own backyard.
To use a field guide, you can read about the organism on the info page to find out how to identify it.
You can also look at the map to see where in your area this organism can be found.
350
Halictidae agapostemon
Cool, thanks.
I'll turn on the internet, too, in case you want to look up more info online.
So what do you say, want to find out what lives in our backyard?

THE BACKYARD QUADRAT!!

MATERIALS

- FOUR STICKS
- GARDEN TWINE OR STRING
- A FIELD GUIDE FOR THE PLANTS, ANIMALS, OR OTHER ORGANISMS YOU'D LIKE TO LOOK FOR
- PEN OR PENCIL
  ↳ TO MAKE OBSERVATIONS
- OPTIONAL: CAMERA, MAGNIFYING GLASS, BINOCULARS, ONLINE RESOURCES

PROCEDURES

Step 1: PICK WHICH ORGANISMS YOU WOULD LIKE TO STUDY. YOU CAN CHOOSE SOMETHING RELATIVELY SIMPLE, SUCH AS ALL "FUNGI", OR SOMETHING MORE COMPLEX, LIKE "ALL VISIBLE LIVING THINGS."

Step 2: GO TO YOUR LIBRARY AND FIND A FIELD GUIDE FOR YOUR AREA AND THE TYPE OF ORGANISMS YOU ARE PLANNING TO LOOK FOR. EXAMPLES MIGHT BE "FIELD GUIDE TO NORTH AMERICAN AMPHIBIANS" OR "FIELD GUIDE TO NATIVE PLANTS OF [YOUR AREA]."

Step 3: FIND AN AREA "IN YOUR BACKYARD" THAT YOU WOULD LIKE TO SURVEY. THIS COULD BE LITERALLY IN YOUR BACKYARD, OR IT COULD BE AT A PARK OR ANOTHER PUBLIC PLACE. IF YOU WOULD LIKE TO DO THIS EXPERIMENT IN A PUBLIC PLACE, BRING AN ADULT TO STAY SAFE.

Step 4: DETERMINE THE TOTAL SQUARE AREA OF YOUR STUDY HABITAT IN SQUARE FEET OR SQUARE METERS. MAKE SURE THE HABITAT YOU CHOOSE IS CONSISTENT. FOR EXAMPLE, IF YOU WOULD LIKE TO LOOK AT A LAWN, MAKE SURE THAT IT IS ONLY LAWN AND NOT A FLOWER BED AS WELL. IF YOU WOULD LIKE TO LOOK AT A FOREST, MAKE SURE THAT YOU DO NOT INCLUDE THE CITY. FOR SMALLER AREAS, YOU CAN USE A STRING OR TAPE MEASURE TO ESTIMATE HOW LARGE THE AREA IS. FOR VERY LARGE AREAS, TRY USING ONLINE MAPS ON THE INTERNET.

Step 5: Make your quadrat. A good size might be 1-2 feet on each side. Place twigs in the corners of your quadrat. You can wrap a piece of twine around them to form a square.

Step 6: Look for your organisms within the quadrat. If you do not recognize a certain type of organism, use your field guide to identify it. If you can't identify it right away, it is a good idea to make a drawing of the organism to search for so you can look it up later, or to take a picture if you have a camera with you. In addition to the name of each species of organism, write down the number of organisms you find in your quadrat.

Step 7: When you are finished making your observations, dismantle your quadrat. If you would like to come back later to make observations in the same area, make a note to yourself or take a picture so you can find the same spot again.

Step 8: Calculate the fraction, or percentage, of the habitat your quadrat represents. For example, if your garden habitat is 10 quadrat squares of area, then your quadrat is 1/10 of the total area.

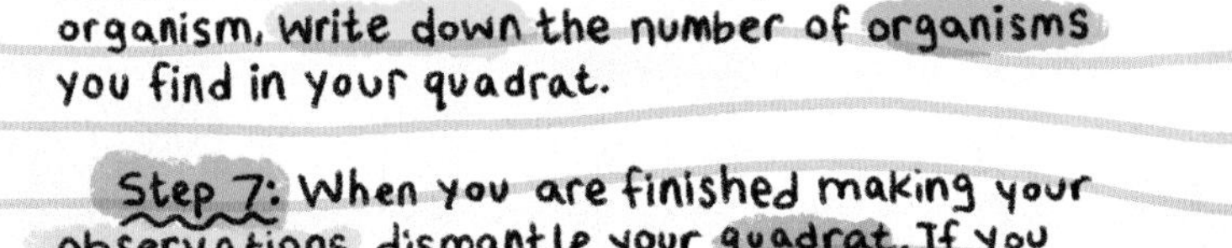

Step 9: Calculate how many organisms you can find in the full habitat.

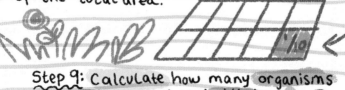

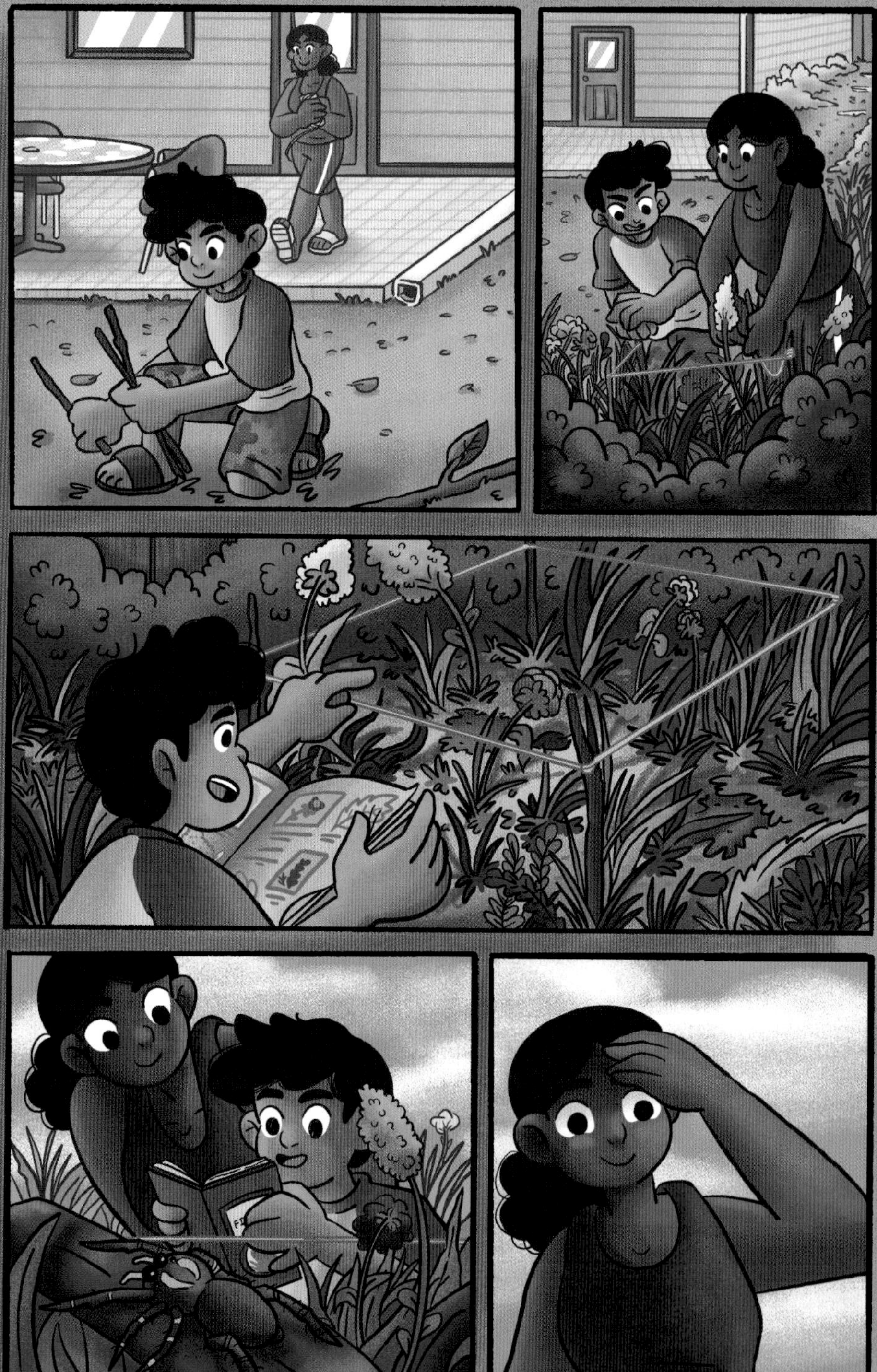

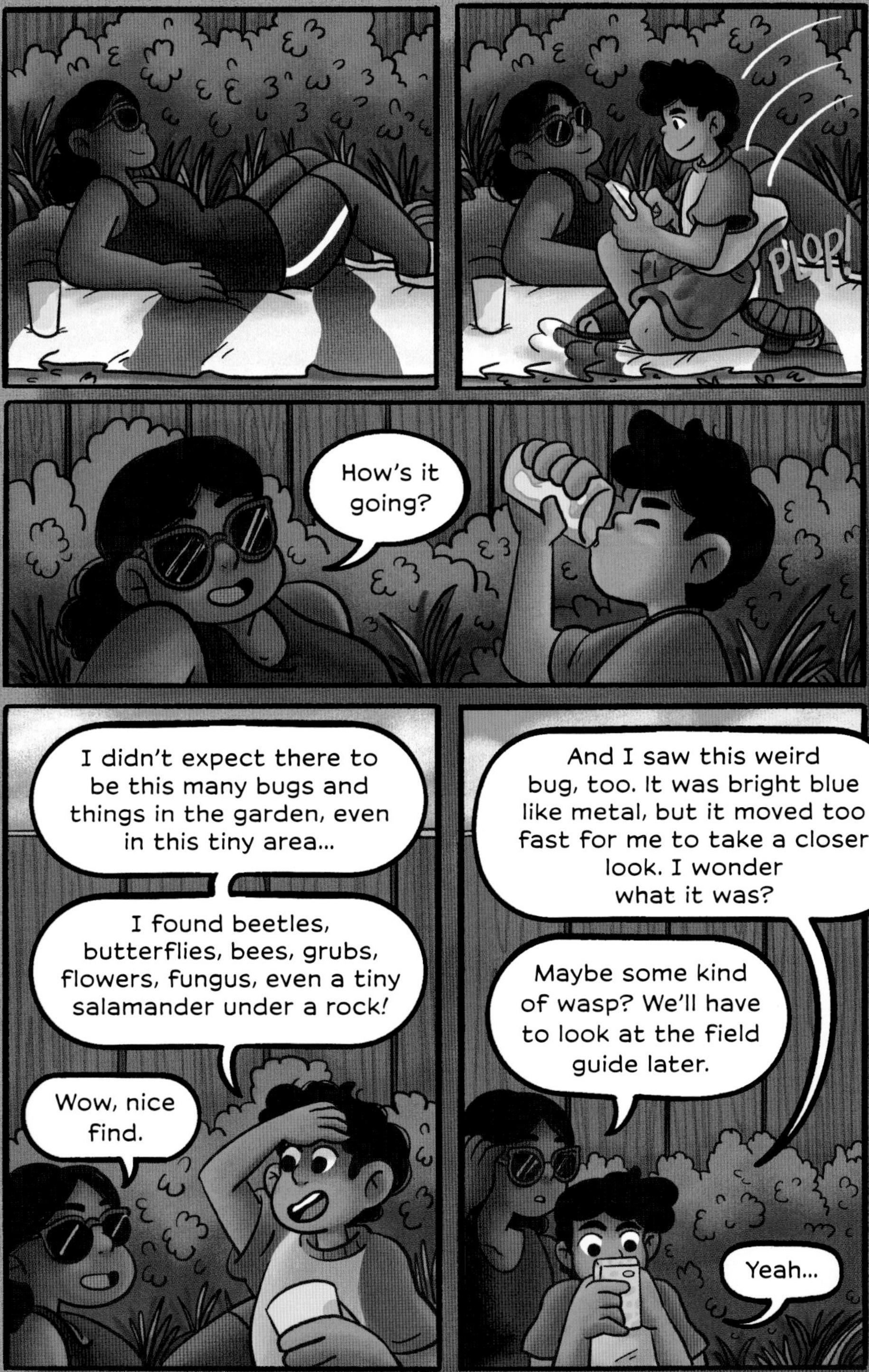
PLOP!
How's it going?
I didn't expect there to be this many bugs and things in the garden, even in this tiny area...
I found beetles, butterflies, bees, grubs, flowers, fungus, even a tiny salamander under a rock!
Wow, nice find.
And I saw this weird bug, too. It was bright blue like metal, but it moved too fast for me to take a closer look. I wonder what it was?
Maybe some kind of wasp? We'll have to look at the field guide later.
Yeah...

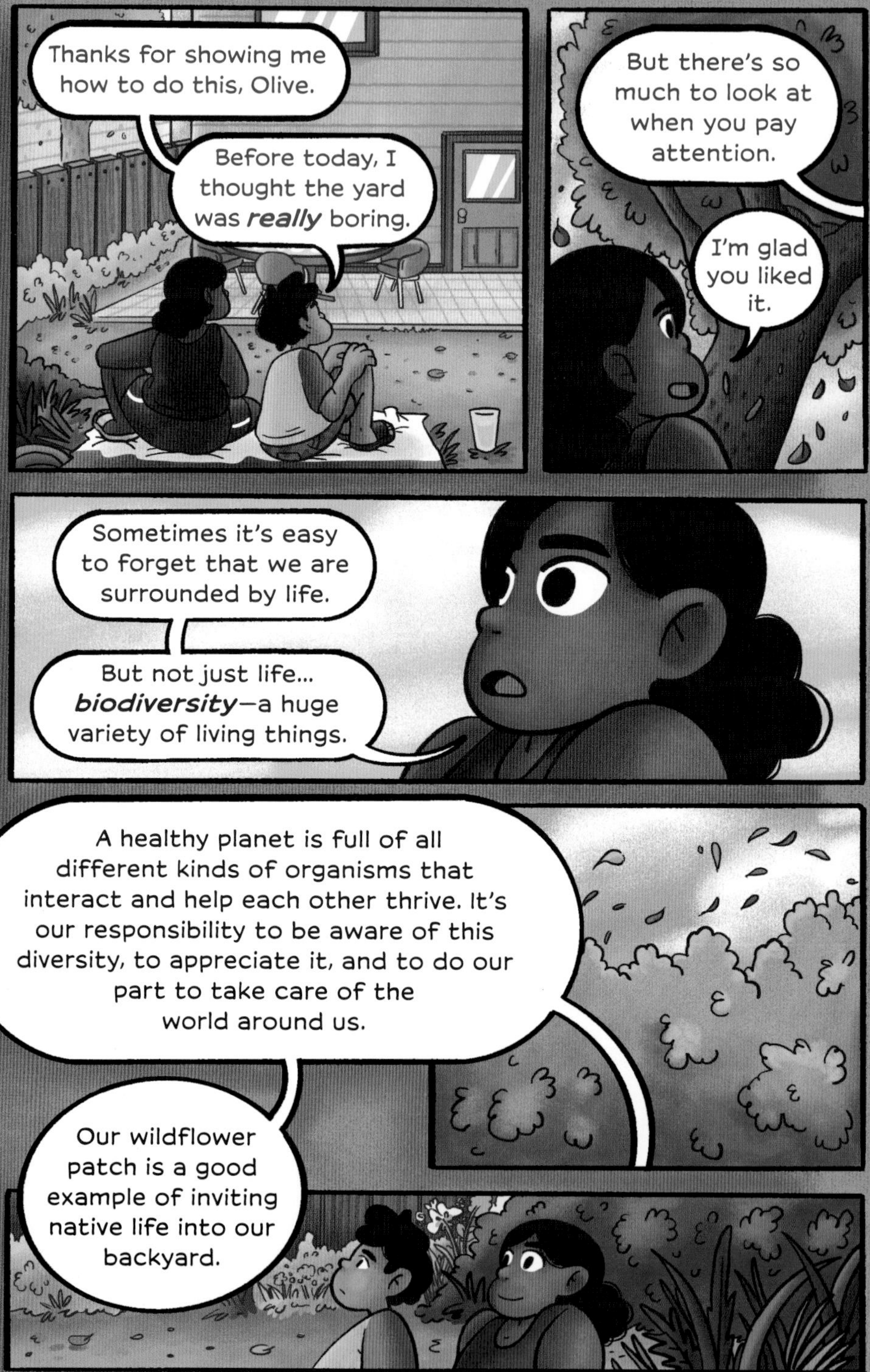
Thanks for showing me how to do this, Olive.
Before today, I thought the yard was *really* boring.
But there's so much to look at when you pay attention.
I'm glad you liked it.
Sometimes it's easy to forget that we are surrounded by life.
But not just life... *biodiversity*—a huge variety of living things.
A healthy planet is full of all different kinds of organisms that interact and help each other thrive. It's our responsibility to be aware of this diversity, to appreciate it, and to do our part to take care of the world around us.
Our wildflower patch is a good example of inviting native life into our backyard.

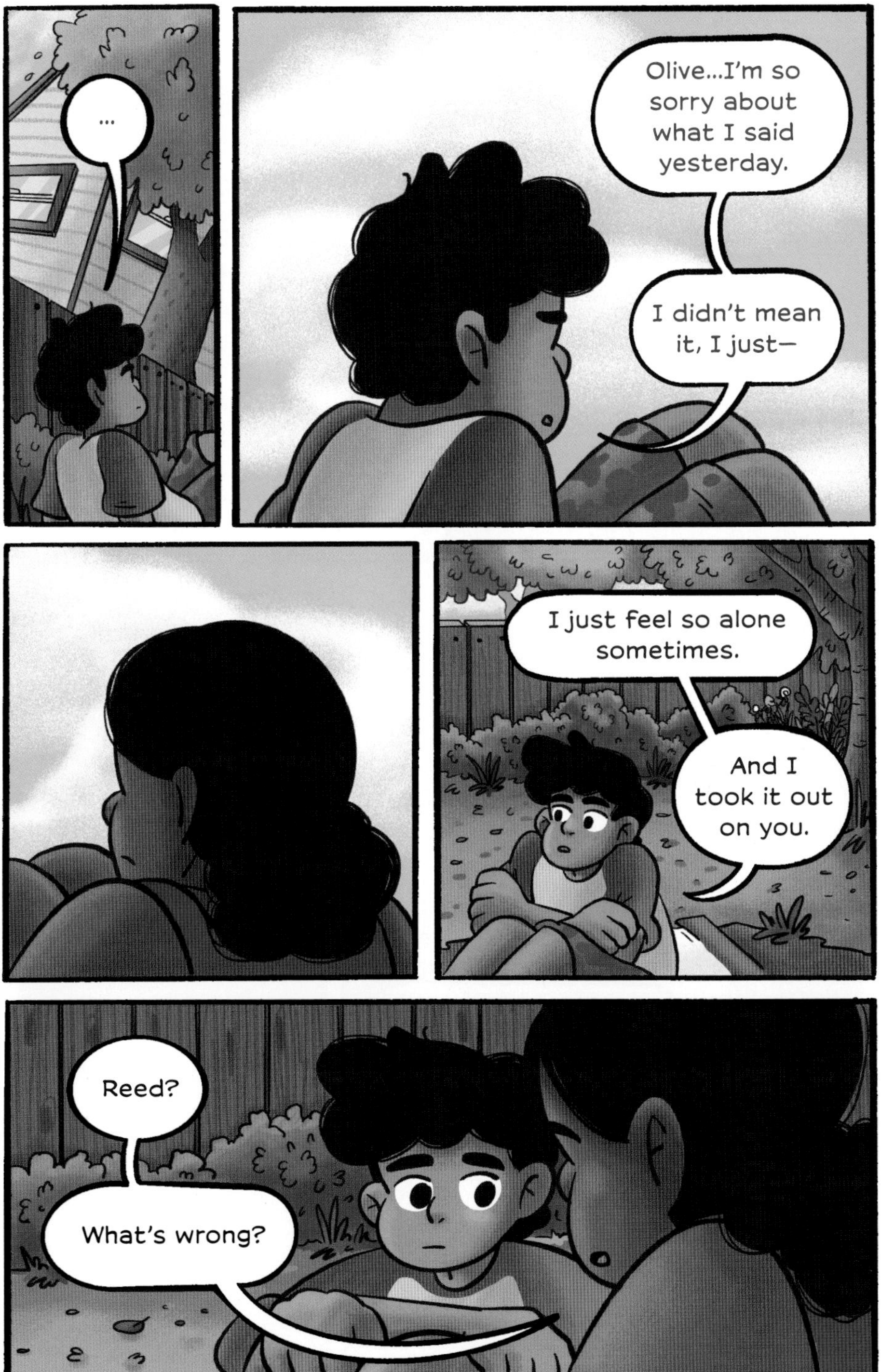
...
Olive...I'm so sorry about what I said yesterday.
I didn't mean it, I just—
I just feel so alone sometimes.
And I took it out on you.
Reed?
What's wrong?

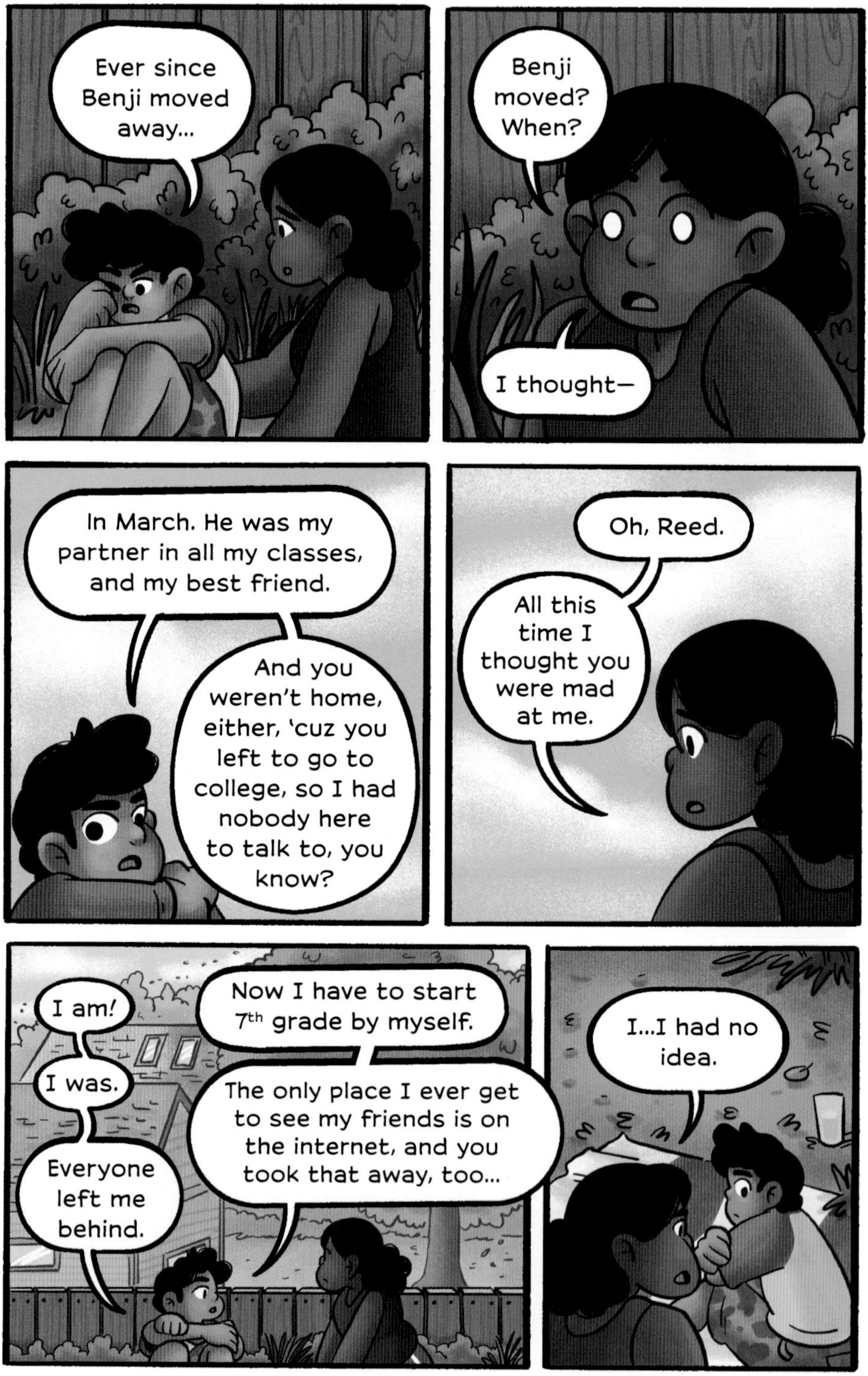
Ever since Benji moved away...
Benji moved? When?
I thought—
In March. He was my partner in all my classes, and my best friend.
And you weren't home, either, 'cuz you left to go to college, so I had nobody here to talk to, you know?
Oh, Reed.
All this time I thought you were mad at me.
I am!
I was.
Everyone left me behind.
Now I have to start 7th grade by myself.
The only place I ever get to see my friends is on the internet, and you took that away, too...
I...I had no idea.

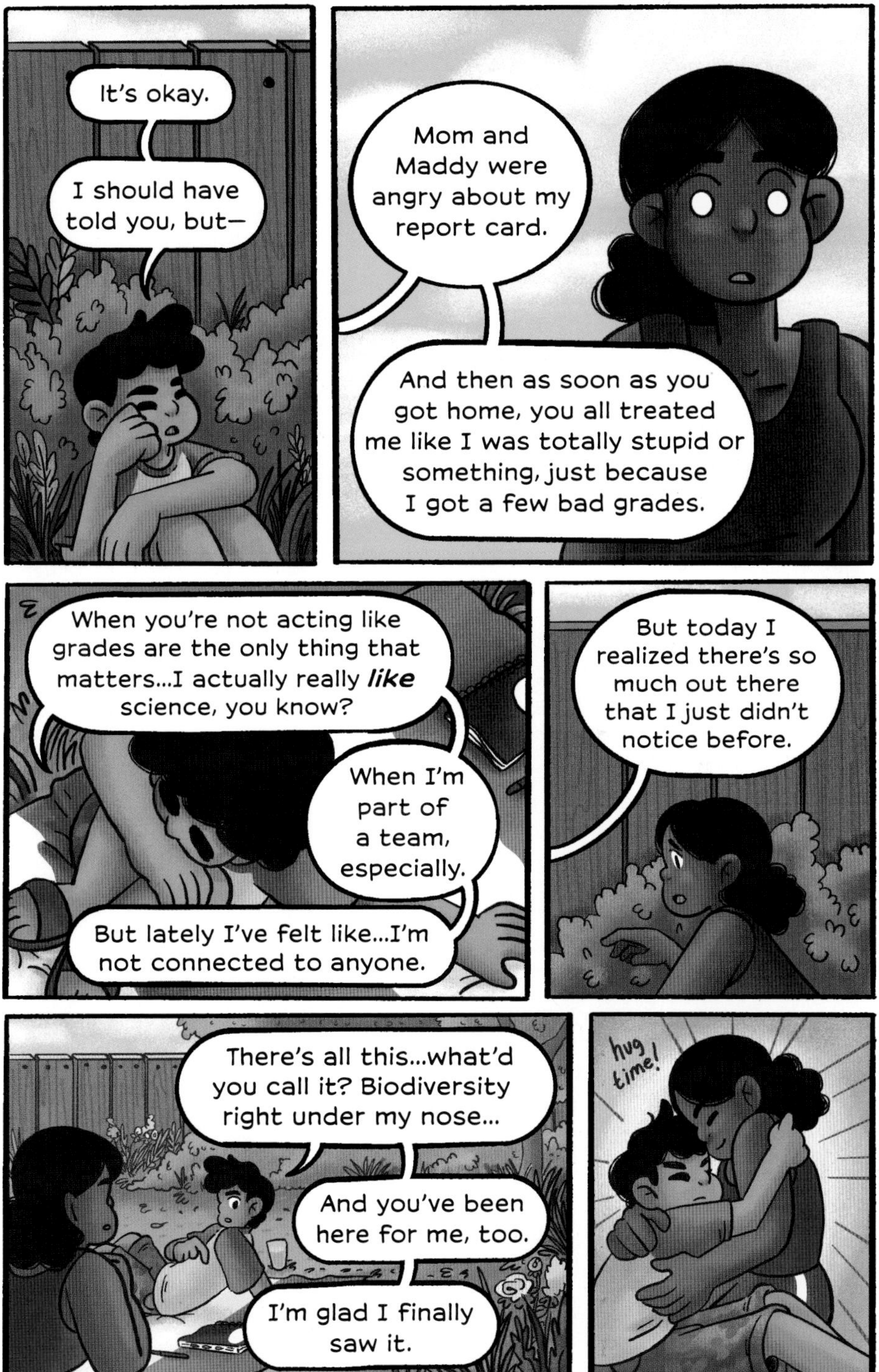
It's okay.
I should have told you, but—
Mom and Maddy were angry about my report card.
And then as soon as you got home, you all treated me like I was totally stupid or something, just because I got a few bad grades.
When you're not acting like grades are the only thing that matters...I actually really *like* science, you know?
When I'm part of a team, especially.
But lately I've felt like...I'm not connected to anyone.
But today I realized there's so much out there that I just didn't notice before.
There's all this...what'd you call it? Biodiversity right under my nose...
And you've been here for me, too.
I'm glad I finally saw it.
hug time!

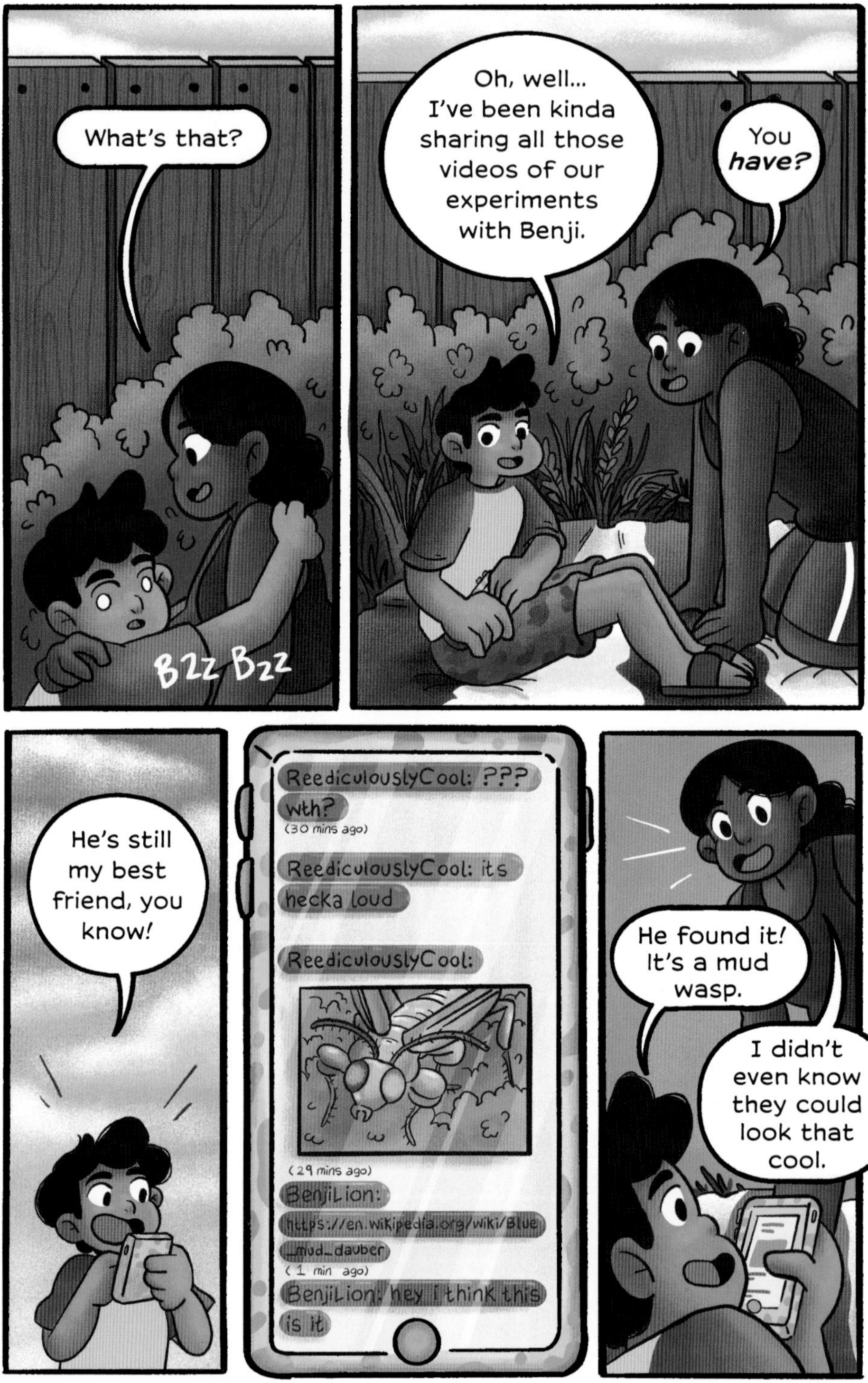
What's that?
BZZ BZZ
Oh, well... I've been kinda sharing all those videos of our experiments with Benji.
You *have?*
He's still my best friend, you know!
ReediculouslyCool: ???
wth?
(30 mins ago)
ReediculouslyCool: its
hecka loud
ReediculouslyCool:
(29 mins ago)
BenjiLion:
https://en.wikipedia.org/wiki/Blue
_mud_dauber
(1 min ago)
BenjiLion: hey i think this
is it
He found it! It's a mud wasp.
I didn't even know they could look that cool.

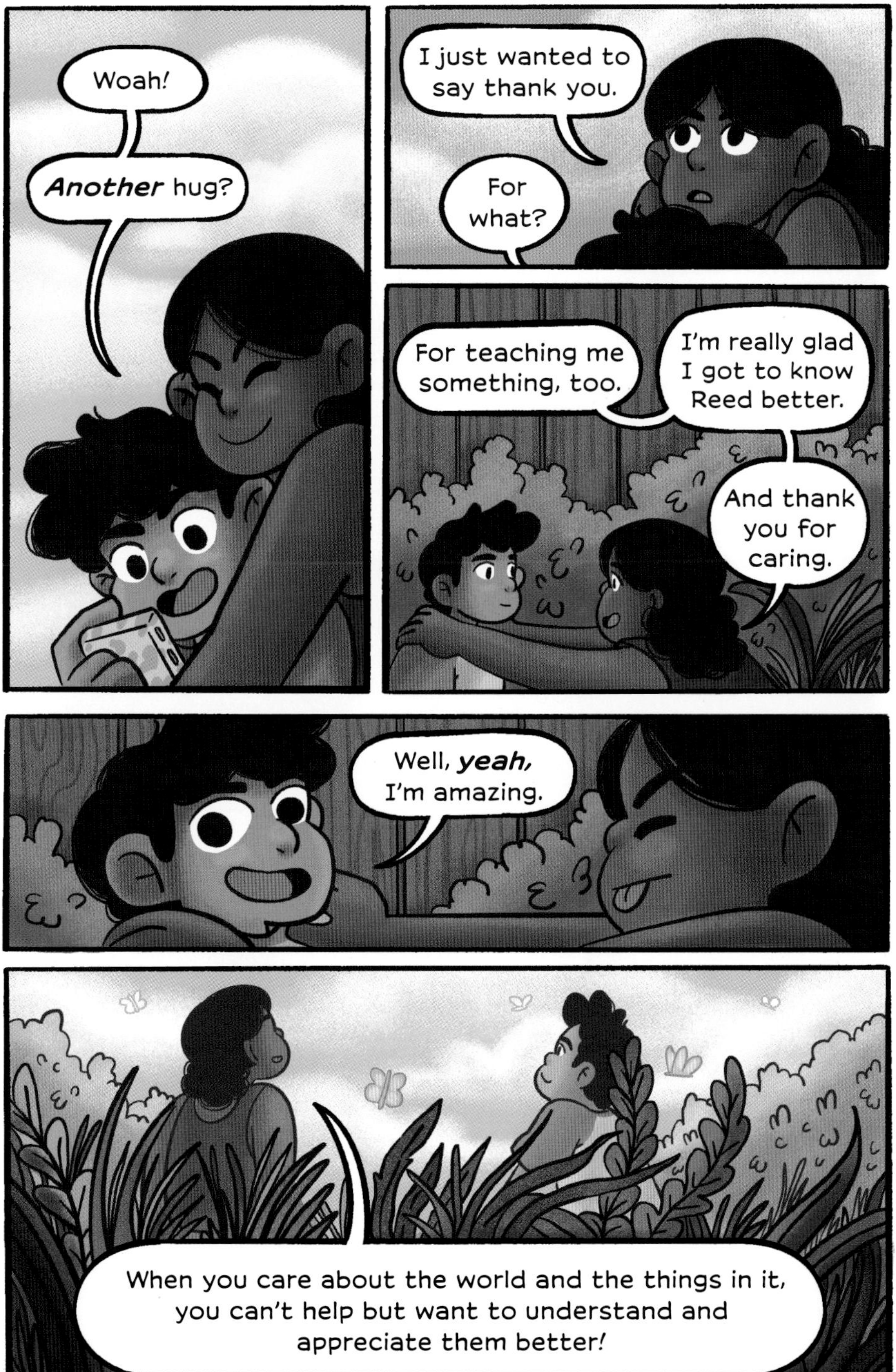
Woah!
Another hug?
I just wanted to say thank you.
For what?
For teaching me something, too.
I'm really glad I got to know Reed better.
And thank you for caring.
Well, *yeah,* I'm amazing.
When you care about the world and the things in it, you can't help but want to understand and appreciate them better!

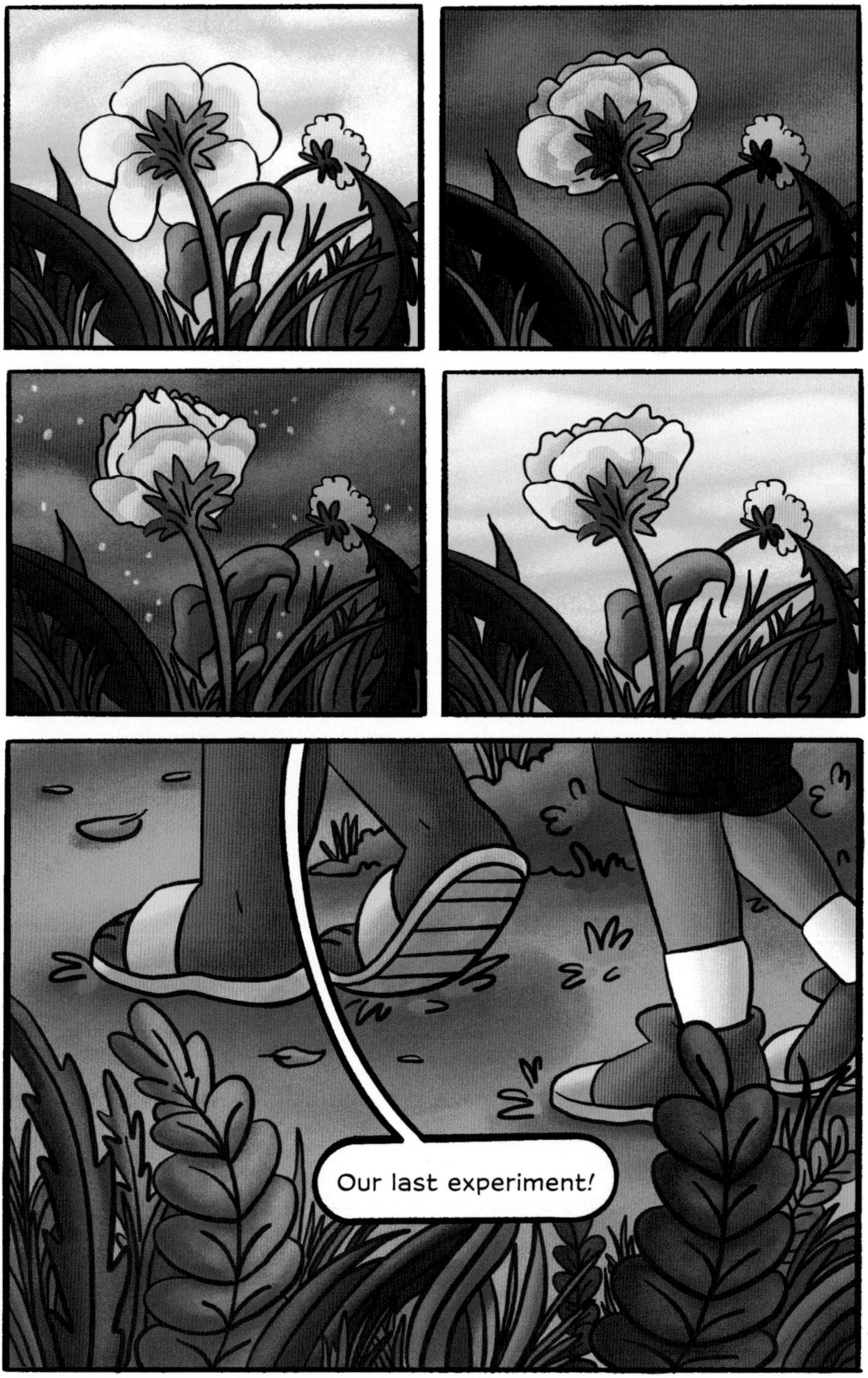
Our last experiment!

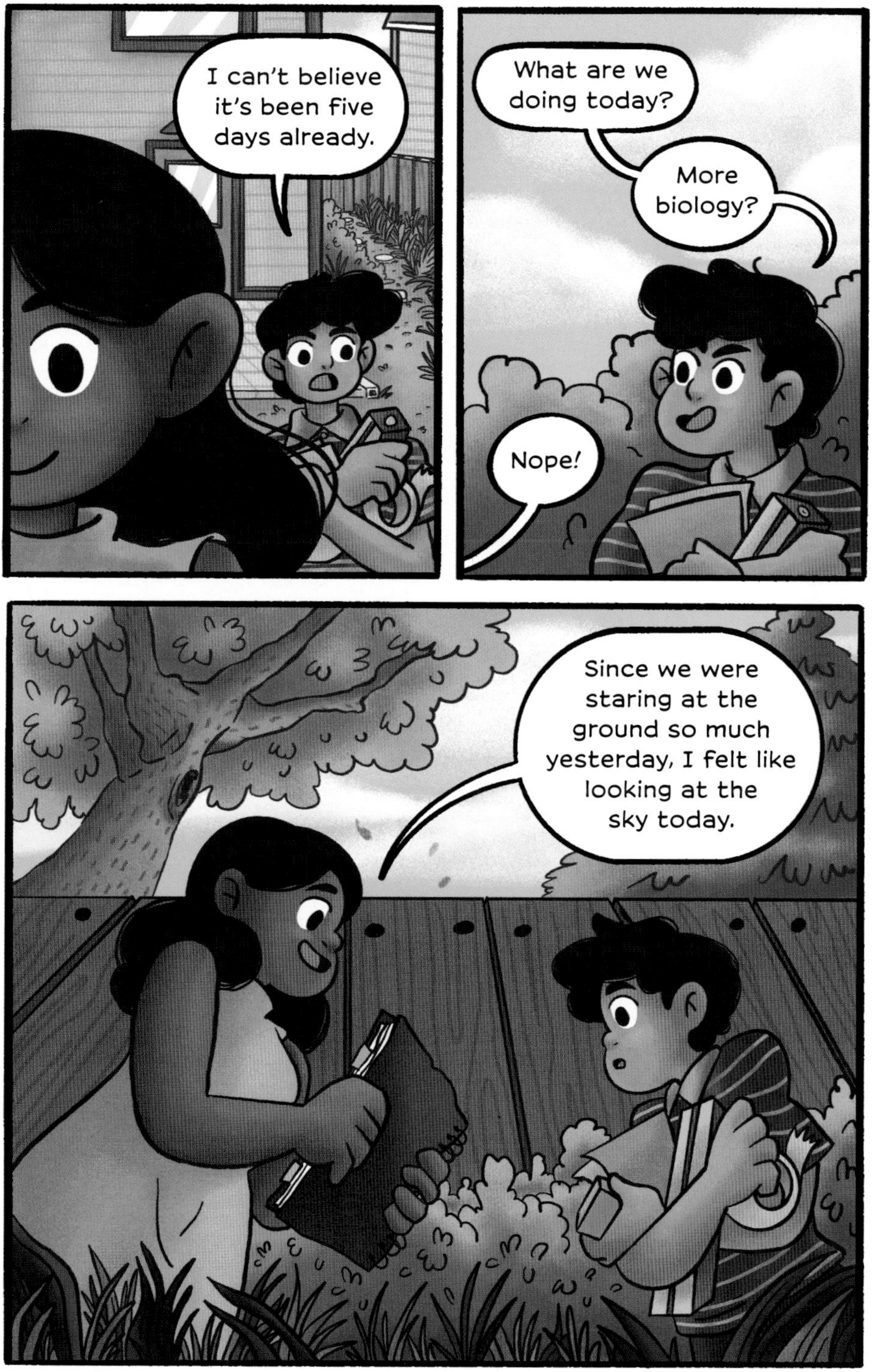
I can't believe it's been five days already.
What are we doing today?
More biology?
Nope!
Since we were staring at the ground so much yesterday, I felt like looking at the sky today.

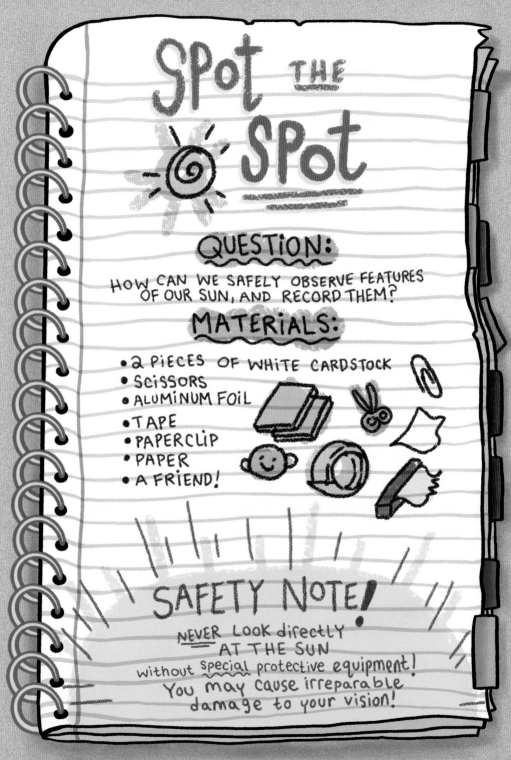

Spot THE Spot

QUESTION:

HOW CAN WE SAFELY OBSERVE FEATURES OF OUR SUN, AND RECORD THEM?

MATERIALS:

- 2 PIECES OF WHITE CARDSTOCK
- SCISSORS
- ALUMINUM FOIL
- TAPE
- PAPERCLIP
- PAPER
- A FRIEND!

SAFETY NOTE!

NEVER LOOK directLY AT THE SUN without special protective equipment! You may cause irreparable damage to your vision!

PROCEDURES

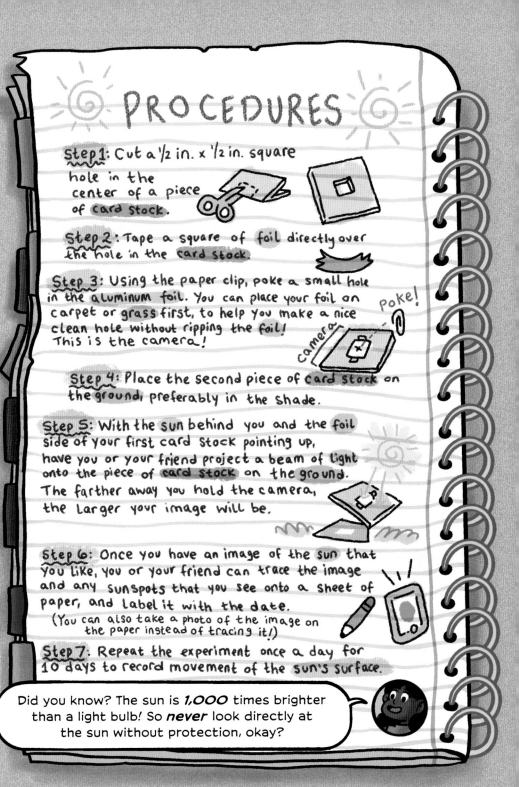

Step 1: Cut a ½ in. x ½ in. square hole in the center of a piece of card stock.

Step 2: Tape a square of foil directly over the hole in the card stock.

Step 3: Using the paper clip, poke a small hole in the aluminum foil. You can place your foil on carpet or grass first, to help you make a nice clean hole without ripping the foil! This is the camera!

Poke!

camera

Step 4: Place the second piece of card stock on the ground, preferably in the shade.

Step 5: With the sun behind you and the foil side of your first card stock pointing up, have you or your friend project a beam of light onto the piece of card stock on the ground. The farther away you hold the camera, the larger your image will be.

Step 6: Once you have an image of the sun that you like, you or your friend can trace the image and any sunspots that you see onto a sheet of paper, and label it with the date.
(You can also take a photo of the image on the paper instead of tracing it!)

Step 7: Repeat the experiment once a day for 10 days to record movement of the sun's surface.

Did you know? The sun is **1,000** times brighter than a light bulb! So **never** look directly at the sun without protection, okay?

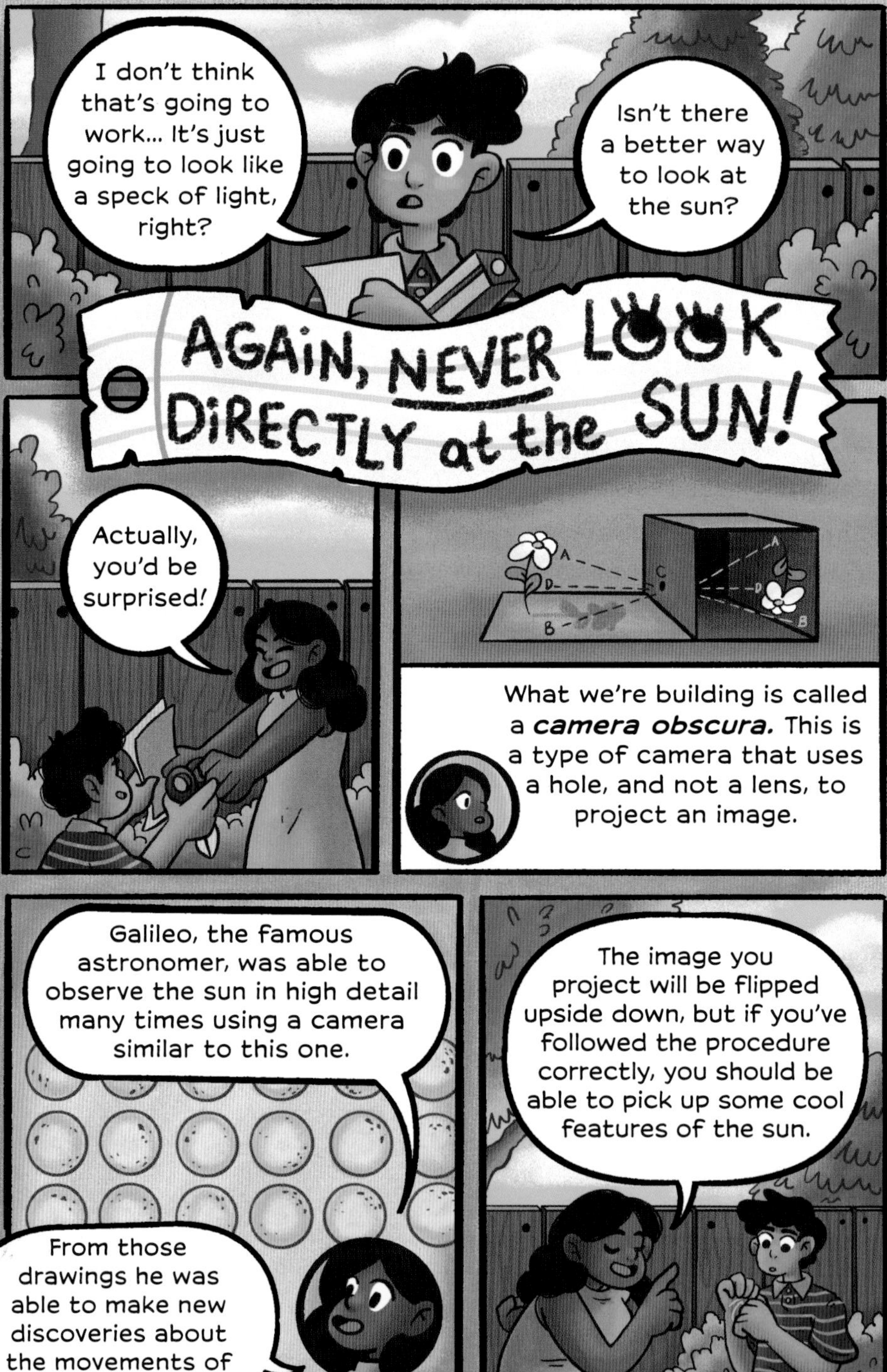
I don't think that's going to work... It's just going to look like a speck of light, right?
Isn't there a better way to look at the sun?
AGAIN, NEVER LOOK DIRECTLY at the SUN!
Actually, you'd be surprised!
A
D
C
B
What we're building is called a ***camera obscura.*** This is a type of camera that uses a hole, and not a lens, to project an image.
Galileo, the famous astronomer, was able to observe the sun in high detail many times using a camera similar to this one.
From those drawings he was able to make new discoveries about the movements of celestial bodies.
The image you project will be flipped upside down, but if you've followed the procedure correctly, you should be able to pick up some cool features of the sun.

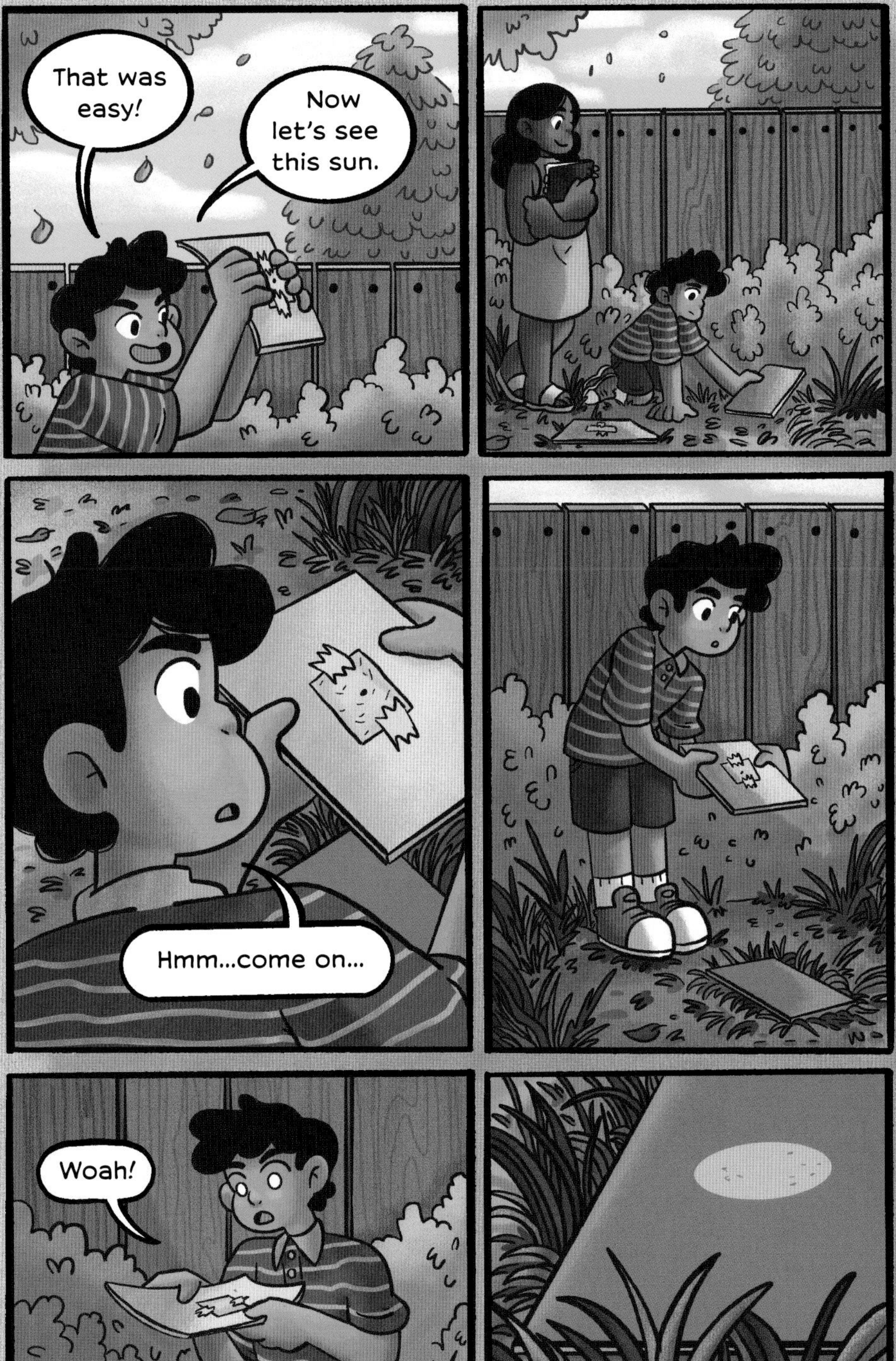
That was easy!
Now let's see this sun.
Hmm...come on...
Woah!

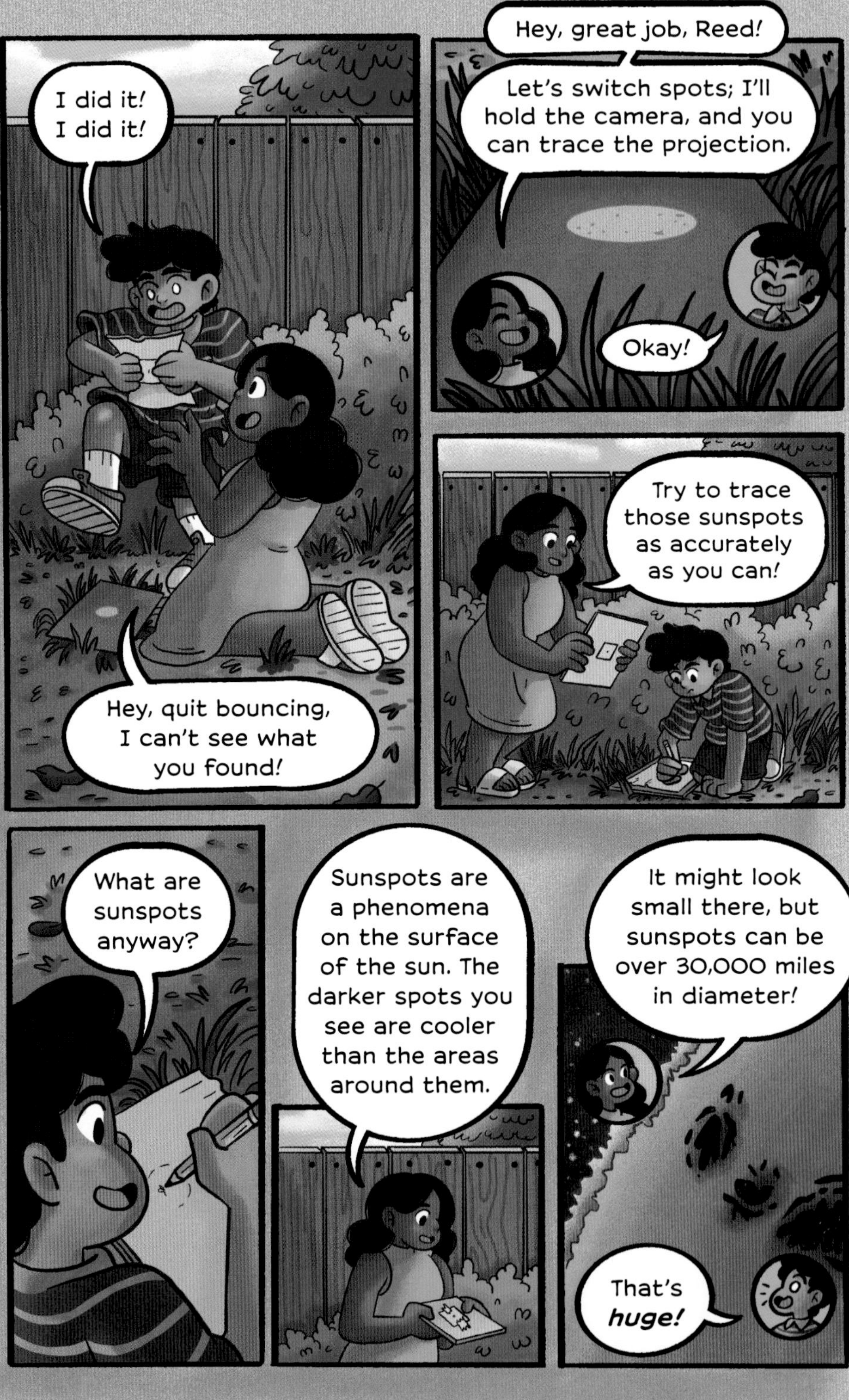
I did it! I did it!
Hey, quit bouncing, I can't see what you found!
Hey, great job, Reed!
Let's switch spots; I'll hold the camera, and you can trace the projection.
Okay!
Try to trace those sunspots as accurately as you can!
What are sunspots anyway?
Sunspots are a phenomena on the surface of the sun. The darker spots you see are cooler than the areas around them.
It might look small there, but sunspots can be over 30,000 miles in diameter!
That's *huge!*

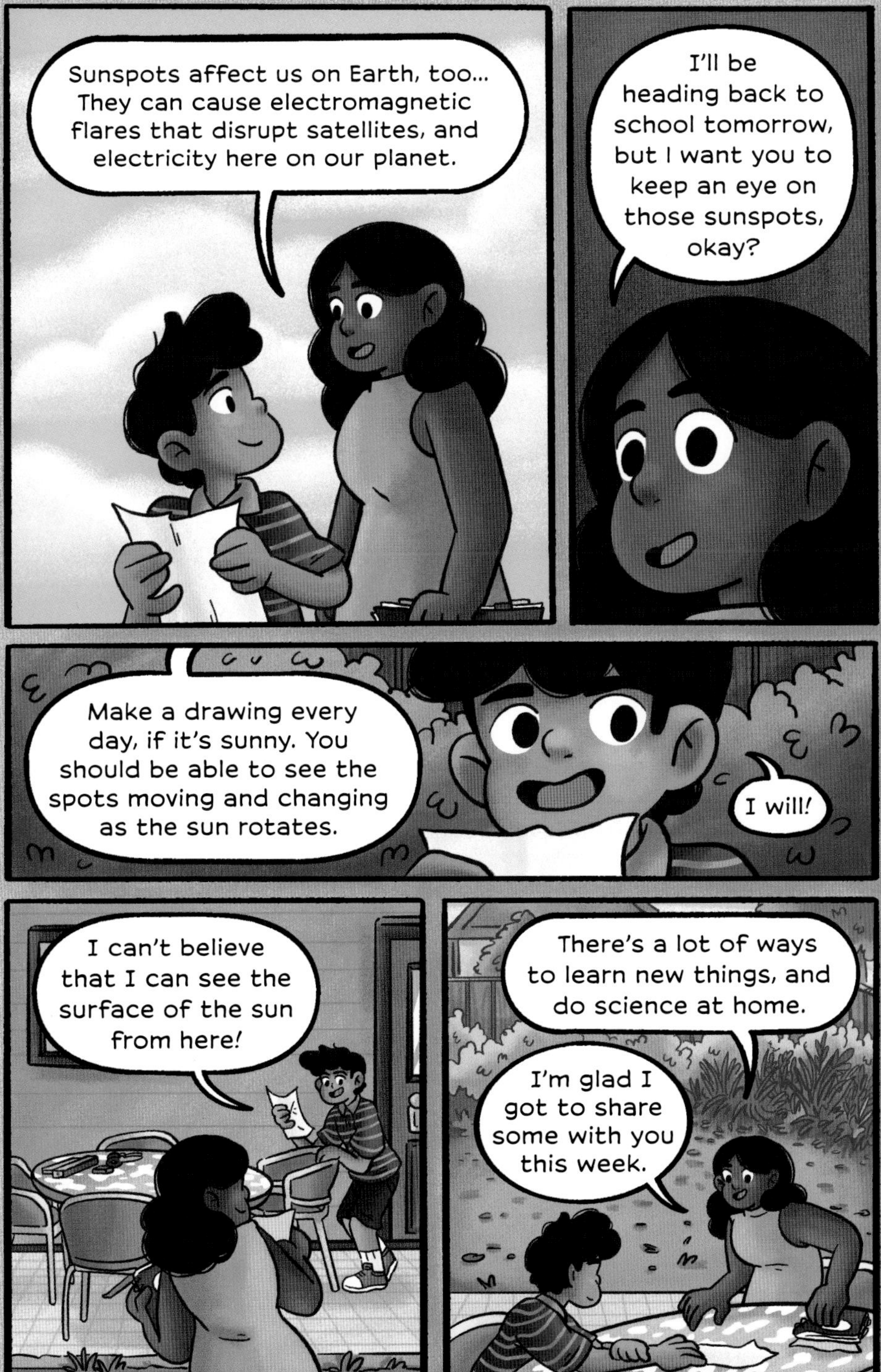
Sunspots affect us on Earth, too... They can cause electromagnetic flares that disrupt satellites, and electricity here on our planet.
I'll be heading back to school tomorrow, but I want you to keep an eye on those sunspots, okay?
Make a drawing every day, if it's sunny. You should be able to see the spots moving and changing as the sun rotates.
I will!
I can't believe that I can see the surface of the sun from here!
There's a lot of ways to learn new things, and do science at home.
I'm glad I got to share some with you this week.

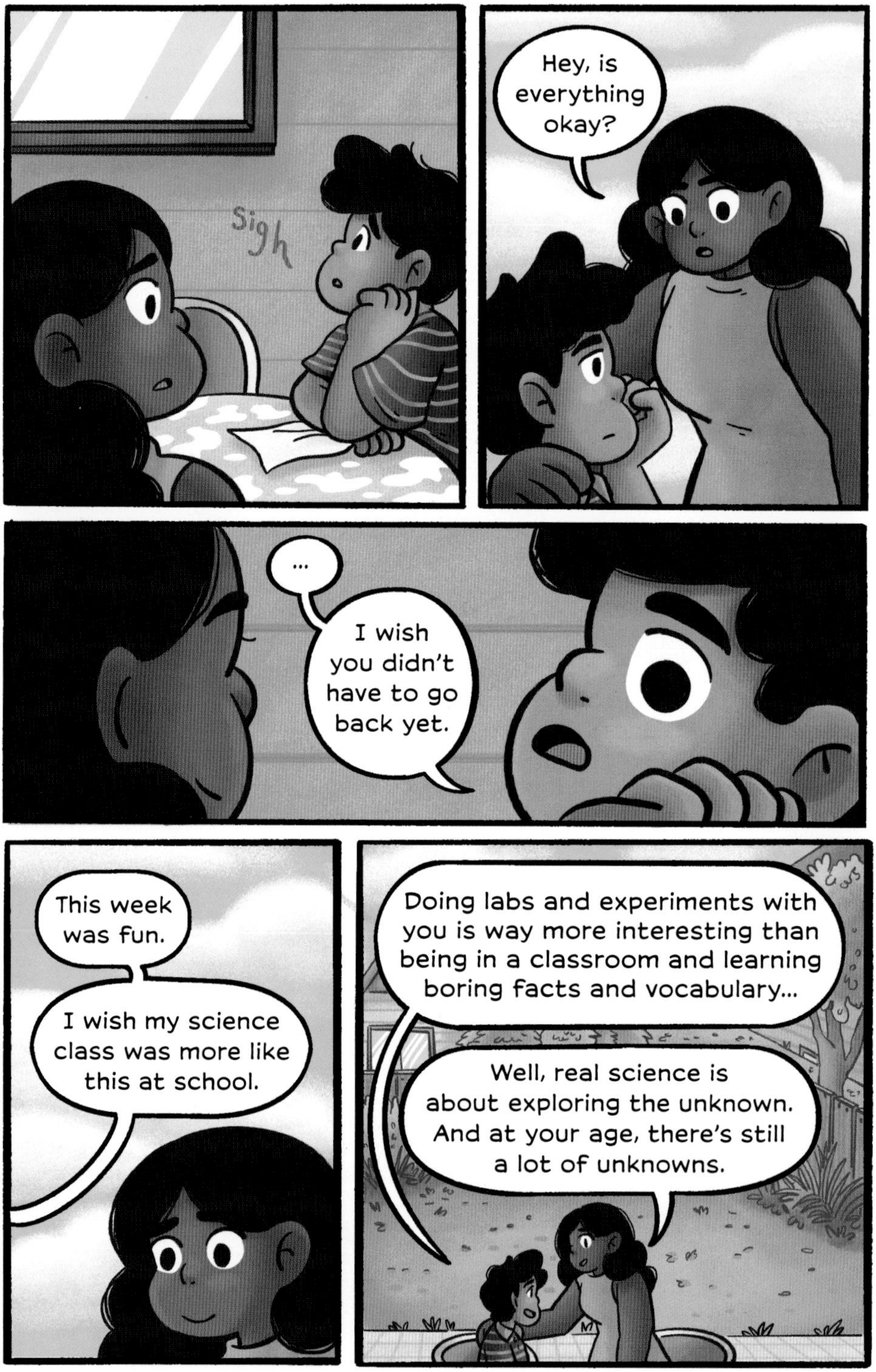
Sigh
Hey, is everything okay?
...
I wish you didn't have to go back yet.
This week was fun.
I wish my science class was more like this at school.
Doing labs and experiments with you is way more interesting than being in a classroom and learning boring facts and vocabulary...
Well, real science is about exploring the unknown. And at your age, there's still a lot of unknowns.

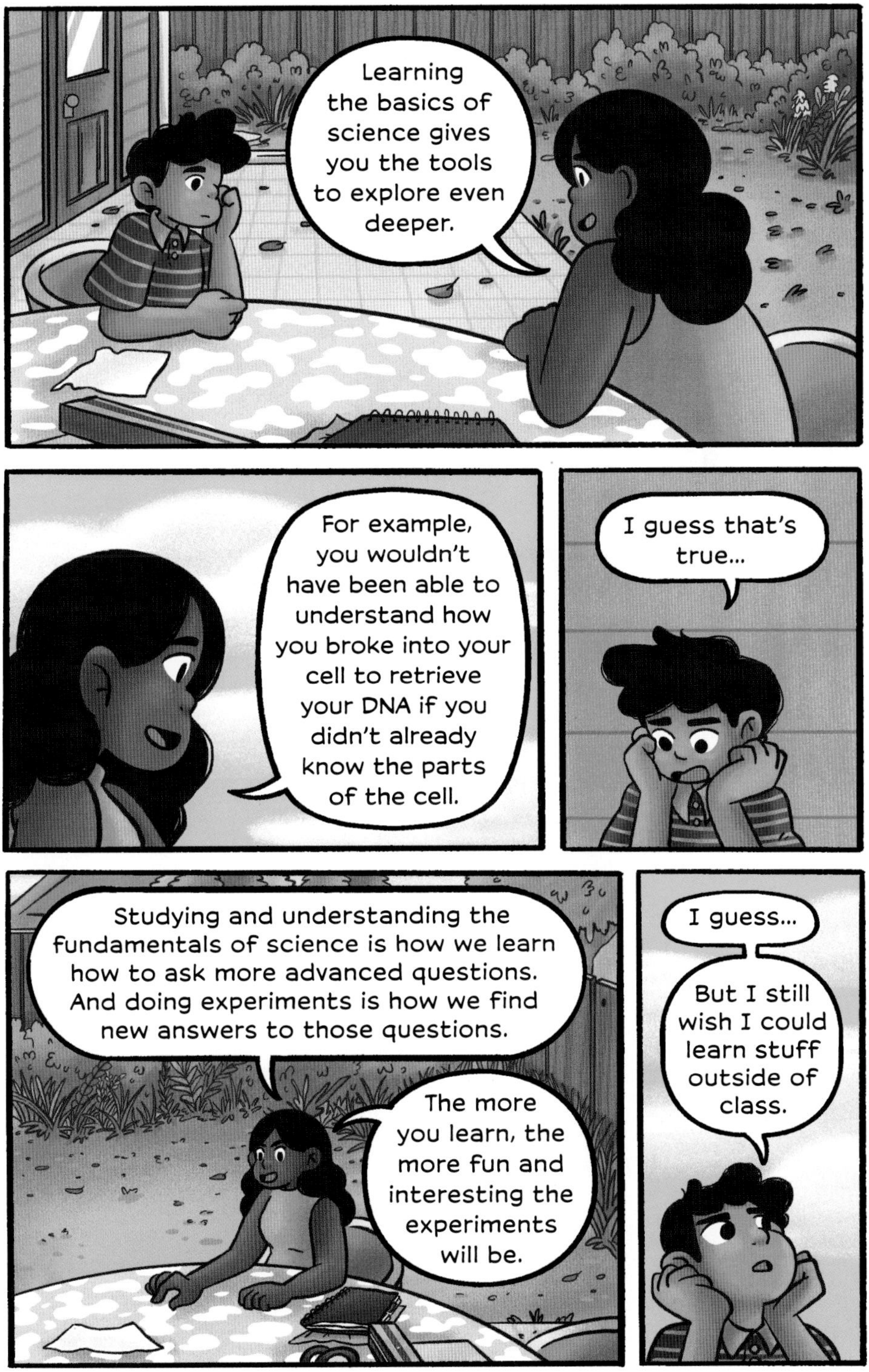
Learning the basics of science gives you the tools to explore even deeper.
For example, you wouldn't have been able to understand how you broke into your cell to retrieve your DNA if you didn't already know the parts of the cell.
I guess that's true...
Studying and understanding the fundamentals of science is how we learn how to ask more advanced questions. And doing experiments is how we find new answers to those questions.
The more you learn, the more fun and interesting the experiments will be.
I guess...
But I still wish I could learn stuff outside of class.

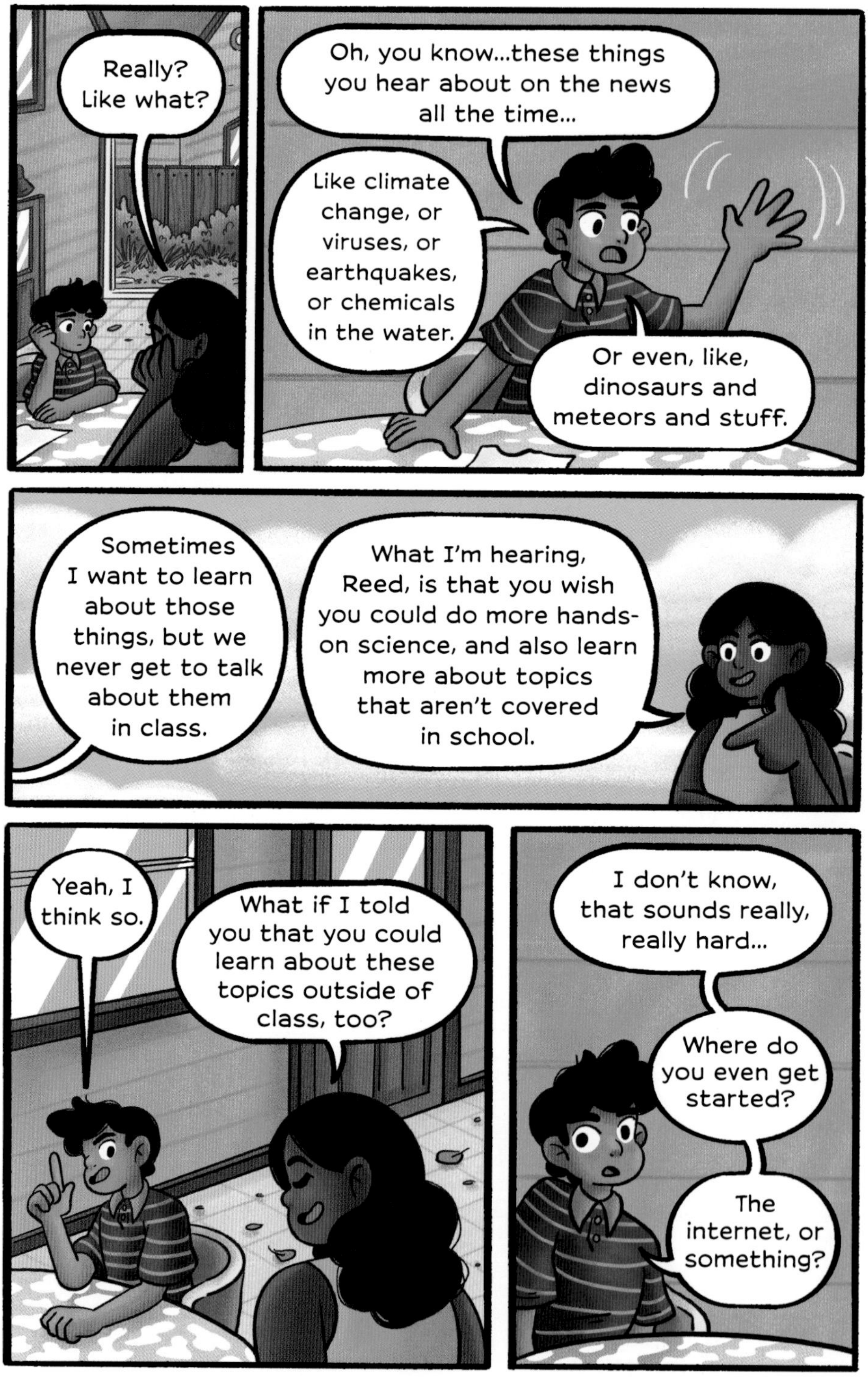
Really? Like what?
Oh, you know...these things you hear about on the news all the time...
Like climate change, or viruses, or earthquakes, or chemicals in the water.
Or even, like, dinosaurs and meteors and stuff.
Sometimes I want to learn about those things, but we never get to talk about them in class.
What I'm hearing, Reed, is that you wish you could do more hands-on science, and also learn more about topics that aren't covered in school.
Yeah, I think so.
What if I told you that you could learn about these topics outside of class, too?
I don't know, that sounds really, really hard...
Where do you even get started?
The internet, or something?

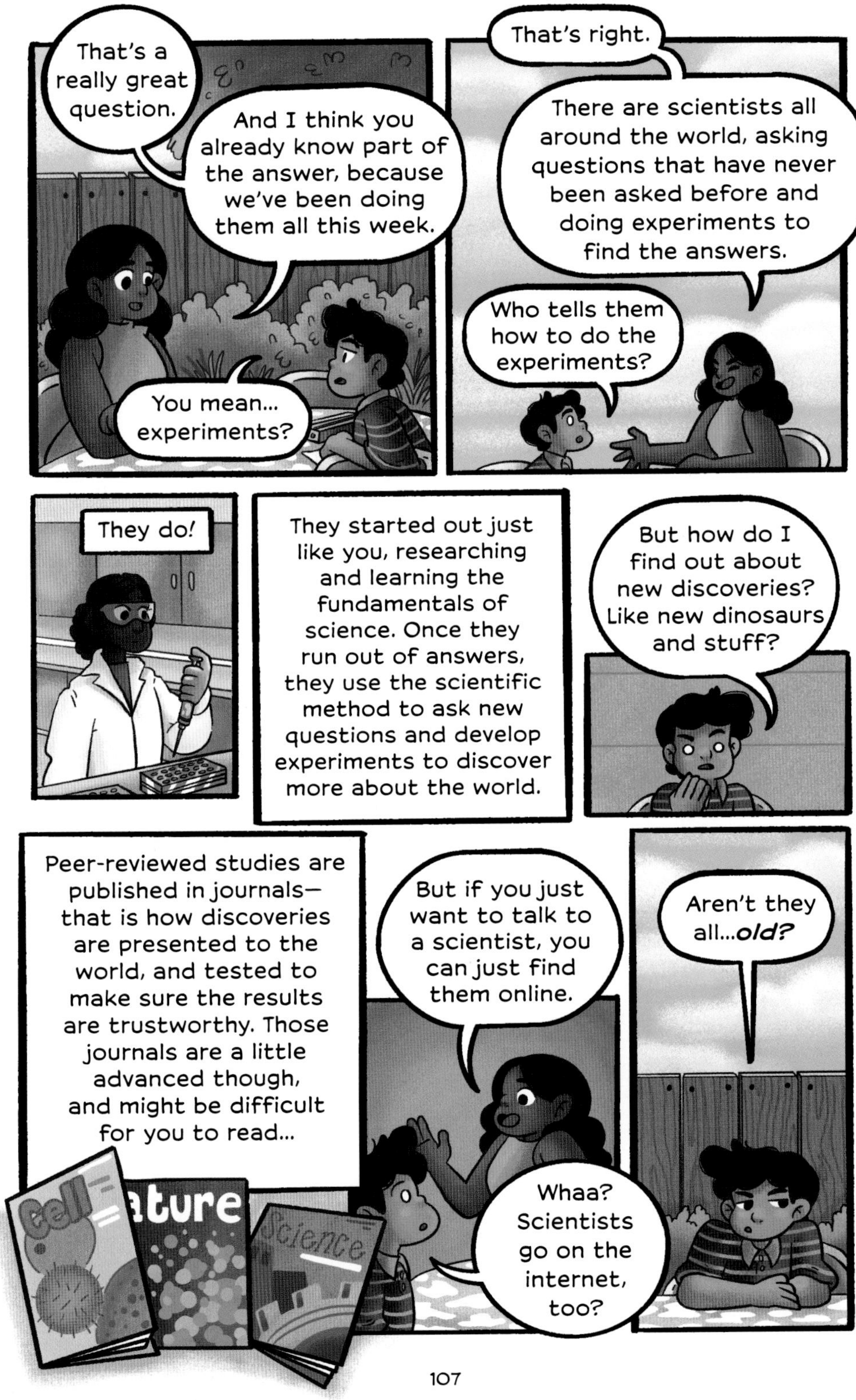
That's a really great question.
And I think you already know part of the answer, because we've been doing them all this week.
You mean... experiments?
That's right.
There are scientists all around the world, asking questions that have never been asked before and doing experiments to find the answers.
Who tells them how to do the experiments?
They do!
They started out just like you, researching and learning the fundamentals of science. Once they run out of answers, they use the scientific method to ask new questions and develop experiments to discover more about the world.
But how do I find out about new discoveries? Like new dinosaurs and stuff?
Peer-reviewed studies are published in journals—that is how discoveries are presented to the world, and tested to make sure the results are trustworthy. Those journals are a little advanced though, and might be difficult for you to read...
Cell
ature
Science
But if you just want to talk to a scientist, you can just find them online.
Whaa? Scientists go on the internet, too?
Aren't they all...*old?*

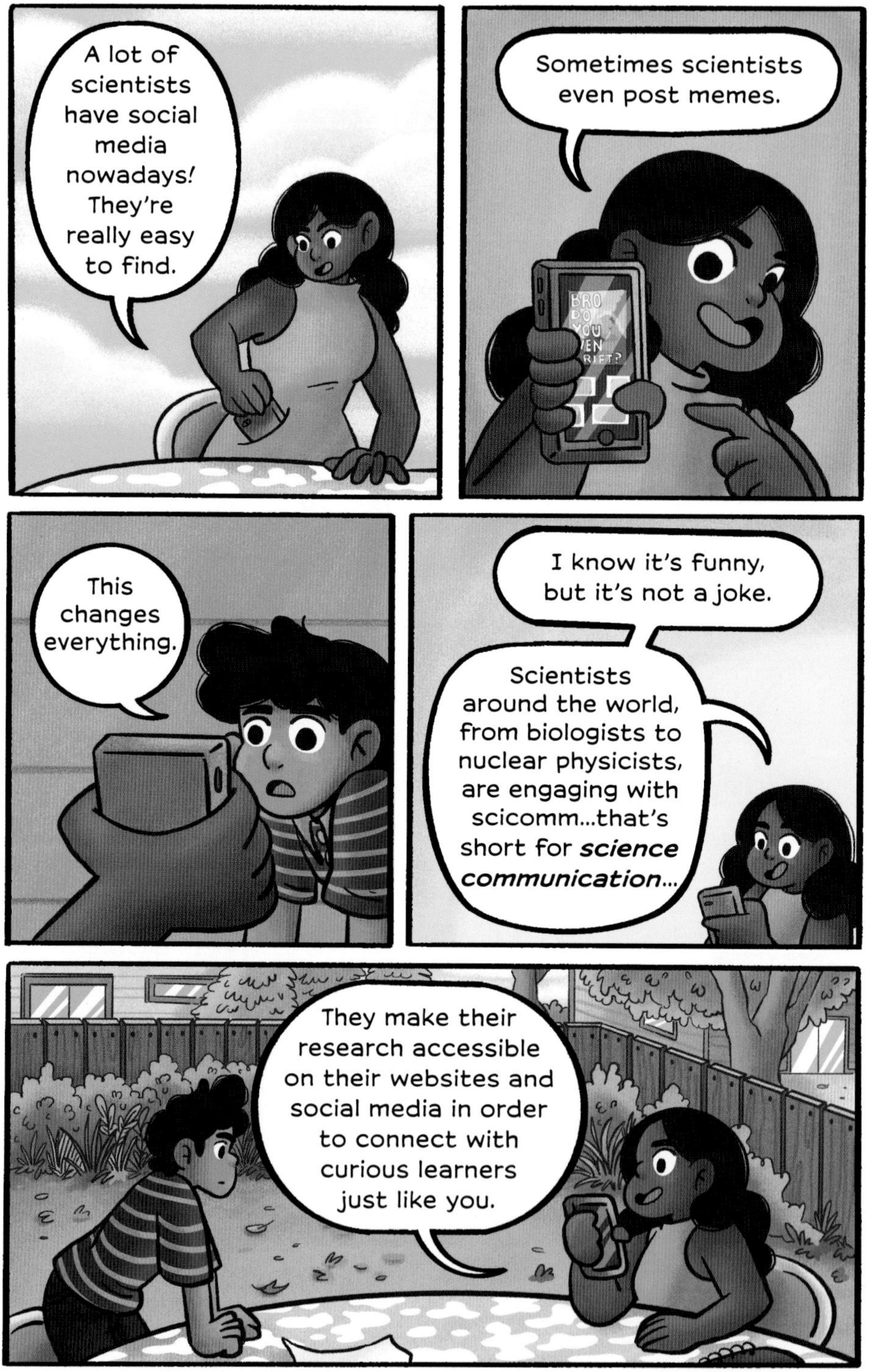
A lot of scientists have social media nowadays! They're really easy to find.
Sometimes scientists even post memes.
This changes everything.
I know it's funny, but it's not a joke.
Scientists around the world, from biologists to nuclear physicists, are engaging with scicomm...that's short for *science communication*...
They make their research accessible on their websites and social media in order to connect with curious learners just like you.

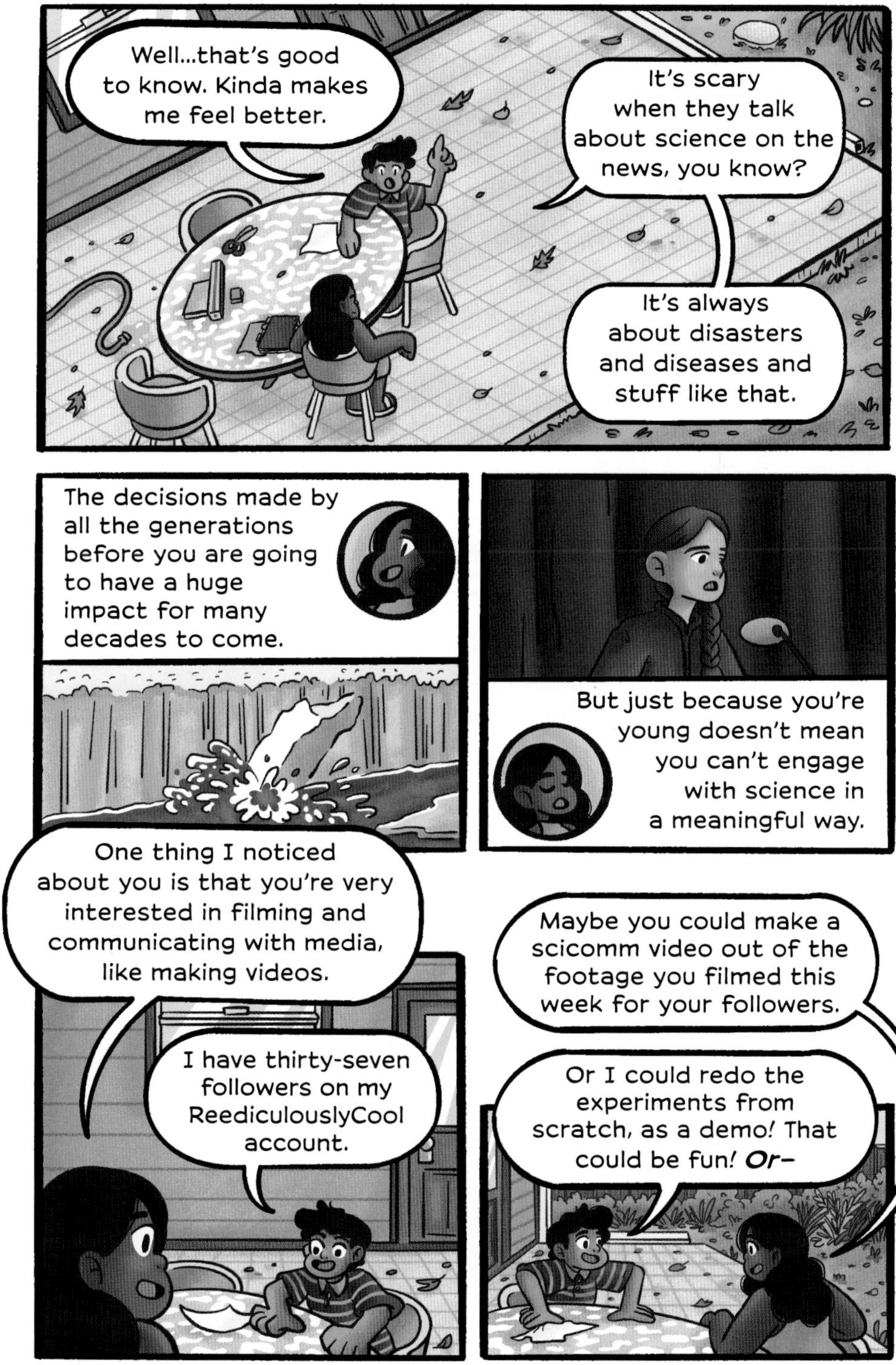
Well...that's good to know. Kinda makes me feel better.
It's scary when they talk about science on the news, you know?
It's always about disasters and diseases and stuff like that.
The decisions made by all the generations before you are going to have a huge impact for many decades to come.
But just because you're young doesn't mean you can't engage with science in a meaningful way.
One thing I noticed about you is that you're very interested in filming and communicating with media, like making videos.
I have thirty-seven followers on my ReediculouslyCool account.
Maybe you could make a scicomm video out of the footage you filmed this week for your followers.
Or I could redo the experiments from scratch, as a demo! That could be fun! *Or–*

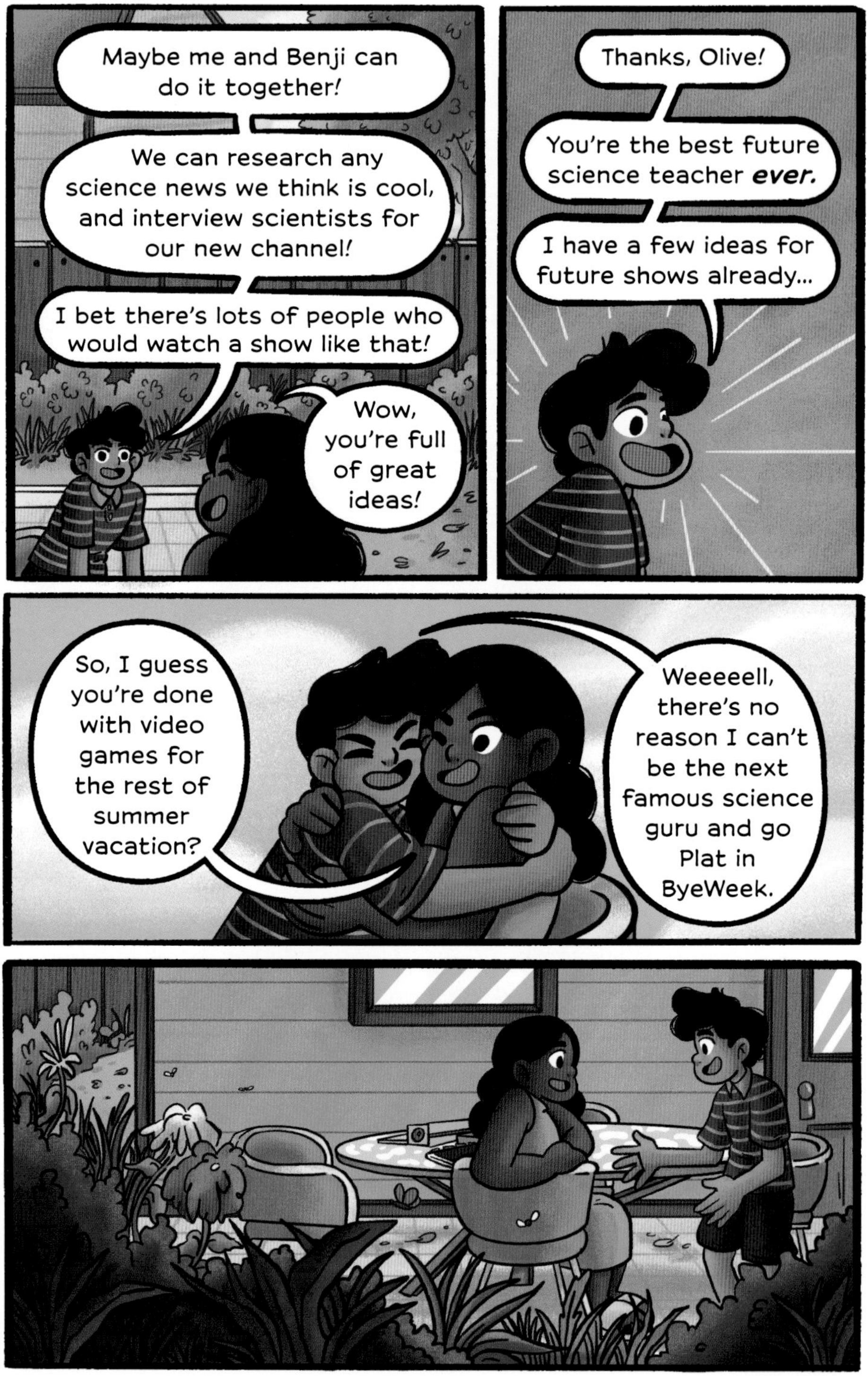
Maybe me and Benji can do it together!
We can research any science news we think is cool, and interview scientists for our new channel!
I bet there's lots of people who would watch a show like that!
Wow, you're full of great ideas!
Thanks, Olive!
You're the best future science teacher ***ever.***
I have a few ideas for future shows already...
So, I guess you're done with video games for the rest of summer vacation?
Weeeeell, there's no reason I can't be the next famous science guru and go Plat in ByeWeek.

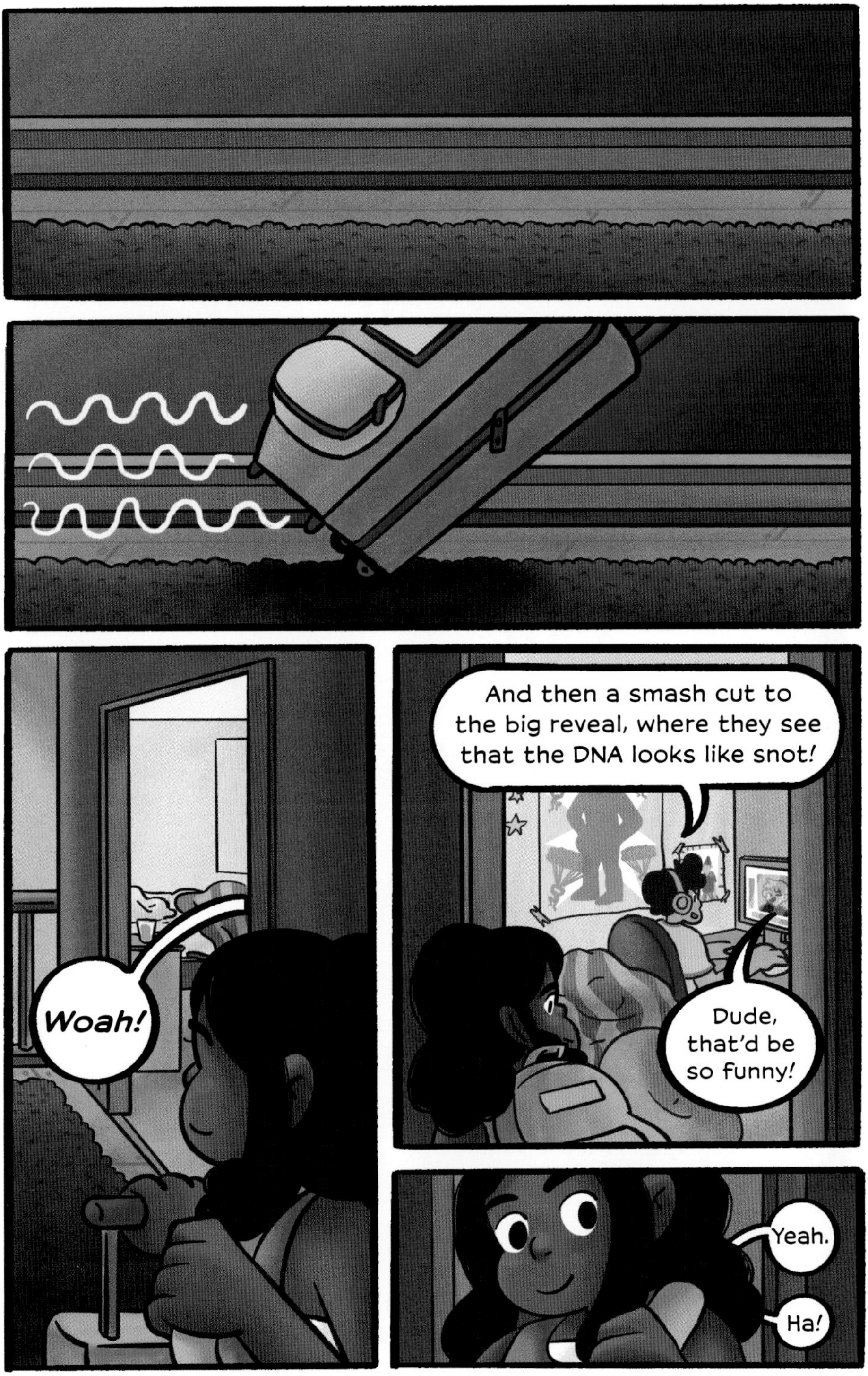
Woah!
And then a smash cut to the big reveal, where they see that the DNA looks like snot!
Dude, that'd be so funny!
Yeah.
Ha!

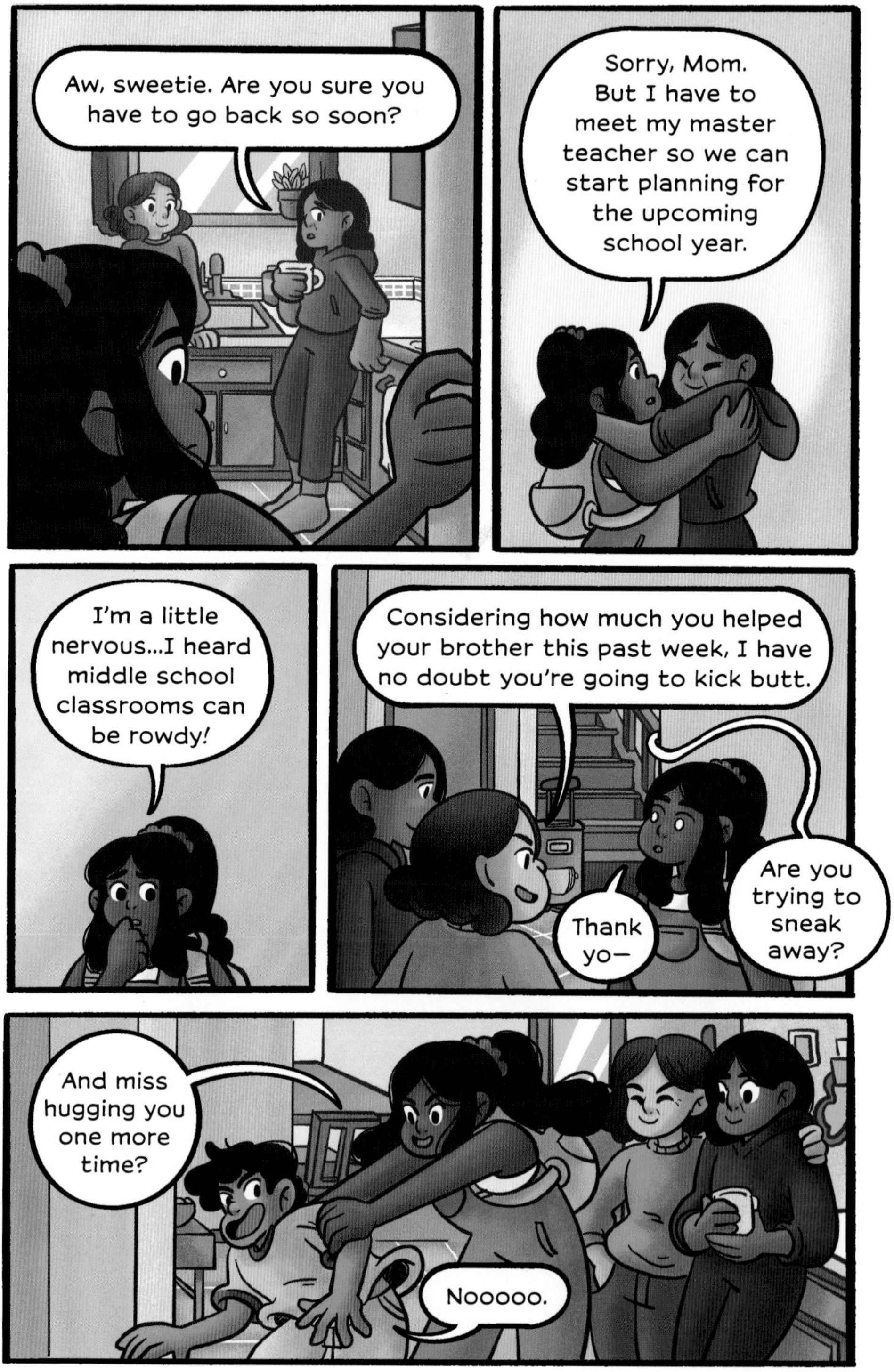
Aw, sweetie. Are you sure you have to go back so soon?
Sorry, Mom. But I have to meet my master teacher so we can start planning for the upcoming school year.
I'm a little nervous...I heard middle school classrooms can be rowdy!
Considering how much you helped your brother this past week, I have no doubt you're going to kick butt.
Thank yo—
Are you trying to sneak away?
And miss hugging you one more time?
Nooooo.

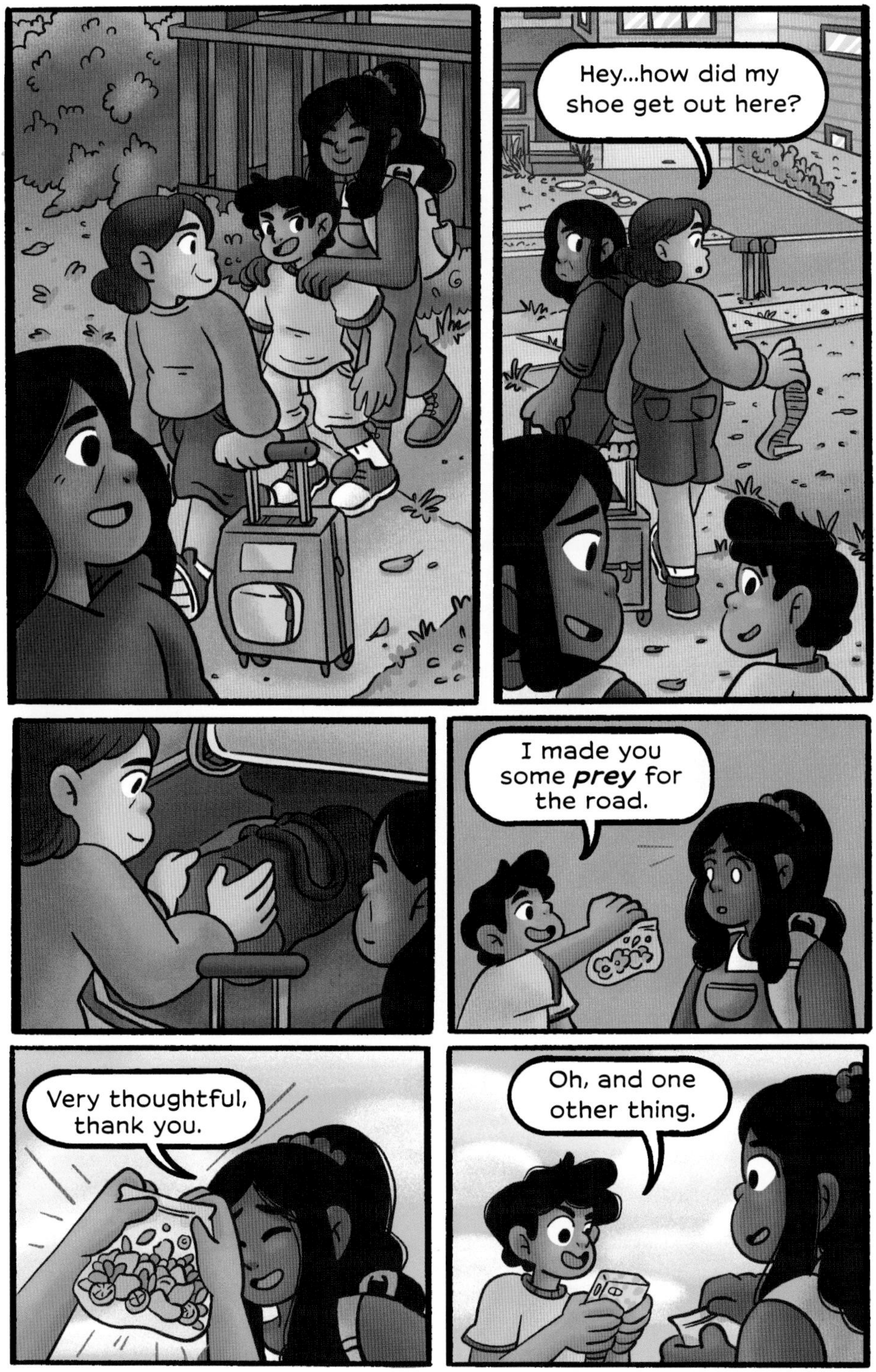
Hey...how did my shoe get out here?
I made you some *prey* for the road.
Very thoughtful, thank you.
Oh, and one other thing.

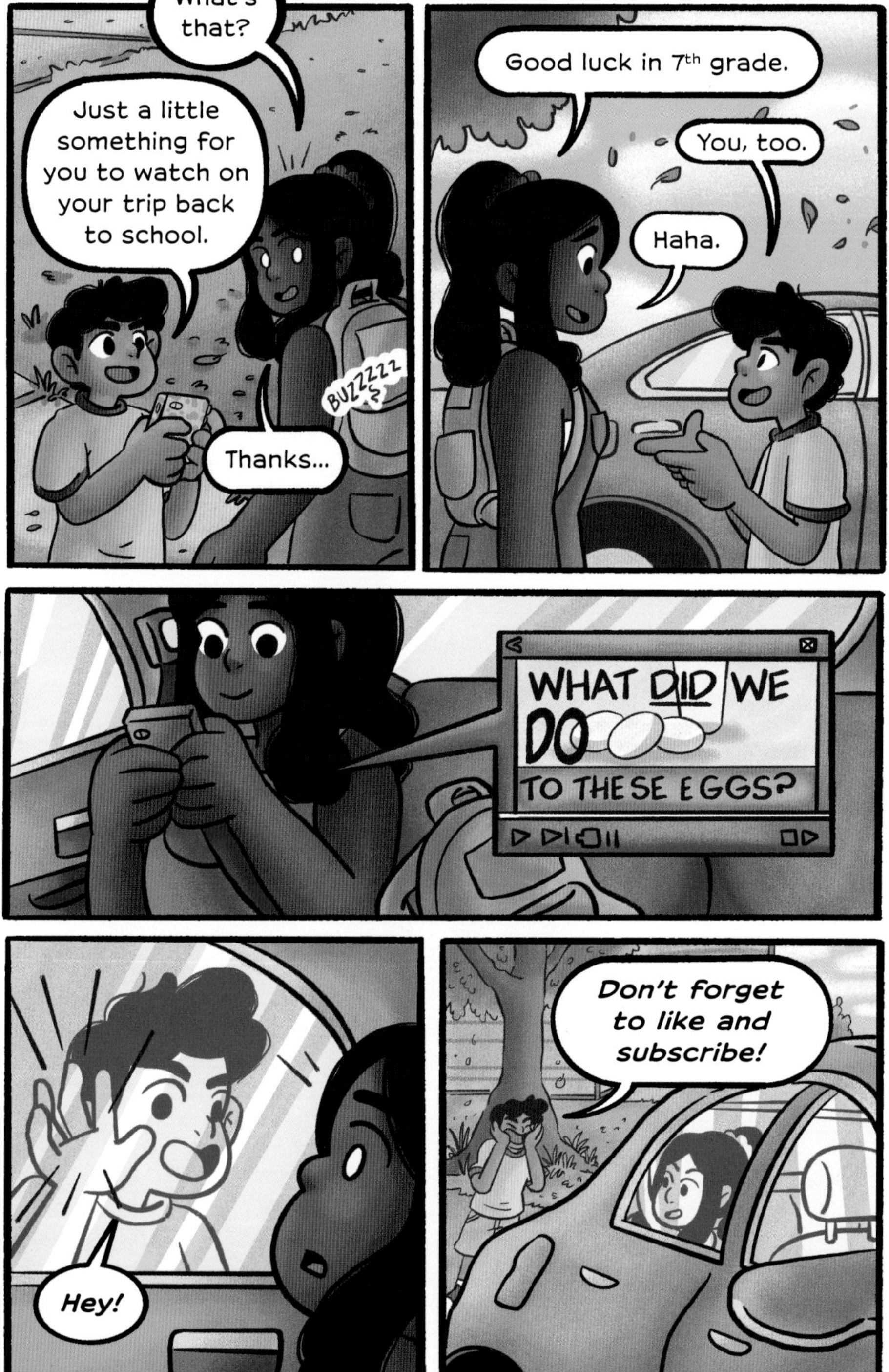
What's that?
Just a little something for you to watch on your trip back to school.
BUZZZZZ
Thanks...
Good luck in 7th grade.
You, too.
Haha.
WHAT DID WE DO TO THESE EGGS?
Hey!
Don't forget to like and subscribe!

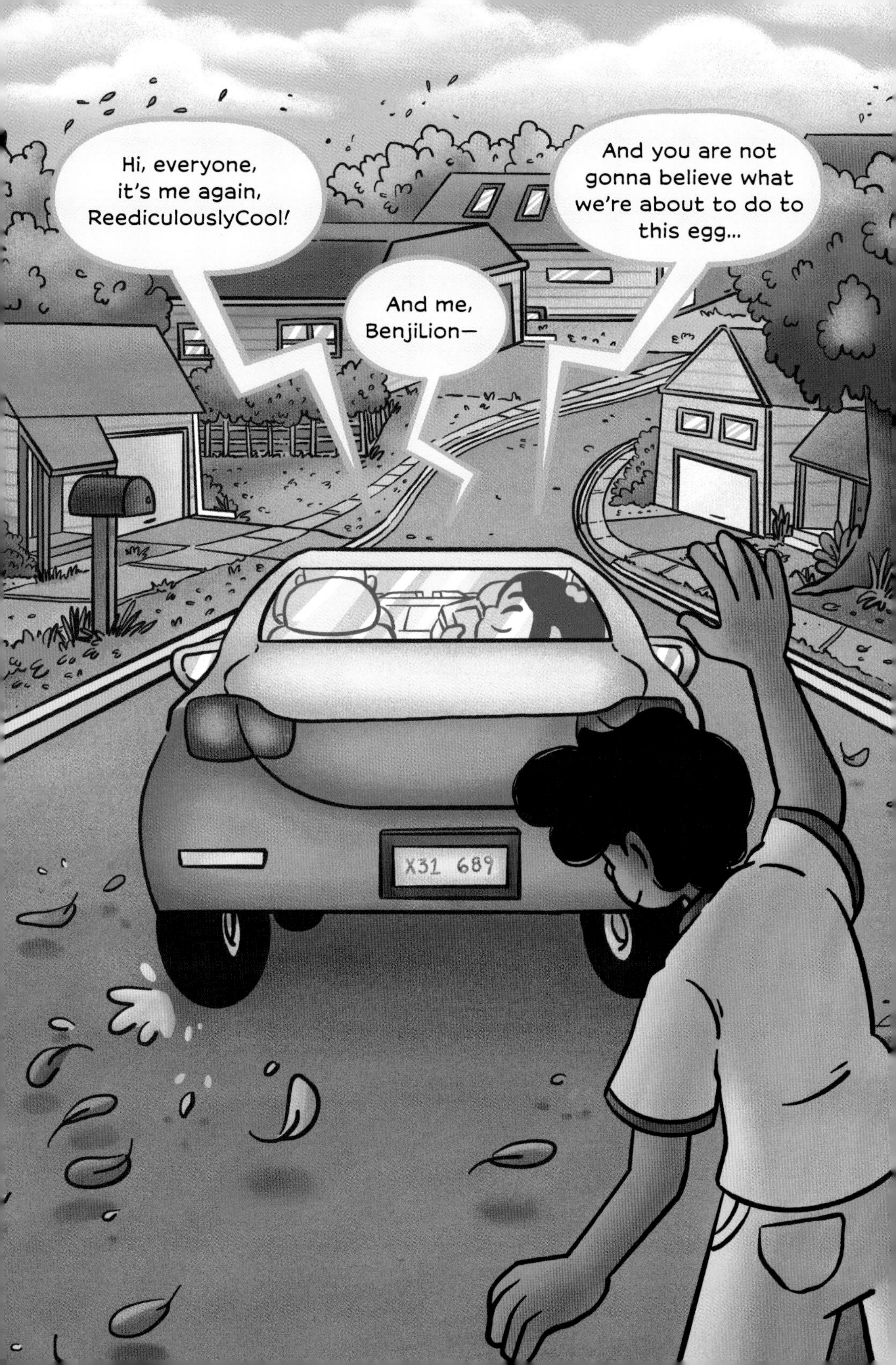
Hi, everyone, it's me again, ReediculouslyCool!
And me, BenjiLion—
And you are not gonna believe what we're about to do to this egg...
X31 689

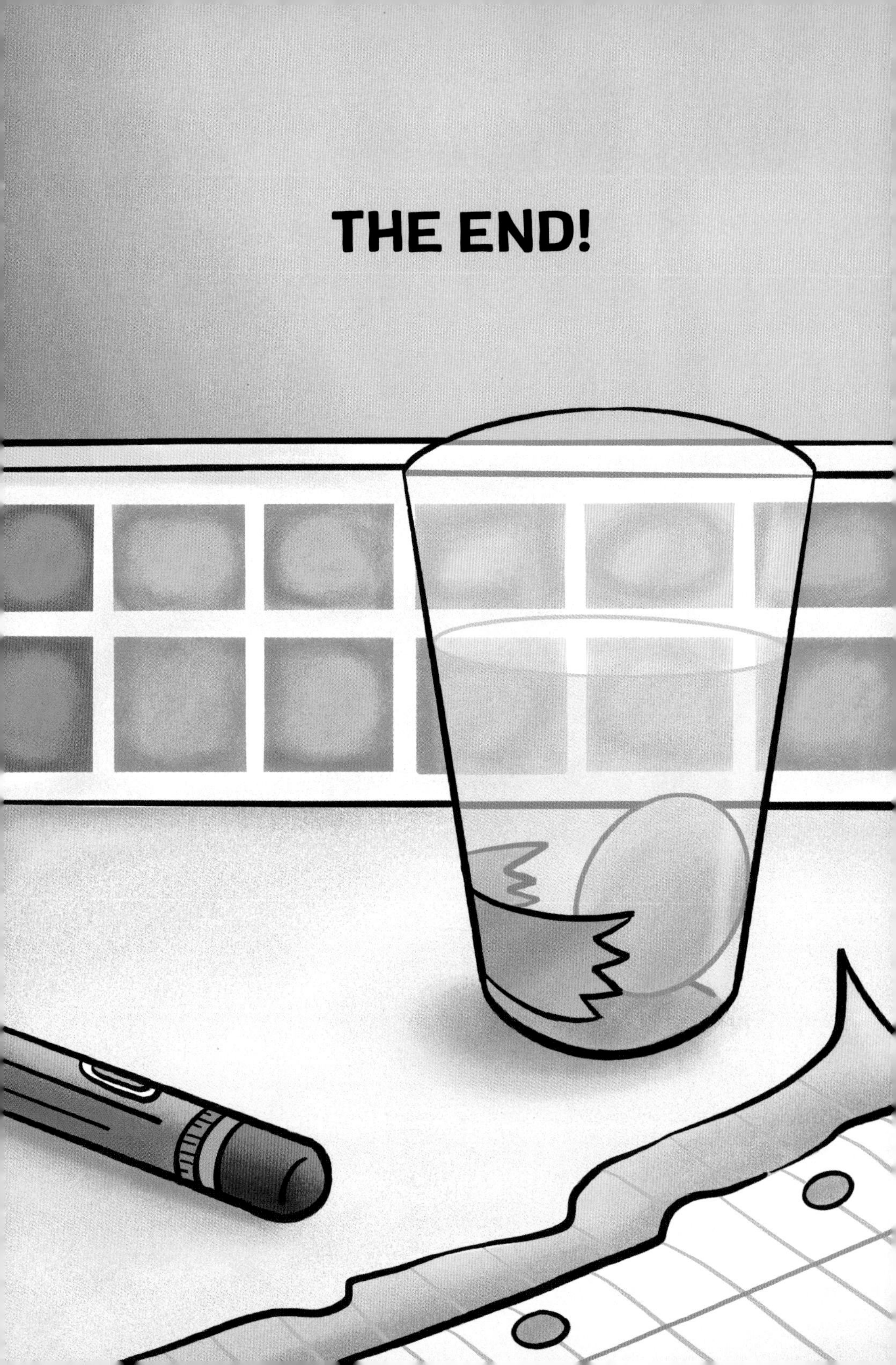
THE END!

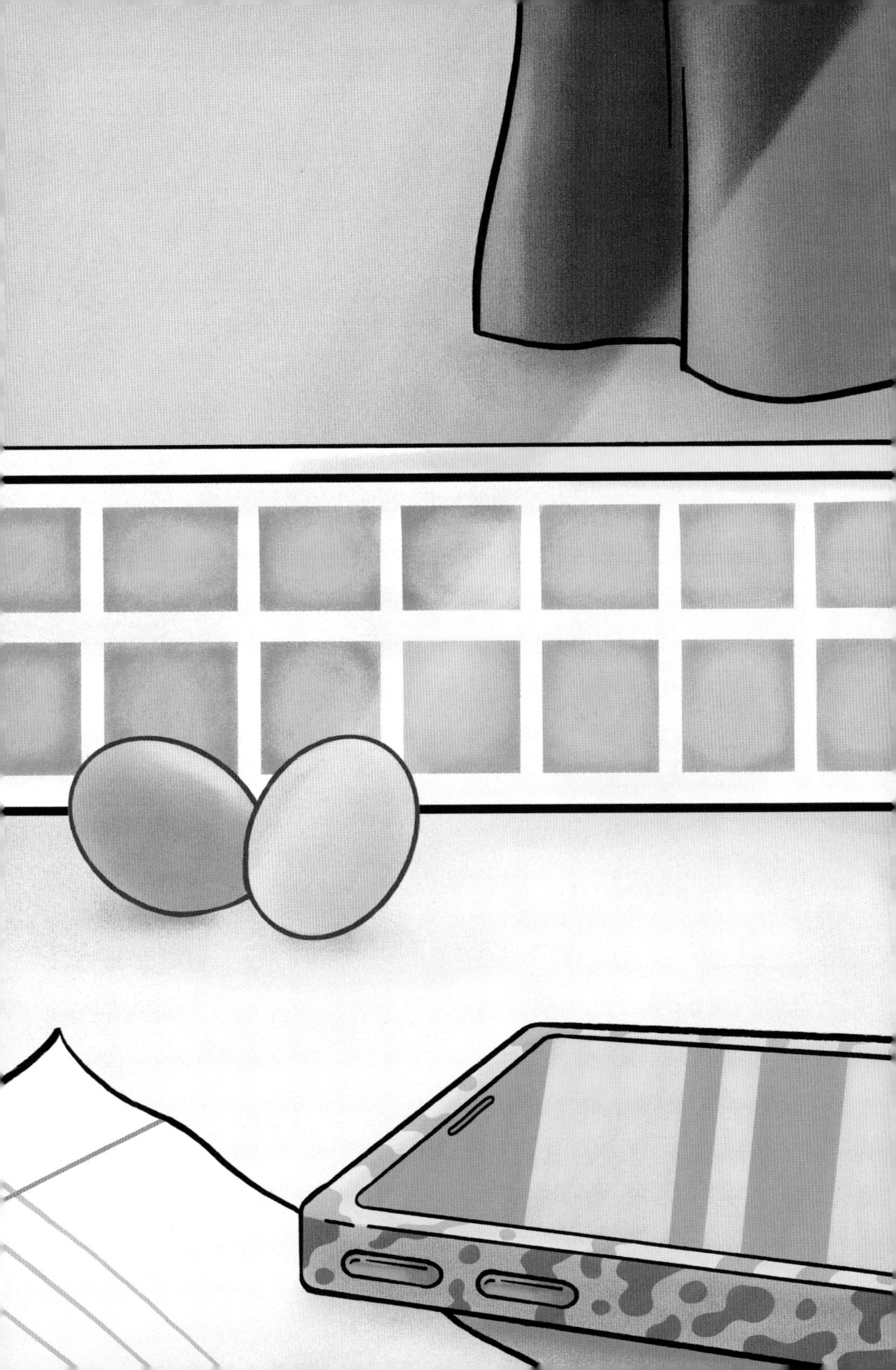

GLOSSARY

- **biodiversity:** the variety of life in a particular habitat
- **camera obscura:** a lensless camera that uses a small hole to project an image onto a surface
- **control:** a version of an experiment performed without any variables present
- **cryptic coloration:** in nature, a type of visual camouflage that animals use to blend in with their environment
- **extraction (DNA):** the isolation of DNA from the rest of the cell
- **friction:** the resistance that one surface or object encounters when moving over another
- **insoluble:** a substance that cannot be made into a solution, or, a substance that cannot be dissolved in a liquid
- **macromolecules:** the four major classes of large molecules that make up living things, which are carbohydrates, lipids, proteins, and nucleic acids

- **organism:** any living creature

- **osmosis:** when water moves from a region of low solute concentration to one of high solute concentration

- **quadrat:** a frame used by scientists to isolate an area for sampling

- **resistance:** when one material rubs against another and slows down the motion

- **semi-permeable membrane:** a membrane that only lets objects of a certain size through it

- **solution:** a liquid with particles that are dissolved in it

- **solute:** the particles in a solution

- **variable:** in an experiment, the only factor that changes

LAB SAFETY

THIS BOOK CONTAINS INSTRUCTIONS ON HOW TO CARRY OUT SCIENTIFIC EXPERIMENTS AND EXERCISES IN YOUR OWN HOME!

BEFORE GETTING STARTED, BE SURE TO REVIEW THIS LAB SAFETY GUIDE TO KEEP YOU AND YOUR EXPERIMENT FUN + SAFE.

- READ THE EXPERIMENT INSTRUCTIONS THOROUGHLY BEFORE DOING THE EXPERIMENT
  ↳ THE BEST WAY TO PREVENT ACCIDENTS IN THE LAB IS TO BE PREPARED, AND KNOW THE PROCEDURES BEFOREHAND TO AVOID CONFUSION OR MISTAKES.

- NO RUNNING OR ROUGHHOUSING DURING THE LAB.
  ↳ MANY LAB ACCIDENTS CAN BE PREVENTED SIMPLY BY BEHAVING MATURELY IN THE LAB. UNLESS MOVEMENT IS A PART OF THE EXPERIMENT. (PLEASE DON'T RUN, POKE, TICKLE, SHOVE, ETC.)

- HANDLE GLASS CAREFULLY
  ↳ GLASSWARE CAN BREAK IF DROPPED OR HANDLED IMPROPERLY! IF YOU BREAK GLASS IN THE HOUSE, GET AN ADULT TO HELP YOU CLEAN IT UP RIGHT AWAY.

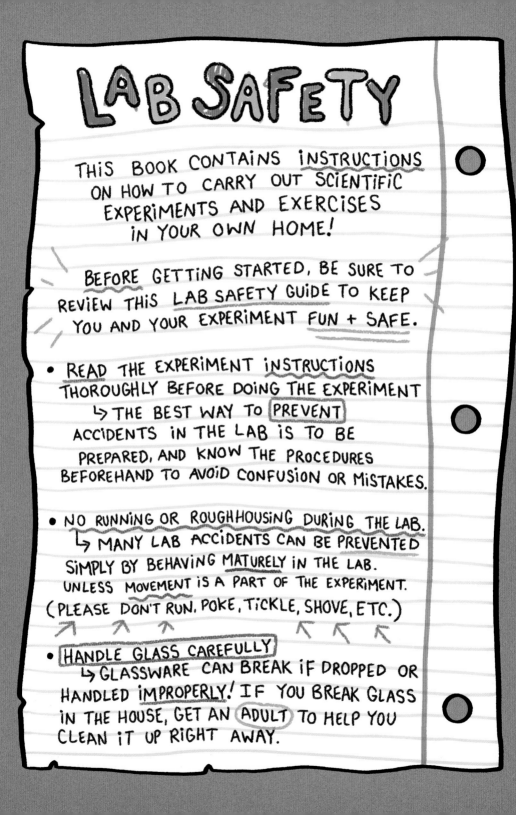

LAB SAFETY
CONTINUED...!

- BRING AN ADULT WHEN PERFORMING EXPERIMENTS IN PUBLIC AREAS.
  ↳ YOU MIGHT WANT TO MAKE OBSERVATIONS IN AN OUTDOOR SPACE AWAY FROM HOME, LIKE A PARK OR A COMMON AREA. IF SO, MAKE SURE YOU GO WITH AN ADULT. THEY CAN HELP YOU CARRY MATERIALS AND SET UP, BUT ALSO CAN LOOK OUT FOR YOU WHILE YOU ARE BUSY LOOKING OUT FOR COOL ORGANISMS.

- NEVER LOOK DIRECTLY INTO THE SUN.
  ↳ YOU MAY BE DOING AN EXPERIMENT WHERE YOU OBSERVE FEATURES OF OUR SUN. NEVER, UNDER ANY CIRCUMSTANCES SHOULD YOU LOOK DIRECTLY AT THE SUN. YOU MAY DO PERMANENT DAMAGE TO YOUR EYES, SO BE SAFE AND FOLLOW THE EXPERIMENT INSTRUCTIONS CAREFULLY.

- CLEAN UP AFTER YOURSELF
  ↳ CLEANLINESS IS AN IMPORTANT PART OF ANY LAB. IF YOU HAVE AN EXPERIMENT GOING OVERNIGHT, CLEARLY LABEL THE CONTENT OF YOUR JARS WITH MARKER ON TAPE SO NOBODY MISTAKES IT FOR SOMETHING ELSE! WIPE UP AFTER YOURSELF IF YOU CREATE A MESS. LEAVE YOUR HOME LAB CLEAN SO THE NEXT PERSON CAN HAVE A SAFE + FUN SCIENCE EXPERIMENT TOO!

HOW to RESEARCH

THE FIRST STEP TO ANSWERING ANY QUESTION IS RESEARCHING A SUBJECT! BUT WHAT SHOULD YOU DO IF YOU HAVE A QUESTION ABOUT SOMETHING YOU HAVEN'T LEARNED IN SCHOOL?

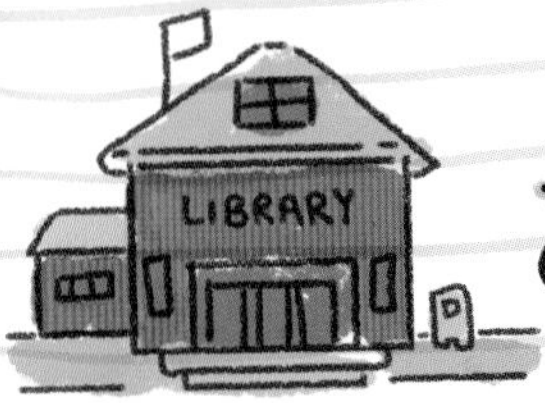
LIBRARY

USE THE LIBRARY

→ YOUR LOCAL LIBRARY IS A GREAT SOURCE OF KNOWLEDGE!

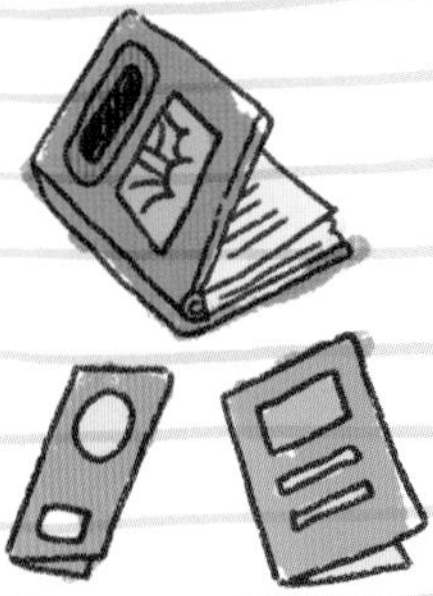

→ ASK YOUR LIBRARIAN TO HELP YOU LOOK FOR BOOKS OR INTERNET ARTICLES ABOUT YOUR SUBJECT, SPECIAL LIBRARY-ONLY REFERENCE TOOLS, AND EVEN INTER-LIBRARY LOANS FROM YOUR LOCAL COLLEGE.

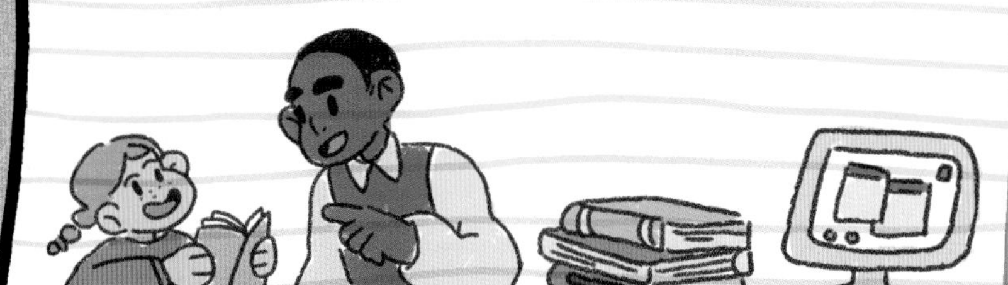

IN ADDITION TO BOOKS, LIBRARIES OFTEN HAVE ACCESS TO SCIENCE JOURNALS, WHICH ARE NEW RESEARCH WRITTEN BY SCIENTISTS THEMSELVES.

HOW to RESEARCH

CONTINUED...!

ASK YOUR TEACHER

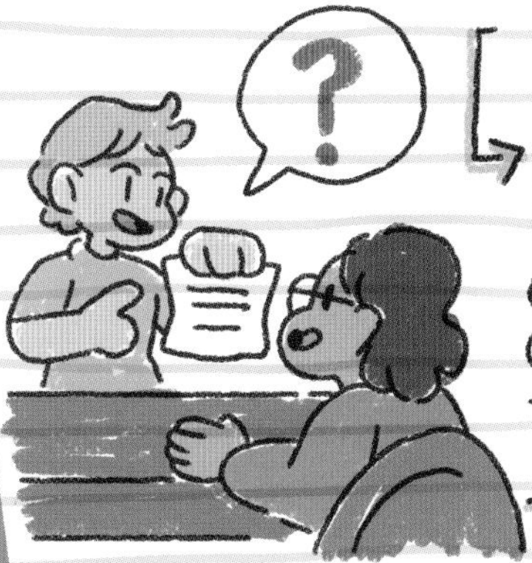

→ EVEN IF YOU HAVEN'T LEARNED SOMETHING IN CLASS YET, YOUR TEACHER CAN OFTEN POINT YOU IN THE RIGHT DIRECTION.

→ NEVER BE AFRAID TO ASK QUESTIONS.

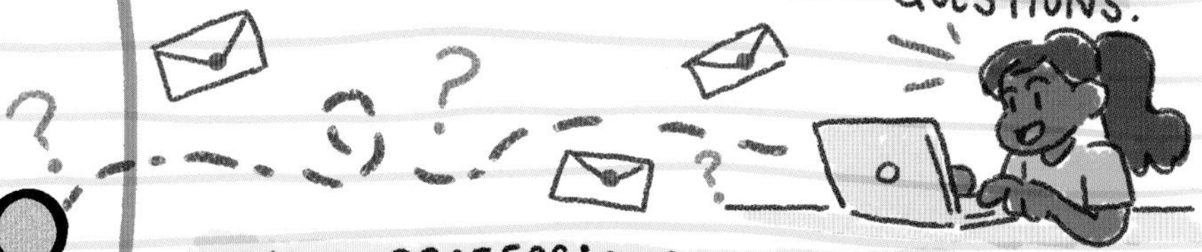

ASK A PROFESSIONAL SCIENTIST

→ DID YOU KNOW? MANY SCIENTISTS USE THE INTERNET AND SOCIAL MEDIA!

→ BE SURE TO LOOK FOR YOUR FAVORITE SCIENTIST'S WEBSITE FOR ANSWERS TO QUESTIONS YOU CAN'T FIND ANYWHERE ELSE.

→ CHECK IF THEY HAVE A SOCIAL MEDIA PAGE, TOO... MANY PROFESSIONAL SCIENTISTS PARTICIPATE IN SCIENCE COMMUNICATION TO RAISE INTEREST IN SCIENCE AND TO ANSWER QUESTIONS FROM FUTURE RESEARCHERS LIKE YOU!

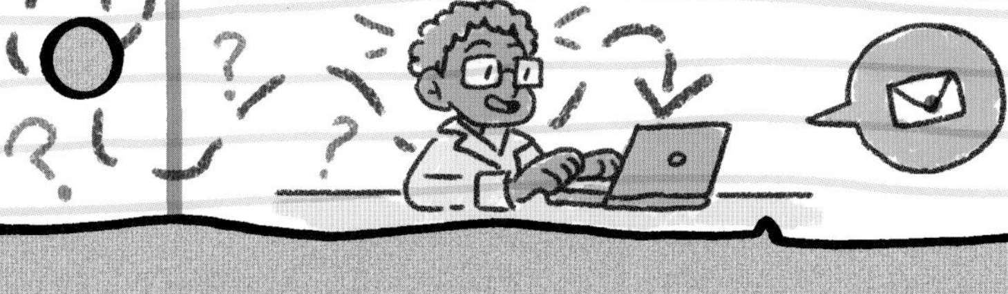

Published by First Second
First Second is an imprint of Roaring Brook Press,
a division of Holtzbrinck Publishing Holdings Limited Partnership
120 Broadway, New York, NY 10271
firstsecondbooks.com
mackids.com

All instructions included in this book are provided as a resource for parents and children.
While all due care has been taken, we recommend that an adult supervise children at all times when following
the instructions in this book. The projects in this book are not recommended for children three years and under
due to potential choking hazard. Neither the authors nor the publisher accept any responsibility for any loss,
injury, or damages sustained by anyone resulting from the instructions contained in this book.

Library of Congress Control Number: 2021906538

Our books may be purchased in bulk for promotional, educational, or business use.
Please contact your local bookseller or the Macmillan Corporate and Premium Sales Department
at (800) 221-7945 ext. 5442 or by email at MacmillanSpecialMarkets@macmillan.com.

First edition, 2021
Edited by Robyn Chapman and Alison Wilgus
Cover and interior book design by Molly Johanson
Science consultant: Kathy Ceceri

Printed in China by 1010 Printing International Limited, Kwun Tong, Hong Kong

ISBN 978-1-250-75481-3 (paperback)
1 3 5 7 9 10 8 6 4 2

ISBN 978-1-250-75480-6 (hardcover)
1 3 5 7 9 10 8 6 4 2

Penciled and inked digitally with an ink brush in Procreate on an iPad Pro.
Colors produced in Photoshop on a Cintiq 13HD, using a grainy, hard airbrush.

Don't miss your next favorite book from First Second!
For the latest updates go to firstsecondnewsletter.com and sign up for our enewsletter.